GRAND EMPORIUM

MERCANTILE MONSTER

Southern Literary Studies

SCOTT ROMINE, SERIES EDITOR

GRAND EMPORIUM

MERCANTILE MONSTER

THE ANTEBELLUM SOUTH'S LOVE-HATE AFFAIR WITH NEW YORK CITY

RITCHIE DEVON WATSON JR.

LOUISIANA STATE UNIVERSITY PRESS

BATON ROUGE

Published by Louisiana State University Press
lsupress.org

Manufactured in the United States of America
FIRST PRINTING

DESIGNER: Andrew Shurtz
TYPEFACES: Benton Modern,
Monotype Grotesque,
Grotesque No. 9

COVER ILLUSTRATION:
Bird's-eye view of New York and Brooklyn, 1851,
drawn from nature and on stone by J. Bachman[n].
Courtesy Library of Congress.

Library of Congress Cataloging-in-Publication Data
ISBN 978-0-8071-7933-8 (cloth)
ISBN 978-0-8071-8006-8 (pdf)
ISBN 978-0-8071-8005-1 (epub)

to Sue, Susan, and Jane Forbes
and to my grandchildren,
Jane Larkin, Thomas, Emma Forbes,
Susan, and Kate,
New York City enthusiasts all

CONTENTS

GRAND EMPORIUM

MERCANTILE MONSTER

ONE

THAT MOST SOUTHERN CONNECTED OF NORTHERN CITIES

ON MAY 13, 1818, Charlestonian Ann Wagner sent a letter to her son Effingham describing with great enthusiasm her experiences as a tourist in the bustling and rapidly growing city of New York. The musical and operatic culture she encountered there ranked particularly high in her estimation. The previous week, for example, she had gone "to hear Phillips sing in the play of the Devil's Bridge." His "Song of Fancy sketch," she raved, had "exceeded anything I ever heard." Indeed, Wagner judged that she had "never seen an opera performed in so great a [style] since I left England." So enraptured was she by the singing that she assured her son she would attend another performance before the artist left the city. The Charleston matron was as impressed with the variety and price of New York's merchandise as she was with its cultural offerings. The food markets especially delighted her. "The meat and fish is beautiful, and the . . . asparagus I am charmed with. I very often go to market and wish I could send you some of the good things. . . . The salmon is the only thing I see high, that is seventy-five cent per pound."[1]

Ann Wagner's travels would take her on to Philadelphia, Providence, and Boston, yet the lure of New York City seems to have surpassed that of the other northern towns. By mid-October, long past the time her son had apparently expected her back in Charleston, she remained in Manhattan—slightly but by no means fully contrite for being away from home for more than five months. Though she was "sorry to think that you have all expected me home before the first of September," Wagner wrote in a letter dated October 17, 1818, she went on to observe somewhat archly that it had not been her "intent when [she] left home to return sooner." In response to her son's complaints that she had not written home often enough she replied: "I am certain I wrote you in Boston and on my return to New York, and in all have written you five times . . . since I left home." As much as she disliked being taken to task for being a lax correspondent, she seems to have been even more offended by her son's implication that she had been seduced into extravagance by the mercantile pleasures of Gotham. With barely concealed resentment she reminded her son that she had "properly acknowledged the receipt of both of your remittances, which I am much indebted to you for. I hope it has been all out of funds received from rents, interest and wages that became due since I left home as I should be much hurt to think I had occasion to call upon you." If she gave the family in Charleston too much trouble she couldn't "help it." She was spending her money as profligate southern tourists would do for years to come. She was enjoying the pleasures of a real city, a "charming place." Compared to Charleston she found New York to be "a new world."[2]

Though she did not realize it, Ann Wagner represented the initiation of what was soon to become a mid-nineteenth century flood of southern visitors to New York. This flood of southerners was in turn facilitated by the flood of southern cotton that was finding its way through the city's port destined for New England and European textile factories. In 1788 sixty-two bales of cotton had been shipped across the Atlantic. By 1825, thanks to the rapid settlement of the interior South, the expansion of slavery, and the development of Eli Whitney's cotton gin, New York was exporting the astonishingly higher total of 153,757 bales.[3] During the second decade of the nineteenth century, a decade during which visitors like Wagner began to descend upon the city for both business and pleasure, Gotham was decisively establishing its commercial dominance over its major rivals for the cotton trade—Philadelphia, Boston, and even Charleston.

In the period of stability that followed the end of the War of 1812 and the defeat of Napoleon, New York merchants quickly recognized the utility and profitability of loading their ships with the southern cotton European manufacturers craved and hauling back the manufactured goods that American consumers coveted. By 1820 New York City had, in the words of David Quigley, "regularized the movement of capital and supplies between the plantations of the black belt and the mill towns of Britain" so efficiently that no other American city, north or south, could compete with it more successfully. In 1822 over half of New York's rapidly increasing exports were produced in the South, and cotton comprised 40 percent of these southern commodities. By 1835, 119 of the 120 ships bound from New York to Liverpool, England carried raw cotton. The hefty profits derived from the cotton trade allowed the city's merchants to devise increasingly efficient shipping lines both to southern ports, where the cotton was first loaded, and to European ports, where it was finally deposited.[4]

Cotton made possible the massive expansion of New York's banks, and the rise of these huge establishments magnified the city's dominance of the lucrative trade. As John Hope Franklin has observed, southern merchants as well as planters could usually secure better credit terms in New York than they could find in Charleston or New Orleans. Gotham could offer its clients "six months of credit interest free and another six months of credit at low interest rates." Smaller southern banks with much smaller resources were in no position to compete with their larger New York rivals. Quigley has observed that the years in which New Orleans led Gotham in cotton exports were "exceptions that affirmed New York's dominance, as New Orleans traders employed New York ships and relied upon New York banks for credit."[5] Ann Wagner had presciently foreseen in 1818 that Gotham would become the center of what she called "a new world," and it was one upon which the antebellum plantation South would find itself increasingly dependent.

The process through which Gotham's merchants would come to dominate the lucrative cotton market is strikingly reflected in business history of the Brown family. Family patriarch Alexander Brown was a Scotch-Irish immigrant who by 1800 owned a thriving linen business in Baltimore. But Alexander was an acute enough businessman to look beyond linen and appreciate both the moneymaking potential of the just developing and rapidly expanding trade in cotton and the centrality of New York City to that trade. In 1825 he dispatched his son James to Manhattan and his son William to Liverpool with the aim of furthering "the interest of Messrs. William and James Brown and Co., of Liverpool, and of affording greater facility, and the choice of markets, to our southern friends who are disposed to give . . . us their business." Within a few years Brown and Company, anchored by siblings in both New York and Liverpool, had established itself among the largest cotton traders in the English market. Brown Brothers achieved its dominance by offering southern planters a variety of services that could not be matched by local traders. The firm provided planters and factors cash advances on future crops. It arranged shipping to Liverpool and provided insurance on the cotton while in transit. It sold large quantities on commission. And through its local agents in New Orleans, Mobile, Savannah, and Charleston it offered credit at relatively low interest as well as currency exchange for its clients. By the flush years of the 1830s Brown Brothers was accruing profits of over $400,000 a year—"enough to buy thirteen one-hundred-foot yachts, or thirteen hundred carriages" for Alexander's numerous progeny. In 1838 James Brown could boast of handling 178,000 bales of cotton, 16 percent of his country's total exports to the United Kingdom.[6] The extraordinary success of Brown Brothers exemplifies the collective entrepreneurial energy of nineteenth-century Gotham's mercantile elite as well as the phenomenal success of an individual family that would over the coming centuries weave itself intimately into the commercial, cultural, and philanthropic life of New York City.

Though the Browns and other New York cotton brokers were businessmen and bankers, the vagaries of the trade not infrequently brought them into direct contact with the institution of slavery. The credit they extended to planters was commonly secured by the future delivery of the slave-cultivated crop or even by the slaves themselves. When crops failed or planters were otherwise unable to pay back their credit advances to firms such as Brown Brothers, they were forced to surrender what they had advanced as security—their land and their slaves. Ultimately the Browns were owners of at least thirteen cotton plantations as well as hundreds of slaves, possessions that constituted a significant portion their wealth. "James Brown sat in his New York office," Sven Beckert writes, "hiring resident managers for slave plantations."[7] Of course pious Scotch Presbyterians like the Browns did not boast or advertise the fact that they were among the nation's largest slave owners; nonetheless they were nearly as entangled with the institution as a Tidewater or Delta planter aristocrat.

Families like the Browns who through their extensive commercial activities in the cotton trade became intimately involved with the institution of slavery could feel more comfortable living in New York than they would have been in Boston or Philadelphia, for from its early origins as Dutch New Amsterdam in the mid-seventeenth century through the British colonial period it had remained much more than its rivals to the north and south undisputedly a slave city. Indeed, on the eve of the revolution only Charleston could boast of containing a larger enslaved population. In the 1740s approximately 20 percent of its ten thousand souls were, in the words of Jill Le Pore, "the souls of black folk." Early English visitors to New York like William Strickland often expressed surprise to find a place whose external appearance, though much smaller than London, bore a remarkable resemblance to the British capital. He noted that the dwellings were "in the stile we are accustomed to; within doors the furniture is all English or made after English fashions. The mode of living is the same." There was, however, one clear and inescapable difference that in the eyes of this traveler separated old world London from new world New York: "the greater number of the Blacks."[8]

Thus, slaves were from the beginning of its founding a significant and integral part of the economic and social fabric of colonial and federal New York City, and, as in the southern colonies, their presence became an increasingly troubling element in the consciousness of the town's free citizens. Indeed, racial trouble arrived early in Gotham's history. On the morning of April 6, 1712, some two dozen male and female slaves, having armed themselves with guns, axes, clubs, and knives, set fire to a building and attacked whites who arrived to fight the fire, killing nine and wounding seven. The rebellious slaves, being a relatively small group, were quickly subdued. Ultimately twenty-one were executed in ways that would have seemed appropriate to fearful and vengeful white citizens. "Some were burned at the stake," write Leslie and Michelle Alexander, "while others were hanged . . . or had their necks snapped. One rebel was strapped to a large stone wheel, each of his bones broken with a wooden mallet."[9]

With the imposition of these hideous punishments New York's first slave insurrection ended with the draconian assertion of white authority. It did, however, predictably generate legislation that sought to maintain white control over New York's potentially restive Blacks. After 1712 the colonial government enacted a series of laws that discouraged masters from freeing slaves and prohibited free Blacks from owning land. Other laws lengthened curfew for the enslaved and imposed further restrictions on Blacks walking the streets at night. For example, no slave over the age of fourteen could be abroad after sunset without carrying a lantern to establish his or her identity. Violators incurred the punishment of thirty-nine lashes.[10]

Such draconian laws, however, were not entirely successful in extinguishing the threat of Black insurrection in Manhattan. In 1741 the city was the setting for a second, even more infamous slave insurrection. In *New York Burning* Jill Le Pore has unearthed and vividly describes weeks of terror during which "ten fires blazed across the city" and "two hundred slaves were suspected of conspiring to burn every building and murder every white." The punishments administered to the participants of this second uprising were more numerous and just as gruesome as those that had been meted out in 1712. Thirty suspects were convicted before the colony's supreme court. Of these unfortunate miscreants "thirteen black men were burned at the stake," and seventeen were hanged, "two of their dead bodies chained to posts not far from the Negroes Burial Ground, left to bloat and rot."[11] Among Britain's North American cities New York bears the dubious distinction of being the setting for two bloody slave uprisings.

As notable and shocking as these northern racial insurrections may appear today, both were promptly buried by eighteenth-century New Yorkers, along with the corpses of the rebels, and practically expunged from the city's collective memory and its recorded history. Their recent unearthing by Le Pore and historians of *The 1619 Project* provide vivid support for the project's creator, Nicole Hannah-Jones, when she observes that "the vision of the past" that she absorbed as a Black Iowa teenager "from high school textbooks, television, and the local history museum depicted a world . . . where Black people did not exist."[12] The history of New York City as it was written well into the twentieth century reflected white America's historical amnesia concerning Black America.

By the early nineteenth century slavery, although very much in evidence in New York City, maintained a progressively lower profile in the rapidly growing metropolis than it had commanded during the colonial period. However, beginning around 1820 the booming market for cotton became a major element in assuring Gotham's continued prosperity, and the lucrative cotton trade thus had the ironic effect of reinforcing slavery's centrality to the city's commercial fortunes. The Brown family's direct solicitation of "southern friends . . . disposed" to doing business with their firm furnishes concrete evidence of the way the burgeoning demand for raw cotton cemented increasingly strong economic and cultural ties between New York City's wealthy businessmen and bankers and the plantation South in the first half of the nineteenth century. From the 1820s through the 1850s the region's merchants and planters—often with their wives and their enslaved in tow—flocked to New York to what John Hope Franklin has characterized as "the hub of trade between the

North and South as well as other parts of the country and, indeed, the world." Ira Berlin and Leslie Harris observe that these southern visitors would "attend to business, seek the latest fashions, and marvel at the great metropolis. It was only natural that their business partners entertained them in their homes, sharing fine wines, sumptuous meals, and perhaps a good cigar. Together they attended New York's theater, took the waters at New York's spas, and cheered the horses at New York's tracks." Such social intimacy and the family connections that not infrequently emerged from it "literally made New York an outpost of Southern culture."[13]

Even though the extensive interregional social contacts occasioned by the highly profitable trade in cotton were largely felicitous for both parties in the decades of the 1820s and 1830s, by the 1840s and 1850s these relations had become more fraught with hostile and ambivalent feelings, especially on the part of southerners. As sectional tensions deepened over the institution of chattel slavery upon which the lucrative cotton trade was established, southern planters became more and more critical of what they considered New York's tepid and inadequate support for the peculiar institution that made the hundreds of thousands of cotton bales possible. At the same time, they could not ignore the reality that they remained dependent on Gotham's merchants to guarantee for their region its "most regular form of interregional connection in the years leading to the Civil War." Like it or not—and often neither southerners nor New Yorkers did like it—Gotham's economic primacy would make the city a crucial "hinge of union," attaching North to South despite the strain of increasingly heavy political pressures exerted by abolitionist forces.[14]

The strong links between New York's merchants and bankers and the South's planter elite had an inevitable effect on the city's culture and politics, assuring that Gotham would remain largely sympathetic to southern economic interests and generally supportive of the slave system upon which the region's plantation economy rested. Though southern journalist James De Bow might have been exaggerating somewhat when he opined that Manhattan's economic fortunes were "almost as dependent on Southern slavery as Charleston itself," few would have disputed the reality that by 1830 Gotham far surpassed both Boston and

Philadelphia in its dependence on its trade with the South. It was thus hardly surprising that by 1835, as Phillip Foner has demonstrated, Gotham's commercial establishment had come overwhelmingly to believe that "the agitation of the slave question and the interference with the right of Southern slave-holders" to own their chattel was "inexpedient, unjust and pregnant with evils." They also had concluded that the dissolution of the Union over the issue of emancipation would lead to disruption of the cotton trade and economic catastrophe.[15] Preservation of New York's economic dominance, they believed, was dependent upon the preservation of the Union; and in the decades preceding the Civil War no group was more diligent than Gotham's commercial elite in urging sectional comity, even if that comity required that the North tolerate the South's peculiar institution.

The willingness of New York's business community to abide slavery in the interests of order and commercial prosperity at least partly explains the glacially slow evolution of the antislavery movement in New York—city and state—during the eighty-year period between national independence and the Civil War. Even before the flourishing of the nineteenth-century cotton trade with the South, Gotham had been distinguished from its rivals, Boston and Philadelphia, by the robust presence of slavery in its economic life. During periods of both the seventeenth and eighteenth centuries it had been home to what Berlin terms "the largest urban slave population in mainland North America, with more slaves than any other city on the continent." Slaves had constituted as much as a quarter of colonial New York's labor force, a reliance that modern New Yorkers, in yet another deft display of historical amnesia, have chosen to ignore. And if slavery was a significant part of the culture and economic life of Manhattan, it was even more in evidence across the East River in Brooklyn and the other Dutch-dominated farming communities that made up King's County on Long Island. Slavery may have declined after the Revolutionary War "in most Northern cities for economic, religious, and philosophical reasons and in response to African American protest." But this decline was hard to detect in the greater New York City area. In 1790 more than half of Brooklyn's residents were slaveholders. And outside Brooklyn the percentage of households owning slaves in 1800 ranged between 70 and 80 percent.[16]

In light of New York's seventeent and eighteenth century dependence on and toleration of slavery and of its nineteenth-century dependence on the southern cotton trade, it is hardly surprising that the process of

emancipating its enslaved required more than half a century of strenuous political effort and was accomplished only through a series of in-
cremental and much-debated legislative measures, suggesting both the
degree to which New York was beholden to slavery and the limited influence of antislavery sentiment in the city. Even as Black New Yorkers
moved slowly toward freedom they faced "vicious popular prejudice,"
both from those supporting slavery and those opposed to it. Though the
state of New York finally moved to abolish slavery in 1817, the law stipu-
lated that slaves born before July 4, 1799, would not be free until July 4,
1827. Even on that date children born to enslaved mothers on the eve
of July 4, 1827, would remain legally apprenticed to their white masters
until they were twenty-one. Thus, some Black New Yorkers remained
without their freedom until 1848. Of all the northern states the only one
to outlast New York in the preservation of slavery was New Jersey.[17]

As New York City slowly disentangled itself from the institution of
slavery, through the early and mid-decades of the nineteenth century,
it remained a relatively hostile place for its Black residents compared
to Philadelphia and Boston. The antagonism was particularly virulent
toward those thought to be runaways. Indeed, as Jonathan Wells has
noted, the municipal police force made no effort to conceal the fact that
it willingly "collected reward money for returning runaways, essentially
serving as a patrol force for southern masters." Black New Yorker David
Ruggles, a prominent participant in Gotham's Underground Railroad,
ironically declared the police and other citizens dedicated to catching
runaways to be members of the "New York Kidnapping Club." Wells describes this loose organization as a "powerful and far-reaching collection
of police officers, political authorities, judges, lawyers, and slave traders
who terrorized the City's Black residents throughout the early nineteenth century." These zealous kidnappers, he charges, were cheered on
by a Wall Street business community, who supported the capturing and
return of fugitives "so that peace with the slave South remained intact."[18]

New York's reputation as an urban center dominated by southern
sympathizers and defenders of the region's peculiar institution was but-
tressed by the fact that during the first half of the nineteenth century
Gotham was not only the plantation South's major commercial partner,
the city was also the epicenter of the nation's illegal slave trade, profitably conveying thousands of enchained Africans to North and South
America right up to the Civil War. From 1800 to 1860 New York built
more slave ships and sent out more slave expeditions than any other port

in the United States. The illegal enterprise was immensely profitable. Ron Soodalter has observed that "with the sale of an average cargo of 800 slaves bringing in as much as $960,000—a sum equaling tens of millions in today's currency—many a [New York] ship owner, investor and captain grew wealthy from the proceeds of a single successful voyage."[19]

The protracted death of slavery in New York and the city's well-earned reputation for supporting and even helping to sustain the system of chattel slavery were reflections of the unique economic bonding between Gotham and the antebellum South's planter elite through the first half of the nineteenth century. It was an economic and cultural attachment that made Gotham much more sympathetic to southern interests than either Boston to the north or Philadelphia to the south, and it was politically confirmed and cemented by the ascendancy of the Democratic Party to dominance both in the South and in Manhattan. David Quigley points out that leading New York Democrats of the prewar period, from Fernando Wood and John O'Sullivan to August Belmont and Samuel Tilden, consistency and unapologetically arose year after year to slavery's defense and unhesitatingly denounced abolitionists. These party leaders organized the Democratic Vigilance Committee in 1859 to help assure increasingly restive and alarmed slave owners that Gotham remained predominately and reliably prosouthern in spirit and in politics. On the eve of Lincoln's inauguration Mayor Fernando Wood urged New Yorkers to respond to the secession of the slave states by declaring its own independence. During the Civil War these prominent members of the city's political leadership became known and were widely condemned as "Copperheads," politicians who opposed the war and advocated a negotiated settlement with the Confederacy. Even after the Civil War Gotham continued to boast politicians like Samuel Tilden, who, serving as governor of the state of New York, continued to sympathize publicly with the plight of the defeated and subjugated white South. His failed 1876 presidential campaign "attracted its most passionate support in South Carolina and elsewhere in the former Confederacy."[20]

The gradual disengagement of New York City's politically dominant commercial elite from northern slave labor did not fundamentally alter its commitment to the preservation of slave labor in the South and the preservation of the commercial union between Gotham merchants and southern planters. One of these merchants explained their position succinctly and rather eloquently to one of Manhattan's most prominent abolitionists, Samuel J. May:

Mr. May, we are not such fools as not to know that slavery is a great evil, a great wrong. But a great portion of the property of the Southerners is invested under its sanction; and the business of the North, as well as of the South, has become adjusted to it. There are millions upon millions of dollars due from Southerners to the merchants and mechanics alone, the payment of which would be jeopardized by any rupture between the North and the South. We cannot afford, sir, to let you and your associates endeavor to overthrow slavery. It is not a matter of principles with us. It is a matter of business necessity. We mean, sir, to put you abolitionists down, by fair means if we can, by foul means if we must.[21]

By the early 1830s southerners were flocking to New York City in ever larger numbers, and many of them would subsequently agree with early tourist Ann Wagner that it was indeed an impressive place to see. Even a confirmed frontiersman like Davy Crockett was moved after a visit to hail the metropolis as "the London of America, the Big Prairie of the north, the Mississippi of commerce." But well before the rise of a strong abolitionist movement and before emotional debates over the issue of slavery created unbridgeable sectional divisions, southerners had begun to nurture deeply ambivalent attitudes toward the place upon which so much of their prosperity had come to depend. Along with the delight and wonder there coexisted a strong and growing hostility to what the South recognized as the growing wealth and power of Gotham and the consequent servitude of southerners to its economic hegemony. Beginning in the late 1830s a series of southern commercial conventions gave formal expression to this antipathy. As one delegate complained, the South stood before New York "in the attitude of feeding from her own bosom a vast population of merchants, ship-owners, capitalists and others, who, without the claim of her progeny, drink up the life-blood of her trade." If some southerners were inclined to view the cosmopolis as a place of marvels and wonder, others condemned it as a vampire-like beast or even as the commercial equivalent of the Whore of Babylon. The New Orleans *Crescent* urged its readers to stay away from a cesspool of "exorbitant profits, reckless . . . character," and "speculation, unflinching fraud and downright robbery."[22]

Southern resentment toward what it perceived as its economic submission to New York City extended to a resentment of the South's cultural and literary subservience to Gotham. Though generally not as intemperate as those who denounced the Manhattan's economic suzerainty, many southerners shared the vexation of Virginian James Heath over their region's subordination to its literary and publishing power. "I wish," Heath complained, "we had energy, capital and enterprise enough in the metropolis of the Old Dominion [Richmond] and in the Old Dominion herself to creep out of the vassalage that we are placed in, to New York literature." Heath's sense of the Old Dominion's cultural "vassalage" to Gotham was not simply an expression of sectional paranoia. John Hope Franklin has convincingly argued that in publishing as in cotton trading there was no real competition between New York and smaller southern publishing centers such as Richmond, Charleston, and New Orleans. Southern presses were so few and so primitive in their operation that they "could scarcely handle any large or complex" printing orders. Prominent southern writers sent their manuscripts to the North for publication, most frequently to Manhattan publishing houses.[23]

The history of the Crescent City's *De Bow's Review,* one of the most influential monthly magazines in the antebellum South, demonstrates the cultural subjection to New York that Heath so resented and deplored. Among southern journalists no one argued more passionately against the South's economic and cultural subservience to Gotham than its publisher, James De Bow. In one of his many columns dedicated to this subject he began his attack, like Heath had done with his Virginia readers, by taking his fellow Southerners to task for their cultural lethargy and their failure to demonstrate to the fullest the "high and liberal spirit of enterprise." This fatal deficiency had condemned the region to a dependence on New York enterprise, a dependence that had resulted in Gotham's ships transporting most of the South's cotton to market. It had brought millions upon millions of dollars into the coffers of Manhattan's merchant elite. Wealth that might have been had been employed to advance the region's development had instead been diverted to New York and "lost to the South." In cultural as well as commercial exchanges, De Bow argued, the South had allowed itself to be impoverished by the same lazy reliance. Southerners had sent their books to New York to be published, and they had visited the city and attended its concerts and theaters. But how many New Yorkers, De Bow asked bitterly, had bothered to read a book published in the South, to attend a southern college, or to visit a southern spa? How many had invested a portion of their "accumulated years" of profits from southern cotton on "Southern improvements"?[24]

Reading James De Bow's editorial one could hardly imagine that he would ever have allowed himself to descend into a relation of dependency with Gotham that he so deplored in his fellow southerners. But it was exactly this kind of dependency to which he seems to have been forced to submit during the years he edited and published his *Review*. In printing his magazine in New Orleans De Bow struggled during the journal's early years with local printers and their unreliable presses, going so far as to purchase an expensive machine on one of his visits to Manhattan. He apparently rationalized his purchase of a northern machine with the consolation that at least his southern magazine would be written and printed by southern hands. Alas, southern workmen were unable to efficiently operate his northern equipment. Ultimately De Bow chose to print in New York City the *Review* that he wrote and edited in New Orleans. Perhaps even more galling to De Bow was the fact that advertisements placed by Manhattan firms supplied his magazine with most of its revenue. As David Quigley ironically observes, this apostle of regional independence was forced to follow in his enterprise "the same New Orleans–New York circuit followed by Southern cotton."[25]

Conservative New Yorkers and Wall Street financiers were certainly not unaware of the verbal strikes lobbed their way by publications such as the New Orleans *Crescent* and *De Bow's Review*. In response, they tended either to ignore or to accept with a degree of complaisance the less intemperate southern complaints about their city, and they remained generally supportive of the South and of its peculiar institution right up to brink of the Civil War. But despite New York's broad accommodation to southern interests and opinion, it could never muster the sort of unqualified and unanimous support that southerners would demand of it with increasing stridency through the 1840s and 1850s. New York simply was not fashioned and never could be fashioned along the economic, political, social, and cultural lines of Charleston or New Orleans.

French aristocrat, abolitionist, and mid-nineteenth-century visitor to the city Agenor de Gasparin astutely recognized the unique political and cultural dynamic that, despite Gotham's marked prosouthern proclivities, sharply distinguished it from towns below the Mason-Dixon Line. He understood "the interests of this great city are bound up to such a degree with those of the cotton States, that, until very lately, New York might have been considered as a prolongation of the South." And he was accordingly not greatly shocked to attend a local Presbyterian church in which the minister declared to a sympathetic congregation that slavery

deserved to prevail "until the return of Jesus Christ." Such "cottony the-
ology" was to be expected in a metropolis knit by close economic ties to
the plantation. But Gasparin also recognized that this theological conservatism expressed only one aspect of the city's complex religious and political temperament. If one walked down the street from the proslavery
Presbyterian Church, for example, one entered a Congregational church
that protested slavery "with holy zeal" as fervently as the Presbyterians
up the street defended it.[26]

New York City's heterodox political atmosphere was recognized not
only by European observers like Gasparin but also by some who, though
born in the South, immigrated to and became citizens of Gotham. One
such immigrant was Abram Dittenhoefer, a native Charlestonian who
moved to Gotham with his "Democratic, pro-slavery parents" as a youth.
His subsequent education at Columbia and his pursuit of a law career
gradually turned him into both a Republican and a fervent supporter of
Abraham Lincoln. In his own words New York transformed him from a
loyal southerner into a "Southerner with Northern principles," a man
who lived ironically in a northern city in which resided "many Northern men with Southern principles." Dittenhoefer sensed not long after
moving to New York that it "was virtually an annex of the South" whose
pro-South orientation could be explained by "New York merchants having extensive and very profitable business relations with the merchants
south of the Mason and Dixon line." He was also acutely aware that Gotham's merchants generally had "for sale on their shelves their principles, together with their merchandise."[27]

From his perspective Abram Dittenhoefer could observe like Gasparin the complex mingling of abolition and proslavery sentiments that
characterized Gotham's culture. New York was a place where one could
attend and hear Boston-bred and Harvard-educated Wendell Phillips
deliver "a radical and brilliant anti-slavery speech at the old Tabernacle,
situated in Broadway below Canal Street." Indeed, that great venue for
abolitionist speakers would be filled, but most of the audience on this
occasion would be, in Dittenhoefer's words, "pro-slavery shouters" who
"rotten-egged Phillips during his address. With some friends I was present and witnessed this performance." And yet as heartened as southerners might be by New York's rough treatment of this emissary of New England abolitionism, they could never be entirely sure of the sympathies
of Gotham's citizens. For Dittenhoefer the confused "condition of things
in this pro-slavery city" was aptly illustrated by the following "amusing

incident." A southern buyer had placed a "large order for combs" with a Manhattan dealer in brushes and toilet articles. Not knowing that the dealer was a Quaker, the buyer had conditioned the purchase on the merchant's exerting "all his influence in favor of the South." In response the Quaker merchant had "coolly replied that the South would have to go lousy for a long time before he would sell his combs to them under any such conditions."[28]

The heterodox social and political climate that both Gasparin and Dittenhoefer observed in this rapidly growing and cosmopolitan American city was reflected in the variety of political opinions expressed in its journals and newspapers, a variety consonant with Manhattan's new-found role as the "nation's information center." If newspapers like James Gordon Bennett's *New York Herald* and William Cullen Bryant's *Evening Post* appealed to readers sympathetic to southern interests and to the region's peculiar institution, other city papers like Horace Greeley's *New York Tribune* and the *New York Times* raised powerful and eloquent anti-slave voices. In a city where Bennett's southern-inflected *Herald* reigned as the nation's most profitable daily newspaper, Greeley's abolitionist *Tribune* ran a very close second and its weekly edition was generally acknowledged to be the most widely distributed journal in America.[29]

It was just this quality of cultural and political heterodoxy that would continually disappoint and ultimately enrage southerners as they demanded New York's unconditional allegiance on the increasingly vexing issue of fugitive slaves. On one hand the business and political establishment of the city strenuously sought to support and enforce the Fugitive Slave Act when it was included as a key part of the Compromise of 1850, and they demonstrated their backing of the South and their commitment to the Union by organizing the Union Safety Committee. The membership of this organization read like a who's who of Gotham society and included names like William Astor, son of John Jacob Astor, and the Brown Brothers, who gave the largest single contribution to the committee's budget. As Eric Foner has pointed out, "only a handful" Gotham's tycoons refused to join. Yet those few but prominent holdouts included William Tappan, wealthy merchant and the city's most prominent abolitionist, and John Jay, grandson of the nation's first chief justice and one of a small number of lawyers willing to defend fugitive slaves in court.

At the same time as the Safety Committee was calling for full enforcement of the law and city police were zealously tracking down runaways, adopted New Yorker Sydney Howard Gay was actively ushering fugitive slaves through the city to safer refuges further north. Indeed, his Record of Fugitives compiled in 1855 and 1856 shows that he sent well over 200 slaves on to freedom. Gay was one of a small but highly effective group of abolitionists who through the New York Vigilance Committee moved three to four thousand slaves through the city north between 1835, the year of the committee's founding, and 1860. He would eventually be hired as a writer for Greeley's *New York Tribune*. Notwithstanding their relatively small numbers, Greeley, Gay, Arthur and Lewis Tappan, William Astor, and other committed New York abolitionists successfully worked to ensure that by the 1850s Gotham along with Philadelphia would function as "the central stations of that glorious humanitarian institution of modern times, the Underground Railroad."[30]

Despite the diligent efforts of Gotham's banking and merchant elite to demonstrate their loyalty to the South's increasingly irate and beleaguered planters by endorsing full enforcement of the Fugitive Slave Act, the case of escaped slave James Hamlet vividly illustrates how impossible it would prove to be for New Yorkers to achieve the broad consensus on the issue of runaway slaves that southerners demanded of them. Hamlet had fled Maryland with his family and resided in the city for two years. Discovering his whereabouts, his owner had waited for the new law to go into effect before having him seized on September 26, 1850, eight days after President Fillmore had signed the act. By the evening of the 26th a speedy hearing before a U.S. commissioner in which Hamlet had not been allowed to testify had ended with his being quickly escorted in handcuffs to a waiting steamboat. By September 27, when Hamlet's family learned of his seizure, he lay in a Baltimore prison.[31]

The response of New Yorkers to the railroading of Hamlet out of the city was immediate and indignant, and it extended across racial lines. Hearing that Hamlet's owner would allow him to purchase his freedom for $800, two thousand African Americans, "with a slight and visible sprinkling of white abolitionists," filled the Methodist Episcopal Zion Church to make contributions toward purchasing his freedom. Even more remarkably the *Journal of Commerce,* Gotham's staunchly prosouthern apologist for slavery, began its own fundraising campaign. The money was quickly procured, and John H. Woodgate, a "respectable" Wall Street businessman, carried it to Baltimore. Exactly one week after his arrest James Hamlet had returned to his family in New York a free man.[32]

The same city that had turned a blind eye to the building and outfitting of slave vessels had collectively—black and white citizens—

organized to purchase the freedom of a black slave. A solid majority of New Yorkers were no doubt content to support the South's "peculiar institution" if it remained decently contained below the Mason-Dixon Line. But on the matter of seizing a runaway like Hamlet—a gainfully employed family man—and peremptorily returning him to slavery, Gotham's citizens were decidedly more ambivalent and divided in their opinions. Despite the ministrations of their merchant elite on behalf of the South, the city's complex political and social culture made it impossible for Gotham's conservative political establishment to marshal the kind of unqualified popular support for slavery that the South demanded of it.

As New York continued to grow at an astonishing rate during the 1840s and 1850s into a large and increasingly cosmopolitan urban center, it grew unattached to its own dismantled institution of domestic slavery, less and less united on the broader issue of slavery in the Union, and consequently less and less culturally bonded to its slave-owning trading partners in the South. While the commitment to slavery grew ever stronger in most slave states through the first half of the nineteenth century, it grew progressively weaker in Gotham. Statistics illustrate this point. In 1790 blacks made up 2,500 of the city's 60,000 residents, a relatively small but quite visible minority in a town where one of every seventeen artisans was still a slave owner. By 1800 the black population had increased modestly to 3,500, but within one decade free black New Yorkers had come to outnumber slaves. At the dawning of a new century and even before the massive influx of southern cotton would weld New York's economy to the South, support for slavery had become, in the words of Edwin Burrows, "thinner and more fragile" than at any time in the previous century. In 1799 the state passed legislation ensuring gradual emancipation, an initiative that brought an unexpectedly rapid decline in slave owning in both state and city. By 1810 84 percent of the state's 9,000 blacks were free, compared to 33 percent in 1790.[33]

New York's gradual disentanglement from the institution of slavery would continue as the nineteenth century progressed. By July 4, 1827, the city's slave system was gone. The withering of demand for slave labor had been encouraged by the ever-increasing supply of cheap labor furnished by immigrants pouring into the metropolis from Europe. Though the free Black population of New York continued to increase briskly, growing from 2,500 in 1790 to 14,000 in 1830, Gotham's total population increased even more dramatically. As a result of this explosive population growth Blacks declined as a percentage of the population, falling from 9 to 7 percent during the single decade of the 1820s.[34] Southerners who visited New York City during the antebellum decades could not have been unaware of the demographic and cultural changes that were making Gotham less and less comfortable with the idea of chattel slavery. New Yorkers continued to vie successfully for southern cotton and to welcome southern visitors with open arms, but they would increasingly view the peculiar institution upon which their southern friends and clients had established their wealth as an unpleasant anachronism.

———————

In August of 1831, at about the time southerners were beginning to question the wisdom of allowing New York to control their region's trade and banking, Nat Turner led a bloody and shocking slave rebellion in Virginia that brutally shattered the South's carefully cultivated myth of benevolent and paternal planter aristocrats lording over placid and contented Negro slaves. Turner's insurrection resulted in what historians have described as the last lengthy and free discussion of slavery south of the Mason-Dixon Line. The debate took place in Richmond in the Virginia legislature during January of 1832. It resulted in the decisive defeat of the state's antislavery forces. For all practical purposes the slave question was closed in the Old Dominion. And as Virginia went, so went all the slaveholding South. With the continued profitability of slavery, especially in the Cotton Belt, and with mounting attacks on the institution from increasingly emboldened abolitionists, the South hunkered down in a defensive intellectual posture, one that grew more belligerent and defiant as the Union moved ever closer to the Civil War. For white southerners the survival of the plantation system seemed to demand absolute racial and ideological unity. The departure of any southerner from the tenets of proslave orthodoxy represented a kind of treason, a betrayal of one's race and an assault on the very foundations of southern society. The defense of slavery would lead tragically to the region's savage intolerance of antislave opinion and to what Fred Hobson has characterized as the closing of the southern mind.[35]

By the politically contentious and increasingly tense 1850s the beleaguered slaveholders of the South looked toward New York City with increased impatience and urgency. Here was a place that for decades had waxed fat off the products of southern slavery and that had welcomed southerners to come and spend their fortunes in its hotels, restaurants, and emporiums. It was time for Gotham to rise with one voice and come to the defense of the South and of slavery. And what sort of resistance to abolitionist attacks on their peculiar institution did the region expect from the merchants and bankers who they assumed ruled Manhattan? To have some idea of the response that the slave states demanded from prosouthern New Yorkers it would be instructive to look at how they themselves had dealt with those fellow southerners who had dared publicly to criticize or question slavery. Precious few had chosen since 1832 to question the South's racial orthodoxy, but of these few the most interesting of the region's antebellum iconoclasts was North Carolina native Hinton Rowan Helper.

Hinton Helper would have seemed an ideal candidate for critiquing and questioning southern slavery. Born and bred in North Carolina, he was no friend of the black race, and he was not much interested in examining the ethical or moral dimensions of the institution. His overriding concern, expressed vigorously in *The Impending Crisis of the South,* was with the calamitous effects of the slave labor system on the economic wellbeing of the white middle and working classes. He argued "that slavery, and nothing but slavery" had "retarded the progress and prosperity of our portion of the Union; depopulated and impoverished our cities by forcing the more industrious and enterprising natives of the soil to emigrate to the Free States; brought our domain under a sparse and inert population by preventing foreign immigration; made us tributary to the North and reduced us to the humiliating condition of mere provincial subjects in fact, though not in name."[36]

Helper was convinced that only by destroying chattel slavery could the "six millions of non-slaveholding whites" liberate themselves from what he described as a "second degree of slavery." And by whom were these nominally free southern yeomen enslaved? They were in bondage to the great planters and their commercial allies who had achieved complete domination over the South's political system. Even though nonslaveholders outnumbered slaveholders by "six to one," he argued, this massive majority had "never yet had any uncontrolled part or lot in framing the laws under which" they lived. Consequently, there was in the southern states "no legislation except for the benefit of slavery, and slaveholders." The planter elite had created "a cunningly devised mockery of freedom," extending to middling southern farmers, laborers, and craftsmen a dubious "privilege," "a shallow and circumscribed participation in the political movements that usher slaveholders into office."[37]

In *The Impending Crisis of the South* Hinton Helper appealed to the mass of fellow white southerners to divorce themselves from the siren call of white racial unity, to see that their economic and social interests would never be furthered by binding themselves loyally to the great planters. Nonslaveholders needed to recognize that slaveholders were "arrogant demagogues whom you have elected to offices of honor and profit," men who had "hoodwinked you, trifled with you, and used you as mere tools for the consummation of their wicked designs." Only when middling southerners understood their true relation to the institution of slavery could they liberate themselves from their own servitude and elect leaders who would level the playing field for white laborers by heavily taxing slave owners and using the revenue to finance the shipment of inferior Blacks back to Africa.[38]

When he published his appeal in 1857 Helper obviously entertained the hope that thoughtful fellow southerners, "true-hearted, candid and intelligent" men, would read his book. Indeed, he allowed himself to imagine that these southern readers might be "legion." In fact, though many people in the South knew about his book, only a very small number read it, and nearly all these readers seem to have found *The Impending Crisis* to be both a hideous and an extremely dangerous text. Indeed, Robert Downs has caustically observed that it was nearly impossible to obtain a copy of Helper's work in any part of the South. Many legislatures passed laws "forbidding its possession or sale." Men were hanged for possessing copies. Mobs in Helper's native North Carolina "drove several ministers out of the state for defending the book, and there was a public book burning in one town. In other slave states men were mobbed and beaten for having Helper's work in their homes." Those select southern critics who reviewed *Impending Crisis* made clear why it was a poisonous work not safe to be placed in the hands of readers. It was "a 'deadly attack' upon their 'peculiar institution'"; it was also "incendiary, insurrectionary, and hostile to the peace and domestic tranquility of the country." Helper himself was the lowest type of man, a despised "traitor to his native sod and native skies." Of humanity's "miserable renegades and mendacious miscreants," he was surely among the worst.[39]

Though idealistically Helper may have hoped for a receptive and large southern audience, practically he seems to have known better than to trust his region's capacity for intelligence and clear thinking on the issue of slavery. By the time his book was published he had conveniently located himself north of the Mason-Dixon in New York City. He had initially intended to publish his work in Baltimore, but slaveholding Maryland forbade the publication of any writing intended to "excite discontent amongst the people of color of this state." Gotham would prove a less hostile milieu for Helper. Prosouthern journalists like James Gordon Bennett warned that his book contained gunpowder enough "to blow the Union to the Devil." But prominent abolitionist editor Horace Greeley praised *The Impending Crisis* and prompted the Republican Party to print and distribute 100,000 copies of an abridged edition during the 1860 presidential campaign.[40] Thanks to his move to New York City, he would find a wide audience and become as celebrated north of the Mason-Dixon as he was reviled in his native South.

Though undoubtedly disappointed by having failed to connect with a southern audience, he could not have been altogether surprised. For in *The Impending Crisis* he had brilliantly identified the homogeneity and conformity of the South's thinking about the issue of slavery and the monolithic solidity of his region's slave culture. He had diagnosed the stultification of "the entire mind of the South" that was the terrible result of its "acquiescence with Slavery," and he fully understood the disastrous consequences of this blind acquiescence for open inquiry and intellectual diversity: "Free speech is an institution almost unknown at the South. Free speech is considered as treason against Slavery; and when people dare neither speak nor print their thoughts, free thought itself is well-nigh extinguished. All that can be said in defense of human bondage, may be spoken freely; but question either its morality or its policy, and the terrors of lynch-law are at once invoked to put down the pestilent heresy." It is extraordinarily ironic that in this passage Hinton Helper anticipated with uncanny accuracy the hysterical response with which his fellow southerners would greet *The Impending Crisis of the South*. He would pay the price for frankly and fearlessly articulating what twentieth century critics of southern culture would come to understand decades hence, the inconvenient truth that "not only had slavery affected Southern prosperity, it had also closed the southern mind."[41]

As we will see in the following chapters, the love-hate affair between New York City and the plantation South that had begun so hopefully for both parties by 1820 was fated to end badly. True, despite initial southern apprehension about Gotham's economic and cultural hegemony, the entente between the two parties had been relatively easy to maintain in the 1820s and 1830s. But as abolitionist sentiment grew stronger in the 1840s and 1850s and as New York rapidly transformed itself into a more cosmopolitan and complexly structured urban center, interregional relations inevitably grew more and more fraught. While slavery led the southern mind to close and retreat from the world—witness the reception to Hinton Helper's book—enormous prosperity brought on by the cotton trade expanded both New York City's challenges and problems and its civic ambitions and cultural horizons. By the 1850s southern defenders of slavery were insistently calling on Gotham to support their cause by behaving politically more like a provincial southern city, the very thing that New York was less and less inclined and able to do.

In *Gotham: A History of New York City from 1898 to 1919* Edwin Burrows and Mike Wallace give a detailed analysis of the way that this "most southern-oriented of northern cities" sought to maintain its alliance with the South in the 1850s by soundly rejecting abolitionist Republicanism. But this same analysis also shows how the political and cultural texture of the metropolis had become too complex to produce the kind of monolithic popular support for slavery that the slave states demanded from New Yorkers. The city Burrows and Wallace describe contained not two but four competing and overlapping political cultures. It was broadly dominated by "Metropolitan Dixiecrats," the shippers, bankers, stockbrokers, wholesalers, and merchants who thrived on the southern trade and pressed for conciliation with the South on the issue of slavery. But this political group was substantially augmented by large numbers of working-class Democrats, men whose economic interests were often in conflict with those of Wall Street. Though they did not share the wealthy merchant's class biases, New York's workers did share the belief that southern trade was vital to their prosperity. In addition, many Irish and German laborers resented the anti-immigrant snobbery of men they considered to be elitist Republicans. They also largely rejected the Republican doctrine that the fledging labor unions that city workers were fighting so hard to establish were a despotic infringement on the principle of "free labor," and they were equally scornful of Black Republicanism's professed concern for the welfare of inferior Blacks.[42] Combining wealthy merchants and humble migrant laborers, this "Dixiecrat" assemblage was not a completely stable political entity, and, whatever their prejudices against those they considered an inferior Black race, neither part of this coalition strongly supported the idea that slavery should be permanently preserved or the proposition that the institution should be allowed to expand into the nation's western territories.

On the other side of the city's political spectrum were two more constituencies, relatively small in numbers but "strategically placed," that would make Gotham's heterogeneous political culture even more complex. "Black Republicans," free men of color, constituted a relatively small minority, but they nonetheless strived mightily and with some success to oppose both segregation within the city and slavery in the nation at large. They were united with "White Republicans," another comparatively small but highly influential group that was composed of journalists, like William Cullen Bryant, ministers, like Henry Ward Beecher, and some of the leading members of the Wall Street business community, such as William Dodge.[43] As described by Burrows and Wallace, New York was by the 1850s a culturally diverse and politically complex city that was incapable of speaking with one voice on any issue, least of all on the thorny issue of slavery.

Amazingly, as slave states moved ever closer to secession in the 1850s, their leaders and molders of opinion seem to have convinced themselves that prosouthern elements in New York City could support them by approximating in Manhattan the homogeneity of opinion about slavery that they had so swiftly attained in their own region after 1830. They deluded themselves with the fanciful conviction that proslave New Yorkers could assert their authority to suppress abolitionist voices with a thoroughness and ruthlessness akin to their own thorough suppression of Hinton Helper's *The Impending Crisis of the South.* The institution of slavery and the survival of the southern way of life rested on the assumption that all whites, slaveholders and non-slaveholders, were destined to hold sway over all Blacks. Southern whites, regardless of wealth or social position, would be unified and vitally sustained in the face of an inferior but potentially restive Black slave population by union in the brotherhood of white-skinned honor and racial superiority.[44] This was a concept so potent that not even a cogent and thought-provoking attack on it by one of their own could induce them to question it. Why could an idea of racial supremacy so evident to the South not be embraced with equal fervor by a city that had benefitted so enormously from the slave system? Why could white New Yorkers not pledge themselves as wholeheartedly as southerners had to the concept of chattel slavery?

The reality that southerners could not recognize was that, as dependent as New York seemed to be on the South's slave-produced cotton, it was an American city, not a southern American city; and it could never be entirely constrained and defined like Charleston or New Orleans or Richmond by the cotton trade or by the institution of slavery. Gotham was rapidly evolving into not only the new nation's largest and grandest metropolis, but also into one of the world's largest urban centers. With its propulsive capitalist dynamism, it represented, for better or worse, America's future. In his *The Island at the Center of the World,* Russell Shorto persuasively proposes the idea that a crucial key to New York's rapid rise into the ranks of great world cities was its general commitment to "tolerance, openness, and free trade," which it had successfully yoked to its remarkable entrepreneurial energy. These were much the same qualities that had impressed Agenor de Gasparin on the eve of the Civil War. A hundred years earlier they had also awed English visitor Andrew Burnaby. Though by 1760 about half of New York's inhabitants remained Dutch, he observed that the other half of the city's population was composed of so many "different nations, different languages, and different religions" that it was "almost impossible to give them any precise or determinate character."[45] To this English vicar the wonder was that such a mongrel mix could fruitfully coexist and collectively build a thriving new American city.

By the 1850s southerners who felt themselves threatened by a rising tide of northern abolitionism seem finally to have concluded that New York's "mongrel mix" was incapable of offering them the resolute support they required for the preservation of their plantation culture. At this point they decisively turned in their polemical writing and in their fictional treatment of Gotham to a full-bore attack on what they considered their erstwhile ally's treachery and hypocrisy. New Yorkers, southern writers concluded, had had their cake and eaten it too, gorging themselves on the profits of slave-produced cotton while refusing to fully endorse the slavery that had produced it. And southerners refined their attacks on Gotham by focusing on what they considered the city's own form of slavery, the wage slavery that had resulted from its embrace of unrestrained industrial capitalism. In their travel diaries and letters home to their kin, southern visitors from Davy Crockett to Edgar Allan Poe would describe these rotten fruits of wage slavery—Gotham's teeming slums and the appalling gulf between opulent wealth and destitute poverty—with shock and disapproval.

The equivalence that defenders of the plantation elite sought to establish between southern slavery and Gotham's wage slavery was most persuasively and cynically articulated by South Carolina senator James

Henry Hammond in 1858 in his speech "On the Admission of Kansas." In "all social systems," Hammond argued, "there must be a class to do the menial duties, to perform the drudgery of life. That is, a class requiring but a low order of intellect and but little skill." This essential and inferior class constituted "the very mud-sill of society and of political government." All societies were built on such a mud-sill social foundation. Fortunately, he informed his Senate audience, the South had "found a race adapted to the purpose" of functioning as a social mud-sill. White southerners had purchased and put to work a race of African slaves, "inferior" to their white masters, "but eminently qualified in temper, in vigor, in docility" to serve their proper "purposes."[46]

Casting his eye over the Senate chamber, Hammond noted that New York senator William Seward had protested that nearly the whole world had abolished slavery. "Aye, the *name*," he cleverly quibbled, "but not the *thing*." In fact, New York's "hireling class of manual laborers," he argued, were "essentially slaves. The difference between us is, that our slaves are hired for life and well compensated; there is no starvation, no begging, no want of employment among our people." Indeed, Hammond concluded, southern chattel slavery was a positive improvement over northern wage slavery. "Why, you meet more beggars in one day, in any single street of the city of New York, than you would meet in a lifetime in the whole South." And while poor urban whites had been dehumanized by their virtual enslavement to a rapacious economic system, black slaves had been "elevated from the condition in which God first created them" by the agency of their benevolent plantation masters.[47]

Hammond was partly correct in his observations about the by-products of wage slavery in New York City. Gotham did indeed contain awful slums, and on its streets one not infrequently encountered beggars. But in his speech the South Carolinian deftly ignored profound differences between Gotham and the plantation South with respect to their treatment of a debased laboring class. The most signal of these distinctions was that the city's menial workers were not chattel slaves. As free American citizens they possessed a significant degree of human agency, and through the middle decades of the nineteenth century they frequently, and sometimes successfully, rose in opposition to their mercantile masters. Moreover, their plight over time stirred the consciences of an increasing number of affluent New Yorkers.

As early as 1808 Gotham's shoemakers had been hauled into court by their "masters" and successfully prosecuted "for uniting to raise their wages." But though the city's merchant masters controlled the courts and the legislature, both skilled and unskilled workers continued to strike for higher wages and better working conditions. The financial panic of 1837 brought both walkouts and expanded union organizing drives. In 1836 two-thirds of New York's workingmen had enrolled in fifty-two confederated unions. Though this nascent labor movement was soon "all but demolished" by the depressed economy of the early 1840s, it resurged in the early 1850s, notably among German cabinetmakers and Irish, German, and American tailors. The worker organizations these men created were not united. They often rose and quickly disappeared. Their strikes were usually broken by scab replacement workers, and they engaged in occasionally bloody clashes with an unsympathetic municipal police force. They never achieved their demands for a ten-hour workday and the abolition of child labor,[48] but neither did their organizations disappear. In fact, they remained a permanent and significant part of New York's mid-nineteenth century social and economic fabric.

As New York's turbulent early labor history suggests, the city's working-class Democrats were a different breed from those Democrats residing south of the Mason-Dixon Line, especially from wealthy slave-owning political figures like James Henry Hammond. Gotham's laboring men generally tolerated the institution of slavery in the South, recognizing that slave-produced cotton was crucial to the flourishing economy of their city and to the business enterprises in which so many of them toiled. But unlike the masses of quiescent white southern laborers who largely supported the political agenda of their region's great planters, the city's working men wanted no part of a slave society. They fully recognized that when James Hammond described the presence in all societies of a class possessing "a low order of intellect" and "little skill" that existed to "perform" the "menial duties" and the "drudgery of life," he was describing them. In the arch-conservative South Carolinian's articulation, they were the "mudsills," and they knew it. They were also intelligent enough realize that slave-owners like Hammond represented a threat to their livelihoods, their dignity, and their liberty.

Despite their understanding of the grave danger that the slavocracy posed to their well-being, New York's laboring class did not desert the party of Jefferson and Jackson. Unlike many workers in other parts of the Union, Gotham's laborers remained distrustful of the Whig-Republican principle of "free labor," and they also scorned what they considered the elitist Republican concern for both enslaved and free

Blacks. Working New Yorkers would never move en masse into the Republican column. But as Michael Woods has observed, they would join their northern brethren in appropriating Hammond's pejorative mudsill label, transforming the "epithet into a humorously subversive badge of regional and class identity." As we shall see, these laborers, like the wealthy merchants and businessmen for whom they worked, would ultimately throw in their lot with the Union, the abolition of slavery, and the dignity of the common worker. In the early days of the Civil War the antislave *New York Tribune* would proudly announce that on the nation's battlefields "the phrase 'I am a mud-sill' is now a common expression of the soldiers who fight for liberty."[49]

The tumultuous but largely fruitless early labor movement in New York City ultimately accomplished something far more significant than the winning of an occasional strike. It succeeded over the decades between 1820 and 1860 in raising the consciences of an increasing number of affluent New Yorkers to the plight of the city's working class. In the 1820s native sons Langton Byllesby (*Observations on the Sources and Effects of Unequal Wealth*) and Thomas Skidmore (*The Rights of Man to Property*) had raised their voices to argue that the new capitalist-industrial order was ushering Gotham into an ominous age of maldistributed wealth and rising social inequality. By 1860 the destitute condition of many of New York's working poor and patently appalling living conditions in the city's slums had combined to alter the consciences of a growing number of well-off, reform-minded New Yorkers. Many of these civic reformers were gravitating toward the melioristic editorial stance of *Harper's Magazine,* a monthly that had been launched in Manhattan in 1850. "It is reasonable and natural," the editor maintained, "that in view of the splendid trappings of our growing houses . . . that the gas-fitters, and cordwainers and ladies' shoemakers, and saloon-servants should hold out their hands for their share of the excess."[50]

Of course, James Henry Hammond would doubtlessly have scoffed at Gotham's reformers by observing that the South had no need to struggle to amend the deplorable misery of its mud-sill laborers. For as he argued in his 1858 Senate speech, a benevolently patriarchal plantation system presided over by a superior white race ruled its inferior Black slaves firmly, justly, and benignly. Unlike New York City's ruthlessly competitive, profit-obsessed business model, the slave South, he confidently declared, had produced a region of happy and contented free whites and equally contented and well-fed Black slaves, a land distinguished by a profound harmony of "political and social institutions." This harmony had vouch-safed the South "a frame of society, the best in the world, and an extent of political freedom, combined with entire security, such as no other people ever enjoyed upon the face of the earth."[51] In contrast to the hellish landscape of Manhattan's urban slums, Hammond projected with what seemed to be complete sincerity the vision of a peaceful, harmonious, and secure southern slavocracy. The region's writers would promptly take their fictional cue from Hammond and others like him, detailing in their essays, travel narratives, and novels the horrors of the city's slums and contrasting them with an Edenic plantation setting in which refined white planter aristocrats ruled humanely over their contented and loyal slaves.

If Hammond's view of New York City's wage slaves might be charita-bly judged as containing an element of truth, the contrasting vision of his native South as a nearly perfect political and social model can be more easily dismissed as a lie. To what extent did he really believe that the harmonious and free South he posited in the Senate was real? We cannot know the answer, but historical analysis has demolished the Eden that Hammond and other like-minded southerners created to justify slavery, secession, Civil War, and the eventual suppression of free Blacks into the straitjacket of second-class citizenship. For over a century historians have labored to show that the plantation system still so alluring to so many Americans was anything but a benign anachronism, and recent scholarship has further clarified that the South's slave-produced cotton was intimately tied to the very capitalistic brutalities that had horrified southerners when they visited antebellum New York City.

In his seminal and massively detailed analysis, *River of Dark Dreams*, historian Walter Johnson focuses on the plantations of the lower Mis-sissippi valley, where the greatest amount of raw cotton was produced at the lowest cost by largest body of slave labor for the highest profit margin. He decisively demonstrates that the cotton economy of the lower South was an integral part of what became one of the world's first global capitalist enterprises. In this highly lucrative market "credit chased cotton from the metropolitan banks of Europe to every plantation outpost," and "the rate of exploitation of slaves in a field in Mississippi, measured in pounds per day, was keyed to the standards of the Exchange in Liverpool, and the labor of the mill-hands in Manchester."[52] Much like modern agribusiness, the production of cotton in the plantation South was capital intensive, and the enslaved were first and foremost for their owners capital, not human beings.

Johnson shows that slaves functioned in the production of mass quantities of cotton as abstract units of production. To maintain maximum production slaves who failed to perform according to their master's standards were subject to discipline, commonly and often harshly applied by the lash of an overseer. Indeed, the lash served "as a sort of universal equivalent, a mechanism by which severity of mistakes could be scaled into an astringent standard measure." In *River of Dark Dreams* the bucolic plantation reveals itself as a brutally exploitive unit of production in which the darker the enslaved laborer's skin color, the more brutal was his or her exploitation. Cotton was harvested in the fields by those with the blackest skin, while light-toned mulattos served their masters in the planter's mansion. Such distinctions were essential to the white aristocracy's distinguishing "between domestic and economic spaces, between the refined lives they lived and the contaminating soil from which they drew their wealth." Hammond's benign plantation patriarchy is banished from Johnson's analysis. It is properly replaced by an understanding of the plantation as a grotesquely capitalistic order, pragmatically and centrally "premised on using people as things to produce other things."[53]

Appearing soon after Walter Johnson's study, Edward Baptist's *The Half Has Never Been Told: Slavery and the Making of American Capitalism* drives another heavy nail into the coffin of Edward Hammond's civilized plantation patriarchy. Baptist's analysis emphasizes the intimate links between the southern plantation and the imperialistic and capitalistic forces that fueled America's westward settlement. It focuses on the expansion of the slave South after the 1780s from a narrow coastal Atlantic strip southwest to a "subcontinental empire." Like Johnson, Baptist emphasizes the essentially capitalist and fundamentally imperialist nature of that savage territorial conquest. "Entrepreneurial enslavers," he observes, "moved more than one million enslaved people by force, from the communities that survivors of the slave trade from Africa had built in the South and in the West to vast territories that were seized—also by force—from their Native American inhabitants." As a result of the explosive growth of the enslaved population from one to five million, the rapidly dilating institution of slavery brought fantastic wealth, not only to the South, but also to a powerful and expanding nation. Both region and nation, Baptist argues, were propelled by the same ruthlessly aggressive entrepreneurial spirit. "White enslavers were able to force enslaved African American migrants to pick cotton faster and more efficiently than free people. Their practices rapidly transformed the southern states into the dominant force in the global cotton market, and cotton was the world's most widely traded commodity at the time, as it was the key raw material during the first century of the industrial revolution."[54]

Thanks to the scholarly work of historians like Johnson and Baptist, James Hammond's Edenic plantation patriarchy lies today in ruins. But his concept was alive and well in 1858, and it would undergird both the South's defense of slavery and its vigorous polemical and fictional attacks on New York City. Sharply alert to Gotham's serious economic and social dissonances, southern apologists and writers remained completely and obstinately blind to the even more profound discordances of their own society. They wrapped the horrors of their peculiar institution into the romantic folds of kindly plantation paternalism. In their minds it was New York, not the South, that was guilty of damnable hypocrisy and double dealing. And it was Gotham, their erstwhile ally and trading partner, that continually disappointed them in the end, failing to fully embrace the Fugitive Slave Act, failing to prevent the election of Abraham Lincoln, and finally failing to assure their region's bloodless exit from the Union.

As armies massed on both sides of the Potomac in the spring of 1861, the South bitterly viewed itself as the aggrieved party in their forty-year love-hate affair with Gotham. The southern mind judged "Execrable New York" to be an inconstant and hypocritical false friend, worthy of being "blotted from the list of cities."[55] Having fully anathematized Gotham, southerners proceeded to follow the path to war, death, destruction, and defeat. After years of futile attempts to placate the slave states, New York City finally turned its back on its former allies and, risking economic disaster, took the path to Union and abolition. Ultimately the South would lie in ruins and a burgeoning, post–Civil War New York would achieve its ambition of becoming one of the modern world's great cities.

TWO

THE GREATEST EMPORIUM OF THE WESTERN HEMISPHERE

THE SOUTH TRAVELS TO GOTHAM

ON THE 17TH of September 1818, at about the same time that Ann Wagner was regaling her son in Charleston with descriptions of the pleasures of New York, young Arthur Morson of Fredericksburg, Virginia, was also describing to his father the wonders of America's fastest-growing city. On his first day in Manhattan, he had gone to see city hall, "a most stupendous building" fronted completely with beautiful marble. Afterward he had visited the state prison to view inmates working industriously at various tasks. "Some," he observed, "were making shoes, boots, saddles, while others were weaving, spinning, winding." Perhaps because the young Virginian would be attending Yale the following year, he seems to have been intent on impressing his father with the educational and self-improving nature of his touristic pursuits. In his letter of September 21, for example, he announced that on Sunday he had visited, not one, but three churches and that he had attended both Presbyterian and Episcopal services.[1]

Whether they traveled, like Arthur Morson, for self-improvement, for business, for pleasure, or for a combination of all these motives, by the 1820s southern planters and their families, buoyed substantially by highly profitable and rapidly increasing sales of cotton, were arriving in ever-increasing numbers to Gotham for both business and pleasure.

But even before the nineteenth-century explosion of cotton production precipitated an annual summer migration of thousands of visitors from the South, southern travelers—especially those living in the Atlantic coastal states—had found their way to New York in significant numbers during the Revolutionary and Postrevolutionary decades of the late eighteenth century. One of these early tourists had been Virginian St. George Tucker, law professor at the College of William and Mary, legal mentor to John Marshall, inventor, poet, horticulturist, supporter of the Revolution, and stepfather to John Randolph of Roanoke. This son of the Enlightenment had been drawn north in 1786 on legal business, and when he arrived with his wife on a hot July morning at the southern tip of Manhattan, he entered a small but thriving city of 30,000 inhabitants, approximately one quarter of the population it would boast roughly thirty years later when Ann Wagner and Arthur Morson visited.

Traveling in the United States during the 1780s was not for the faint of heart. Tucker's wife, Frances Bland Randolph, was in frail health, and as a result of a rough sea voyage when she stepped off the boat, she was extremely seasick and fatigued. Nonetheless both she and her husband were obliged to "to walk above a mile" over "horrid pavement" to lodgings in "intolerably hot" rooms. Tucker's disagreeable surprise at encountering Gotham's frequently torrid and humid summer weather was one that would be shared by countless southern guests over the coming centuries. Fortunately, the couple's spirits rapidly improved, partly because they found so many congenial Virginians already in the city and partly because they found more suitable rooms nearer the center of town amid many attractions and activities. Since New York was at that time the seat of the national government they quickly met Virginia political leaders like Henry Lee and James Monroe. Tucker even ran into a Williamsburg neighbor, a "Mrs. Finnic." From their new Maiden Lane quarters, they ventured forth to services at St. Paul's Chapel on the corner of Broadway and Fulton Streets and to a dramatic production by Nathaniel Lee entitled *The Death of Alexander the Great,* then being performed nearby at the John Street Theater.[2]

St. George Tucker can be counted among the party of future southern travelers who would be charmed and stimulated rather than repelled by the bustle and congestion of New York City. Roughly a week after his arrival this loyal resident of the small Virginia capital of Williamsburg confessed in his travel diary that he liked "the hurly burly and bustle of a large town. . . . You may stand in one place in this City and see as great

a variety of faces, figures, and Characters as Hogarth . . . ever drew."
Beyond his satisfaction at meeting fellow Virginians, he was generally
pleased with the hospitality extended to him and his wife by Gotham's
gentry. "I shall not descend to an Enumeration of the Invitations or visits
we received from many of the Genteel people of New York," he wrote
with obvious gratification in one entry. "Suffice it to say I was obliged
twice to decline the honor of dining with the president of Congress, by
previous Engagements." Though not exceedingly impressed with the
town houses of New York's elite, he was completely charmed by their
pleasant country seats that, interspersed amid fields and scattered forests, dotted the landscape of mid- and upper Manhattan Island. In an
admiring description of a bucolic terrain that would be within seventy
years almost entirely obliterated by incredibly rapid urban development,
Tucker stood on the heights of Fort Washington—present-day Washington Heights—and marveled at a "prospect . . . infinitely varied. On
one side the lofty Cliffs of the north [Hudson] river . . . give Grandeur
to the prospect far superior to any that I have seen. The beautiful plain
of Haarlem, the meanderings of that little river, with the various inter-
spersions of the Waters of the East river, beyond which is an extensive
view of Long Island, form a striking contrast to the bold and noble view
which I have just described."[3]

During a mid-August excursion across the East River to Long Island
Tucker was greatly impressed by the agricultural bounty on display
within the city's environs. To the Tidewater Virginian's eyes New York's
farms seemed relatively small, but he also found them "delightful" and
well-maintained. Indeed, he acknowledged that the typical Long Island
farm was "equally productive" to Virginia plantations "ten times their
extent." And he was charmed with villages such as Jamaica and Flushing
that lay scattered across western Long Island's rich breast, each marked
by the steeples of its quaint Dutch and English churches. It was hard for
him to believe that such pleasantly bucolic scenes flourished within a few
miles of a bustling and rapidly expanding city.[4]

Like many southerners who would come after him, Tucker felt "not
a little regret" when he and his wife left Gotham on the morning of
August 27, 1786. He had enjoyed his first and last taste of city life and
had luxuriated in the varied society he had met there. Certainly, there
were valid objections to living in New York. He could name plenty of
them. "The water for example is execrable. There are more flies than
in most places; nor is there a scarcity of muskettoes. Their houses are

ill-constructed: the rooms are often very small. They have not an inch of garden, nay, hardly of yard, in most parts of Town; the streets in general are very narrow—illy paved, and crooked. Their Butter and Meats are far inferior to Philadelphia." Even after this unflattering compilation of civic inadequacies, however, there remained something deeply alluring to Tucker about Gotham's energy and its "hurly burly." "Under all these Circumstances," he concluded, "if my fortune would permit it I would live on the Island of New York in preference to any spot I have ever seen." It was a wish that other southern cosmopolites would echo in the centuries to come.[5]

Thirty years after Tucker's visit southern tourists in New York had become significantly more plentiful. By the 1820s, however, they were as likely to have hailed from the Deep South and the Gulf states as from the Atlantic seaboard. And they were often flush with cotton money—money that allowed for more ambitious travel itineraries. St. George Tucker's resources had confined him to excursions to upper Manhattan and Long Island. But three decades later a visit to the city was often part of a more encompassing northern tour for southern travelers. As we have seen in chapter 1, in her nearly six-month sojourn in the North Ann Wagner had gone on from New York to Providence and Boston before returning to Manhattan. Visiting the city four years later in 1822 Georgia lawyer J. A. Maxwell began in New York and then proceeded on to Saratoga and New Haven, before ending his travels in Newport, Rhode Island. Other southerners saw the growing metropolis briefly on their way to or from England and the continent. Judith Page Rives of Albemarle County, Virginia, never set foot in Manhattan, but in a diary entry of August 12, 1829, she was obviously impressed with her water view of the shore. She was amazed by "the innumerable masts of the vessels lying at the navy yard" and the adjacent docks, which resembled "a forest of leafless trees." Even from a distance New York struck her as an impressively prosperous place. "There are," she observed, "very handsome houses on each side of the sound near the city, which, with their tastefully ornamented grounds, heighten the beauty of the scene very much."[6]

For southern travelers the lure of New York had to have been strong in the opening decades of the nineteenth century, for getting to Gotham in the presteamboat age was not significantly easier, cheaper, or freer from dangers than it had been for St. George Tucker and his wife in 1786. Maxwell's 1822 journey from Georgia required a seven-day sea voyage from Charleston, and it was followed by a four-day quarantine on Staten Island necessitated by widespread sickness in the city. "Being something of a lawyer," Maxwell bragged, he had been successful in persuading officials to shorten his confinement to two days. But other dangers lurked beyond Staten Island. During one of his first meals in Manhattan, "having an unusually good appetite," he had "made a violent attack upon one of these indigestible clam-and-crayfish looking fellows called lobster." Alas, his gastronomic intemperance had done the Georgia tourist "much injury."[7]

One year before Maxwell's trip a young Presbyterian minister named Daniel Allen Penick had embarked for New York at Richmond on Thursday, November 15, with his father and other family members. Their sail down the James River had been agonizingly slow. By Sunday the eighteenth they remained moored at Hampton Roads, their captain having spent the Sabbath below deck in what the pious Penick described as a "drunk" condition. On Monday the ship finally sailed into the Atlantic, but the three-day sea voyage that took them to Gotham was harrowing to the youthful minister and to all his family. The following passage from his travel diary details quite vividly the miseries on board: "Vomited at dark—dropped into a doze—awoke in a fright, the vessel pitching—the wind blowing—the sails rattling . . . the passengers alarmed—some asking what is the matter—others vomiting." Two years after Penick's journey in 1824 his future wife, Agnes Tinsley, would undertake a similar four-day sea passage from Virginia to New York, one that seems to have been as wretched as that undertaken by her future husband. The majority of the twenty-five passengers on board with her were seasick by the time the boat reached Hampton Roads, and at Cape Henry a "dreadful wind" had forced the captain to lower the sails and had set the vessel rocking "like a cradle." The frightened Agnes "felt several times as if the vessel would sink." When they arrived in New York harbor she and the other ashen-faced and nauseated passengers were conducted, as J. A. Maxwell had been, to the "quarantine ground," where an officer "called out our name and looked at our faces" while the captain swore that all on board were "in good health."[8]

Despite the miseries and dangers attendant upon the sea passage to New York in the years before the advent of the steamboat and the railroad, southerners of means not uncommonly made multiple trips to Gotham. One of these frequent sailors was William Elliott, a Beaufort planter and member of the South Carolina legislature. In a letter dated July 29, 1823, he announced excitedly to his wife: "We have made the passage in three days!!" Completing the Charleston–New York voyage in three days—about half the time normally required—was indeed remark-able. But there had been a price paid for the astonishing speed. Elliott professed that he had "never seen more suffering from sea sickness." On the worst day he had witnessed "thirty persons of both sexes . . . strewed at a time along the deck, unable to hold each other's heads at the time of most need." Five years later Elliott would again make the sea passage. He remained unlucky. The trip took six days, but it was just as "boisterous" as the earlier three-day sail had been. His traveling companion, William Smith, had been terribly ill with "spasms from the confined atmosphere of the cabin, and was revived by the application of laudanum in quantity that would have destroyed an ordinary person." As bad as affairs had been in his cabin, however, conditions in the nearby ladies' cabin had been worse. "With the accompaniment of nurses and children, seasick-ness and squalling," they had "suffered horribly."[9]

Upon successfully and safely negotiating the often-harrowing sea voyage to Gotham southern visitors frequently revived themselves by following the pattern set by Ann Wagner of spending sums of money in Manhattan far larger than their families back home had anticipated. A prime example of such extravagance was South Carolinian Hugh Ball, who had come to New York in 1825 with the serious purpose of studying medicine. While pursuing his studies, however, Ball made frequent re-quests for funds to his obliging brother in Charleston. Indeed, he seems to have spent more money partaking in the pleasures of New York and Saratoga Springs than in advancing his medical career. A year after arriving in Manhattan, as his brother John observed with some asperity in a letter written in October of 1826, the spendthrift had received over the past year from his hardworking brother's hand "the aggregate sum of three thousand three hundred and fifty dollars."[10] Considering the fact that Hugh Ball had burned through the modern equivalent of seventy to eighty thousand dollars in his single year of study in New York, his elder brother's admonishment strikes one as remarkably restrained.

New York City was an expensive destination and not by modern stan-dards an easy one for travelers below the Mason-Dixon Line to reach, yet by the opening decades of the nineteenth century it was a place that certain types of southerners—especially wealthy men and women of flexible and engaging intellects and temperaments—seemed bound to come to and enjoy. North Carolinian James Jeffreys was certainly an appealing example of this type of tourist. Writing to his wife from Man-hattan in 1826 he assured her that a visit of a month or even of a year would be insufficient to satisfy one's curiosity or acquaint him with "one half of the most interesting objects" contained within the metropolis. He himself had seen more "superb establishments" and encountered "more extravagance" in "one day . . . than I ever expect to see in all my life." Unlike those southerners who were intimidated or put off by Gotham's diversity and "extravagance," Jeffreys clearly basked in the city's manifold pleasures. How fine, he wrote his wife, to stand on "Broadway" and watch "the beauty and fashionable stand arrayed in all their splendor." How marvelous to walk down a boulevard "completely alive with people." He realized that it must appear "simple and foolish" to his wife "to be amazed" by New York's "gaudy trappings." But amazed this southern gentleman truly was—and delighted as well.[11]

Even as early as the 1820s southerners like James Jeffreys were dazzled by the size, the variety, the lights, and the energy of America's most rapidly growing city. For William Elliott it hardly mattered that one was forced to march in a semi-nauseated condition to the "Quarantine Ground" to be "examined by the visiting physician" before being "permitted to proceed to the great city." One could "scarcely look on the beautiful prospects" of New York harbor, he wrote admiringly, "and remember anything of these discomforts." Before the visitor's eyes there lay "the beautiful and picturesque scenery of Statin Island on one hand and Long Island on the other." The South Carolina planter was captivated by the "neat white fences and tasteful summer houses—the green hills sloping—the ripened wheat fields falling before the sickle—the cheerfulness, the life and animation of everything around, even before we approach the great metropolis." All of these stimulating and charming sights evoked "a correspondingly buoyant feeling to the beholder."[12]

Like William Elliott, Agnes Tinsley had experienced a rough and stressful voyage to Gotham; but she also was quickly revived by the "beautiful" city that spread before her, punctuated by numerous church spires. She was delighted by concerts at the Castle Garden on the Battery, a circular stone fortification that in the 1820s had been topped by a roof and transformed into a large concert hall. She agreed with visitors like Arthur Morson that city hall was, "one of the handsomest buildings" she had ever seen. And she was excited by the presence of a Revolutionary hero, the Marquis de Lafayette, who was visiting the city in August and September of 1824 while she was there. Three years later fellow Virginian Elizabeth Ruffin arrived with her half-brother, the future rabid secessionist Edmund Ruffin. She too was impressed with Castle Garden, where she had viewed a fireworks exhibition. She wrote in her diary that she had never imagined "that such transcendent beauty and splendor could be presented by an explosion of gunpowder." She was also astonished and delighted by the brightly lighted shops on Broadway. All the stores, she observed, were brilliantly "illuminated, but the brightness of the glass establishments [was] dazzling almost to blindness." This properly bred Virginia belle was puzzled, however, by the reversal in gender roles she observed in Manhattan. The Broadway stores were managed "entirely by its females." Although there was "not a man to be seen behind many counters," one had merely to step to the shop door and see "one single man seated up in a fine carriage . . . riding about for pleasure—a singular reversal of things to me."[13]

More than twenty years after this early wave of southern tourists, enthusiastic visitors like Virginian John C. Myers continued to affirm that the city was "the greatest emporium of the western hemisphere, and after London, the greatest in the world." But by the 1840s travelers from below the Mason-Dixon were not simply amazed by the variety and scale of the city's commercial enterprise and cultural offerings. They were also mightily impressed by a burgeoning list of public works. Perhaps the most impressive of these was the Croton Waterworks with its magnificent system of reservoirs and aqueducts and the massive High Bridge that, when completed in 1848, enabled the city to transport clean water forty miles from upper Westchester County across the Harlem River and down Manhattan to the 42nd Street reservoir. In 1841 a writer for Richmond's *Southern Literary Messenger* traveled to New York expressly to describe another of New York's impressive establishments, the new buildings and the recently assembled faculty of New York University's medical school. For the Virginia visitor the building of this educational institution was evidence of Gotham's ambition to transform itself into a cosmopolitan city of national and even world significance. It was a venture determinedly nonprovincial in its spirit, "not intended alone for the City or the State of New York," but one that extended "at once all its advantages to every part of the Union."[14]

A reader is today struck by the generous and admiring tone of the *Southern Literary Messenger* article. Certainly, the South's premier literary magazine could never have allowed itself the expression of such unalloyed approval for Gotham's public investments twenty years later with the nation on the verge of the Civil War. In the early 1840s, however, it was still possible for southerners to "delight to see the North . . .

advancing in these things" and to applaud New York City's establishment of a medical "institution of overwhelming influence . . . an institution which will assuredly assume the aspect of a national one." Even more remarkably, it was possible for a Virginian to wonder whether the Old Dominion might not advance its own educational establishments "in generous emulation" of the nation's largest and most ambitious city. "We have seen what New York has done," the *Messenger* article concluded. "It becomes Virginia to imitate her example."[15]

Well into the nineteenth century thoughtful southern visitors like the *Southern Literary Messenger* writer who visited New York City were able to engage its dynamics thoughtfully and to examine sharply its import to the nation. They were sometimes confounded by the habits of a place in which men were "crowded together in dense masses,—men of all countries, and colors, and conditions." They were often amazed to observe in the booming metropolis "the workings of commerce on the great scale—slips crowded with fleets of merchantmen,—and streets of banking houses." And they marveled at the "almost infinity of mercantile affairs" that transpired "in this market-house of the Union." But beneath the "bustle of political and mercantile affairs in this City of Adventurers" they also intuited what the *Messenger* writer termed "gleamings of the better part" of the American character. A significant portion of New York's enormous wealth accumulated through its dedication to "individual enterprise" had been tithed in return to the city and designated for the improvement of public works, educational and cultural institutions, and charities. With its unique devotion to both personal aggrandizement and initiative and to civic improvement Gotham epitomized "not alone the hand," but also the beating "heart of the Union."[16]

As willing as some southern visitors were to be impressed by the splendors of Gotham, others found reason to be appalled by what they encountered there. Interestingly one of the more caustic early descriptions of New York was penned by frontier hero and politician Davy Crockett. Though Crockett had anointed Manhattan as "the London of America," his view of the city was also colored more darkly by his politics. He was a fierce antagonist of President Andrew Jackson and of Jackson's 1832 vice-presidential running mate, New York native Martin Van Buren. Crockett's identification with the common man of agrarian and frontier

America did not extend to the urban lower classes. Indeed, his disgust with Gotham's hoi polloi mirrored that of many conservative New Yorkers; even the city's own *Evening Post* had unsparingly described these slum dwellers as the "vilest rabble, black and white, mixt together."[17] Crockett additionally despised them for being members of the debased northern constituency of Jackson's Democratic Party.

Crockett luridly expressed his aversion to Gotham's poor in his fulsome description of the Five Points neighborhood found in his 1835 *Tour to the North and Down East.* Within this section of the city—located just west and south of present-day Chinatown in lower Manhattan—waves of newly arrived Irish and other European immigrants lived and mingled in teeming tenements with thousands of free Blacks. From Five Points in 1832, Crockett observed with decided hostility, "Van Buren's warriors came . . . during the election, when the wild Irish, with their clubs and bludgeons, knocked down every one they could find that would not huzza for Jackson." In the shabby, filthy, and overcrowded houses he observed "cellars . . . jam full of people; and such fiddling and dancing nobody ever saw before in this world . . . black and white, white and black, all hug-em-snug together, happy as lords and ladies, sitting sometimes round in a ring, with a jug of liquor between them." It is difficult to tell whether Crockett was more disgusted by the seemingly casual blending of Black and white races or by the vileness of the immigrant Irish who predominated among the whites of Five Points. In the South, he averred, when one met an Irishman, he met "a first-rate gentleman." But New York's Irish were "worse than savages . . . too mean to swab hell's kitchen." "God deliver me," the anti-Jacksonian Crockett pronounced, "from such constituents, or from a party supported by such."[18]

Davy Crockett concluded his visit to Five Points by musing more generally on what "a miserable place a city is for poor people: they are half starved, poorly clothed, and perished for fire. I sometimes wonder they don't clear out to a new country, where every skin hangs by its own tail."[19] His pungently unsophisticated assessment of the misery of urban poverty would echo that of many other southern visitors to Gotham in the decades to come. Indeed, as northern denunciations of the evils of slavery grew more intense during the 1840s and 1850s southern condemnations of the stark contrast between extreme wealth and abject poverty in Manhattan would grow equally vehement and bitter. Crockett had at least attempted to cloak his indictment of Gotham in the garb of backwoods language and frontier humor. He had presented himself as an amazed country bumpkin come to town. Later writers would ditch the bumpkin persona in favor of the loftier condemnations of southern gentlemen. These gentlemen would censure again and again what they considered to be New York's fundamental and profound moral hypocrisy—the uneasy, squeamish, and at-best lukewarm endorsement of slavery by the city's commercial and political leaders matched with their complaisant acceptance of Gotham's own grotesque extremes of social and economic inequality.

Fifteen years after Crockett's veiled indictment of Gotham's urban destitution in an 1850 speech given before the House of Representatives John McQueen of South Carolina launched a more direct and scathing attack on New York City's moral deceitfulness that was typical of many made by southern politicians in the increasingly contentious 1850s. McQueen began reasonably enough by inviting his northern listeners to cast aside their prejudices and presumptions and to personally visit the South, and he assured them that if they but chose to visit the South they would be moved to acknowledge the truth about the region of which they had been so censorious. Most significantly they would see with their own eyes "the African, fed, clothed, and happy." In the face of this reality—benign white masters ruling mildly over the South's contented enslaved—the "false clamor" of hysterical northern abolitionists would stand "rebuked forever."[20]

In contrast to northerners, who had been loath to venture south of the Mason-Dixon, McQueen observed that southerners had chosen by the tens of thousands to venture north, especially to New York City. But what reality had they encountered when they visited Gotham? They had become acquainted with the staggering disparity that existed between the colossal wealth of the few and the stark and dehumanizing poverty of the many. This inequality was one that northern abolitionists, despite their supposed concern for the welfare of the South's enslaved, seemed entirely contented to ignore among their own lower social orders. Less than three years before delivering his speech McQueen averred that he personally had travelled North and observed in Gotham "scenes such as my eyes had never beheld, and such, I trust, as I may be spared seeing again." Two vignettes remained starkly etched in his memory.

One was a blind man, led amid the throng attached to a dog, (who seemed to me to have been his deepest sympathizer). He held in his hand a plate, as he passed, that had nothing in it as bright as sliver, when I stopped to add a trifle. The other was a woman, seated on the steps of the notorious Astor House, with a shriveled and writhing infant on her knee, and whilst I was in the act of giving her a pittance, I was accosted by a citizen, who said she was doubtless an imposter, who had borrowed the child and bandaged it with bands to impose upon strangers.

McQueen concluded by arguing with apparently genuine conviction that if the miserably impoverished black and white inhabitants of a heartless city like New York could miraculously be transformed into southern slaves and be elevated to the enslaved's "scale of happiness and contentment, they would be more improved in their condition than the philanthropy of the North will accomplish for them whilst they remain on this earth."[21]

Even southerners more kindly disposed toward New York City than John McQueen seem sometimes to have been sincerely shocked by the squalor that underlay the luxury of Manhattan's surface. South Carolina poet and critic Paul Hamilton Hayne, staying at the high-end Clarendon Hotel on Union Square in 1854, assured his worried wife back in Charleston that he was enjoying his visit and that reports of cholera in the city had been greatly exaggerated. The pestilence had been confined to "those horrible localities" where the destitute were known to seize "on the carcass of a fowl thrown out for the scavenger" and take it to their squalid homes "for the purpose of eating the atrocious thing at dinner." Others were less disposed than Hayne to tolerate Gotham's urban indecencies and more inclined to agree with McQueen's blanket condemnations. Planter and lawyer Albert James Pickett, having spent weeks in New York fruitlessly negotiating with the potential publisher of his history of Alabama, pronounced himself at the end of his stay thoroughly revolted by the ubiquitous and yawning gap between Gotham's wealthy and its destitute: "Since I have seen the splendor, the meanness, the selfishness and the ridiculous moneyed aristocracy of the North on the one side, and the poverty distress and destitution of the lower classes on the other, I am content to live in Alabama the balance of my days and *never go out of it.*"[22]

Southern disenchantment with New York extended beyond disgust with its extremes of wealth and poverty. James Thomas Harrison, having assumed responsibility for the welfare of three southern ladies traveling with him to Gotham in the summer of 1853, acquired by the end of his northern excursion a hearty distaste for the Yankee traveling public. Some of his disenchantment seems to have been produced not so much by being in New York, but by the strain and pressure of squiring about and assuming responsibility for three southern damsels traveling far from their homeland into a congested and alien urban setting. "For *one* gentleman," he fretted, "to have to take care not only of himself, but of three ladies and their baggage, is a downright impossibility." Manhattan hotels were so jammed with summer visitors, he complained, that his party had been forced to "take to water, and sleep in a steamboat." But Harrison left no doubt that the general discourtesy of New Yorkers had added considerably to the strain of being a tour director. "All Yankee land" seemed to have "broken loose" for the summer "and a more ill-mannerly set never travelled in any country."[23]

Harrison was most repelled by the lack of manners and the absence of respect exhibited in public by lower social orders toward the more refined among them. In New York his southern sense of social hierarchy, especially the strict segregation of Black and white, had been thoroughly and unsettlingly deranged. But he did not so much "blame the free negroes here for their independence and want of politeness" as he blamed "their *white brethren*" who had "set the example" by their own incivility: "I have seen men who set themselves up for gentlemen in the free states ride inside of the stagecoach and compel ladies to ride *on top of the vehicle;* and compel ladies to *stand up* and ride in the railroad cars for miles, whilst the dogs squared themselves off on the seats with the most complacent air of *triumphant success.* I have seen *free negroes* refuse to exchange seats (much less give them up) to accommodate a party of ladies who desired to get together as one company." After guiding his charges through what he judged to be New York's anarchic public transport systems Harrison had seen "as much of Yankeedom as I wish to see and shall never undertake to travel here with ladies again and mix up with free negroes and Sam Slicks of Yankees. There are many good, clean, and genteel people here," he conceded, "but in travelling you are overcome by the masses of the 'traveling Yankee.'"[24]

For William Adams of Albemarle County in Virginia the absence of gentility among the city's traveling masses that J. T. Harrison had wrathfully excoriated was exacerbated by the brusque, ill-mannered, and conniving natures of the serving classes of the metropolis—men who ought to have been duly deferential toward their southern guests. Returning through Manhattan from a trip to the Midwest in the summer of 1858, he was "very much annoyed by hack men and porters." Indeed, in the process of leaving by boat for the city of Philadelphia he observed bitterly that he had been "swindled out of six dollars by a ticket agent and his accomplices." It is hardly surprising that Adams returned to his native state harboring "a poor opinion of many New Yorkers."[25]

Southerners who were not tourists like Harrison and Adams and who resided in New York City for any length of time might have been expected to grow inured to what they considered the brusque incivility of many of its inhabitants. What some of them could not grow used to, however, was the pervasively condescending attitude of New Yorkers toward the South's people and its culture that rankled and occasionally enraged them. One of these proud and embittered southerners was Francis Hawks. A native Tar Heel and a distinguished alumnus of the University of North Carolina, he served from the 1830s to the 1860s as a prominent and popular Episcopal minister in Manhattan; yet even he seems to have felt the sting of Yankee condescension and to have been resentful of it. As he explained in a letter to David Swain, former governor and long-time president of the University of North Carolina, most northerners judged southerners to be "a set of craven imbeciles" and looked upon them "as *inferiors,* morally, physically and intellectually." Once at a party, he told Swain, he was asked where he had been educated. When he answered that he had attended the University of North Carolina someone asked him how "it was *possible* I could have acquired *there* such an education as they knew me to possess?" Some guests, Hawks resentfully observed, did not even know that the state of North Carolina contained a university, much less one that had been established in the 1790s and that could boast "400 undergraduates with as good a set of professors and instructors as Yale could show."[26]

Nearly two hundred years ago well-bred southerners like Hawkes were complaining about New Yorkers in terms almost identical to those many southerners use today to describe contemporary residents of the city. They not uncommonly believed that most if not all Gothamites were ill-mannered and uncivil, socially brusque, and ethically conniving. And to add insult to injury they were also condescending, treating proud southerners as if they were products of some backward, second-rate, and provincial culture. For a writer for the *Southern Lady's Companion* the possibility that a gullible southern tourist might come to accept New York's opinion of the inferiority of her native region's culture was a concern serious enough to merit discouraging altogether travel to the North. The author of this essay, a self-identified "Methodist preacher," believed that young southern ladies were particularly vulnerable to the corrupting influences of Manhattan. The *Lady's Companion* article furnished as its cautionary example "Eliza," an uncommonly bright, "amiable and vivacious," "affectionate," and "obedient daughter," whose one ill-fated visit to Gotham had ruined her innocent, charming, and ingenuous southern nature. During her time in the city Eliza had become a "frequent visitor" to balls, parties, and theatrical performances, and the effects of these activities on her character were on clear and disturbing display when she returned to her native soil. "Alas," the minister-journalist lamented, "how changed" she was and what an unfortunate change this northern exposure had wrought. "Home, with its quietness and many endearments alone, could not now satisfy her perverted taste. The furniture was too old fashioned—they must have new carpets . . . must have 'whist parties, sitting parties, and dancing parties.'"[27] Eliza's New York experience had brought calamitous consequences. It had turned an exquisite and highly desirable southern belle into a shallow and unstable woman fit to be neither the daughter nor the wife of a southern gentleman.

Because he appreciated the potentially corrupting consequences of travel to Gotham, Alabama lawyer Clement Claiborne Clay was especially appalled and disgusted in the summer of 1850 by the spectacle of thousands of southern tourists, male and female, descending upon New York to disburse with apparent abandon a large share of their cotton wealth to northern merchants, many of whom had already grown rich conveying the South's prime export to market. In a letter to his brother and law associate Hugh Clay, he pronounced himself "reluctant to spend a cent" with New Yorkers. And he was completely discouraged during his 1850 summer visit to observe the city "swarming with southern tourists and invalids, seeking pleasure and health in the midst of our enemies, and disbursing among them 2,000,000 annually . . . instead of expending it in the South to aid and advance our own institutions and our own people!"[28] Clay had almost certainly read and taken to heart the anti-Yankee fulminations of southern journalists like James De Bow, but he also seems to have been as beholden as De Bow to the Yankees he so resented. Just as De Bow had relied on New York businesses to obtain crucial advertising revenue for his *Review,* so Clay seems to have felt himself compelled to journey north from Alabama to Manhattan to procure lucrative legal clients.

Clement Clay must have felt a bit uneasy about drumming up business in a place he so obviously disliked, for he was careful to assure his brother that not for all the legal fees he might generate by his trip to the heart of the Yankee empire would he compromise his loyalty to native state and region. With stubborn pride he boasted that he would not, like other more foolish southern travelers, waste his "time and money" in Gotham. Though his abstemiousness might result in his failing "to pick up any law cases," he would return home poorer but "more attached to the South and more resolved than ever to stand by her first and the union next." Before he concluded the letter to his brother, however, this proud southern nationalist blithely announced—apparently without the least sense of irony—that he had "found some law books here at less than half the catalogue prices." Indeed, he had purchased six volumes at prices cheaper than he would have been forced to pay at home. In this instance Clay seems to have been more than willing to leave his southern dollars behind in New York City. In fact, he frankly admitted to his brother that had he possessed the wherewithal he would have spent much more and added substantially to their legal library.[29]

As Clement Clay's enthusiastic description of book buying suggests, even the most hostile and skeptical southern travelers to New York City frequently and unwittingly revealed conflicted and ambivalent attitudes toward Gotham in their letters home. Albert James Pickett's letters from Gotham furnish further remarkable evidence of this ambivalence. As we have seen earlier, his failure to secure a publisher for his Alabama history had left him toward the end of his stay thoroughly disillusioned and disgusted with the city and resolved never to return. Yet earlier in his visit he had pronounced Manhattan a "brilliant" place, and he had been entirely charmed by its elegance and vivacity. "Everybody looks cheerful and happy," he enthused in a tone that contrasts remarkably with that of his later missives, "and the ladies are adorned with the richest and most elegant apparel, and they walk the streets from ten o'clock until twelve o'clock at night, not minding the coldness of the weather."[30]

Though they did not share the engaging and less censorious attitudes of the more cosmopolitan southern visitors, even staunch southern nationalists like Clay and Pickett could recognize and acknowledge the magnetic force of what John C. Myers described as a "dusty, smoky, noisy, busy, great and animating emporium." They too were able to admire Manhattan's "fine buildings, its long streets and handsome places; its dense throngs of inhabitants, its immense shipping and its enormous trade." But they also shuddered, as did Myers, at the city's "poverty . . . filth . . . extreme misery and degradation." And they looked with a combination of awe and great unease upon Gotham's "never-ending turbulence and commotion" as well as upon its confusing and "mingled crowds," in which one might discern the faces of "Frenchmen, Spaniards, Italians, Austrians, Swiss, Germans, Russians, Chinese, Jews, Turks, Africans, Portuguese, English, Southrons and Yankees: all commingling in the same hour, in the same street, in the same scene. . . ." It was this anonymous, turbulent, and impersonal quality that had disturbed conservative southerners like Clay, Pickett, and Myers from the very beginning of their treks to New York City. Earlier in the 1820s Elizabeth Ruffin had been dazzled by the lights of Broadway's shops, but she had also been disturbed and put off by Gotham's variety and density. She was uneasy about not being able to recognize "a familiar face" among thousands of pedestrians crowding the streets. And she was unsettled even at this early date by onslaught the of hack carriages "ready to run over you at every step" of a street crossing.[31]

Yet though conservative southerners like Clement Clay and Elizabeth Ruffin appreciated and were comforted by the slower pace of life and the sense of social stability that their native plantation South vouchsafed them, even the most loyal and contented sometimes returned from Gotham with a nagging if infrequently expressed doubt as to the adequacy of their own rather soporific culture. One writer for *De Bow's Review* was frank enough to admit that after visiting a city that excited, bewildered, and delighted them it was possible for southerners to feel depressed by "a painful sense of inferiority" when they returned home. "The difference," this writer rather ambiguously observed, was "between a magnificent panoramic view, and a dark still landscape; life in action and life in repose."[32]

Southern visitors to New York were molded by a plantation culture that had married itself economically and socially during the colonial period to chattel slavery, an institution that as the nineteenth century progressed more and more of their fellow Americans were coming to view as an anachronism. In the face of the nation's growing unease with and antipathy toward slavery the great majority of white southerners chose to embrace with uncritical fervor the idealized vision of their homeland crafted by their region's writers and politicians, men like John McQueen. In this fantastical rendering the plantation South was a stable, ordered, and Edenic society in which landed aristocrats held absolute sway over masses of contented black slaves and were deferred to and supported by submissive and loyal masses of more humble non-slaveholding whites. But southerners who carried this glorified image of their harmonious and ordered culture to the North often responded with confusion and insecurity when they arrived in Gotham. Here their ordered cultural perspective was assaulted by a city that seemed to possess no inherent order, a place where, as Myers observed, "nothing" was "fixed . . . nothing permanently settled." In Manhattan all was "moving and removing, organizing and disorganizing, building up and tearing down." The continually active "spirit of change" pervaded "all bodies, all things and all places in this mighty metropolis."[33]

Those southern visitors who firmly resisted the intoxicating allure of Manhattan and who decried the breakneck pace of the city's life and its heedless rush into the future were in fact giving voice to anxieties that native New Yorkers themselves not infrequently expressed during the antebellum decades. In 1853, the year of the triumphant opening of the Chrystal Palace Exhibition, *Putnam's* magazine lamented that the city was moving north up the island with such "astounding" rapidity that everything "old and venerable" was being utterly obliterated. Scarcely "a single land-mark" had been preserved "in token of the former position of the dwelling-places of our ancestors." Three years after the *Putnam's* editorial *Harper's Monthly* declared Gotham to be "notoriously the largest and least loved of any of our great cities." And why should it be admired, the magazine asked. "It is never the same city for a dozen years together. A man born in New York forty years ago finds nothing, absolutely nothing, of the New York he knew."[34]

Perhaps the most revealing and fascinating expression of the individual New Yorker's lifelong sense of dislocation and dispossession can be found in the diary of Philip Hone, the son of a German immigrant carpenter who was born in 1780, amassed considerable wealth in the auction business, and as the city's mayor became a prominent member of New York's political, commercial, and social elite. As his diary reveals, even Hone's secure position in the power structure of the burgeoning metropolis could not immunize him from feeling at times helplessly swept along by the extraordinarily strong tides of New York's explosive nineteenth-century expansion up Manhattan Island. In 1836, eight years after beginning his diary, he announced in one of his entries that he had sold his fine townhouse at 235 Broadway that stood opposite City Hall Park. He was leaving this "delightful" property "with feelings of deep regret," wondering what was to become of the "splendid rooms, the fine situation, my snug library, well arranged books, handsome pictures." But, having bought the house fifteen years earlier for $25,000, how could he resist the "large profit" that he had accrued by selling it for $60,000 to a developer who was planning to convert the lovely home into shops below and part of a hotel above.[35]

Rather glumly Hone admitted that he was no different from any other prominent New Yorker living in lower Manhattan in the 1830s; the surge of the city's growth northward was irresistible. "Almost everybody downtown," he lamented, was "in the same predicament." All were "tempted with prices so exorbitantly high" that none could resist selling. He predicted that even Dutch "burgomasters, who have fixed to one spot all their lives" would soon be seen "in flocks, marching reluctantly north to pitch their tents in places which, in their time, were orchards, cornfields, or morasses a pretty smart distance from town." A mere three years after writing this entry the diarist announced in a tone of real distress that the "poor dear house" he had sold at such a profit to developers was "coming down forthwith" and that within a few weeks "the home of my happy days will be incontinently swept from the earth." As he resignedly observed, "The spirit of pulling down and building up is abroad. The whole of New York is rebuilt about once in ten years."[36] Some decades later the site of Hone's residence would be razed again and replaced by one of Gotham's earliest and most elegant skyscrapers, the Woolworth Building.

By the end of the 1830s Hone and his family had retreated several miles north to a house in the East Village on the corner of Broadway and Great Jones Street. But even there he was overtaken by the relentless destruction and reconstruction that accompanied New York's staggering nineteenth-century expansion. In a diary entry penned not long before his death in 1851 he lamented that houses were being "pulled down" all around him "in the annual renovation of Broadway." Indeed, one house that had been insufficiently underpropped had fallen of its own accord "with a crash so astounding that the girls, with whom I was sitting in the library, imagined for a moment that it was caused by an earthquake." Even this far from Wall Street and city hall "the mania for converting Broadway into a street of shops" proceeded unchecked, and there was no part of it in his neighborhood that was "not in a state of transmutation." On a more positive note, he granted that most of these new structures were very fine ones, such as "a grand concert and exhibition establishment" that was being erected nearby.[37]

As this late diary entry suggests Hone remained to the end of his life decidedly ambivalent about his hometown's transformation, torn between pride in its dynamism and its rise to be "one of the 'wonders' of the Western World" and dismay at the destruction of the past that accompanied its stunning growth. Yet ultimately there was more than a little sourness in his estimation of Gotham's heedless rushing into the future. "Overturn, overturn, overturn! is the maxim of New York. The very bones of our ancestors are not permitted to lie quiet a quarter of a century, and one generation of men seem studious to remove all relics of those which preceded them." If a lifelong, prosperous, and well-connected New Yorker like Philip Hone could find himself toward the end of his life disoriented and alienated by a city so altered from the scene of his early years that he could barely recognize it, one can hardly be surprised that many conservative southern visitors found themselves even more at sea in Gotham and that they frequently resolved, like Alfred James Pickett in one of his more gloomy moods, to return home as fast as they could and *never go out of it again.*"[38]

As the national debate over slavery grew more heated and bitter it is not surprising that southern tourists traveling to the North found themselves more and more frequently the recipients of unflattering remarks about their peculiar institution, even in places like New York City that had traditionally been congenial to southern interests and sensibilities. By the mid-1850s publications like *De Bow's Review* had had enough of Yankee condescension and faultfinding. The journal declared that it was time for the South to issue a touristic declaration of independence. Insolent northerners who insulted their well-bred southern guests with impunity must now "reap the whirlwind." Lines of southern travel to the North should be broken, and southerners should resolve to enjoy future summers "on our own coasts, in our own mountains," where they assuredly would enjoy "health, pleasure, intellectual pastime, and fashion, when it was vainly imagined they existed only afar off." The editorial espoused for the region's travelers both southern "reaction" and southern "revolution," and it charged its readers to turn their worship away from Gotham's "strange gods" and to embrace the South's own guardian deities of hearth and home. "Stand by your Lares and Penates," it exhorted, "stand by them in all the future!"[39]

A contemporary reader of the *De Bow's Review* editorial might well imagine that it heralded a new and revolutionary situation in which wealthy southerners would declare themselves free from their expensive and heretofore obligatory summer pilgrimages to northern locales, chief among them New York City. But exhortations by southern journalists to the contrary, the idea that the South's tourists were eschewing en masse the pleasures of Manhattan was, in the words of John Hope Franklin, "wishful thinking."[40] In reality southern travelers remained just as addicted to Gotham's numerous delights in the 1850s as southern businessmen and planters remained dependent on its shipping lines, banks, and financial institutions to grow and ship their region's cotton. As late as the summer of 1860, less than six months before the election of Abraham Lincoln and less than a year before the Confederate attack on Fort Sumter, southerners continued to flock to Gotham by the tens of thousands, jamming its hotels, theaters, shops, and restaurants. For every southern visitor who pronounced himself alienated by the city and finished with it, there seems to have been at least one adventurer who was entirely willing to take the naysayer's place on Manhattan's crowded avenues.

South Carolinian Paul Hamilton Hayne was one of those travelers whose desire to visit Gotham during the summer of 1854 could not be deterred, as we have earlier observed, even by a bit of cholera. His rather jaunty attitude toward the pestilence—which he had assured his wife back in Charleston had been confined to the poorest neighborhoods—might have been predicted by the unalloyed enthusiasm with which he had embraced the city during his initial visit in 1843. Then he had first laid eyes on New York accompanied by his mother and aunt at the end of a five-day sea voyage. As he wrote to his cousin, Susan Hayne, he had been struck immediately by the beauty of the harbor, and once in Manhattan he had quickly launched himself into its streets, rambling "all over Broadway" on his first day off the boat. In his wanderings he had found much to admire. One could stand on the shore and see "more steamboats than you can count" linking the vibrant urban core to the numerous towns that surrounded its capacious harbor. One could purchase "a knife or anything of that kind for half the price you can in Charleston." As for the hubbub and the cacophony of street life, he found the "omnibuses" and "other conveyances rattling over the stony streets" to be such "sweet music" to his ears that he claimed he found it hard to keep himself awake at night. Hayne embraced Manhattan with enthusiasm and exhibited in his letters none of his cousin's defensive provincialism. In reply to his initial letter describing Gotham's harbor, Susan had informed him that a friend had assured her that Charleston harbor was every bit "as beautiful as that of New York." Hayne insisted that Susan's friend could not have seen New York's harbor with his own eyes but had merely "judged from report alone." Otherwise, he would never have made so chauvinistic an assertion.[41]

Those southerners like Paul Hamilton Hayne who responded with excitement and wonder to New York City seemed to have been most galvanized by Gotham's size and remarkable diversity, combined with an appreciation for its economic and cultural dynamism that vividly contrasted with the relatively static and quiet atmosphere of the rural southern life they came from. As we have seen, even the most skeptical and hostile southern visitors sometimes grudgingly acknowledged Gotham's energy and vigor. But culturally sophisticated southerners like Hayne encountered New York without the bitter defensiveness and anxiety displayed by more conservative fellow travelers like Pickett and Clay. In this respect Ann Wagner's 1818 effusions about the wonders of Manhattan are very close in tone to the almost giddy excitement upon reaching his destination that Hayne communicated to his cousin in 1843. Both Wagner and Hayne hailed from Charleston, South Carolina, a not inconsiderable southern port city. Yet compared to Charleston, New York struck both as representing an entirely "new world." To visit a place of comparable urban scale and diversity one would have to cross thousands of miles of Atlantic waters to the grand capitals of Europe. Suffusing Haynes's letters to his cousin is an attitude of engagement comparable to Wagner's, a delighted apprehension that America was in the process of creating an international cosmopolis of its own, one for which there was no equivalent either in the South or in any other part of the United States.

The awe and the enthusiasm of southern tourists like Ann Wagner and Paul Hamilton Hayne was perhaps most fully and manifestly articulated in a letter written by Louisiana native Abram F. Rightor to his cousin Andrew McCollum in 1851.

> What an empire, or rather what a world is this New York City, and how insignificant do all other places appear when compared to this, with its thousand omnibuses thundering through the streets eighteen hours out of the twenty four, its many thousand hacks and countless drays, with its hundreds of magnificent hotels crowded with the travelling millions, with its forest of shipping that line her fifteen miles of wharves, and its numerous steam boats, constantly arriving loaded with passengers, also the rail roads that radiate from the city with their long train of cars,

arriving and departing at every hour of the day (except the very small hours of the morning) filled with the arriving multitude.

Rightor observed that if one walked through Gotham's "endless streets" he would marvel at "the vastness of her constantly increasing commerce, the miles of sidewalk filled up with boxes and bales of merchandise, turned out to be shipped to all parts of the world." He concluded by confidently and presciently predicting that if New York continued "increasing in the nation for the next fifty years, London [would] only be the second city while New York [would] be first in every respect."[42]

The hundreds of thousands of southern visitors who came, saw, and were conquered by the multifarious attractions of antebellum Gotham were as a rule even wealthier than the southerners who have subsequently flocked to the city in the twentieth and twenty-first centuries. They were moneyed plantation owners, merchants, bankers, and lawyers and they represented the highest levels of southern society. Though in the earlier decades of the 1820s and 1830s they tended to hail from Virginia and the Carolinas, by the 1840s and 1850s more and more of them were members of the new cotton aristocracy of the interior and Gulf Coast South. They often could afford to spend lavishly on their travels; and though New York City was their primary destination in America, it was for a significant number of them only part of far more ambitious itineraries. For example, Georgia native Sarah Gayle Crawford casually observed in her 1853 travel diary that after seeing New York and Saratoga Springs some of her friends were proceeding on to Liverpool, London, Boulogne, and Paris.[43]

Letters and diaries indicate that as a rule southern tourists chose to stay at the city's best and most exclusive hotels. By the late 1830s the Girard House and the Astor House on lower Broadway near City Hall were de rigueur choices for discriminating travelers. And as New York's development exploded north up Manhattan Island southerners followed, choosing a select number of elegant new hostelries, but always remaining within a few blocks of Broadway. In antebellum New York this famous street was the equivalent of modern-day Times Square and Fifth Avenue combined, and visitors from the South were determined to quarter themselves in the center of elegance and entertainment. "But Broadway—Broadway," enthused one guest in 1831, "how pleasant to walk on Broadway about 12 or 1—the sun shining highly in the meantime. They slander New York, when they say there are no beauties here. There are hundreds of them."[44] Among the hundreds of beauties that dazzled the eyes of this southern gentleman, there were no doubt a significant number of southern belles who were themselves enjoying the sights and sounds of the America's most elegant nineteenth-century thoroughfare.

The wealthiest and most widely traveled southerners generally agreed that Gotham's accommodations were equal in luxury to the finest European hotels. Visiting New York in the fall of 1853, Tennessee native John Stewart Oxley was especially eloquent in his praise of the city's amenities, and he affirmed that its hotels were "of course . . . first rate, both as regards splendor of decoration and excellence of cooking." Indeed, he judged Manhattan's "various table d'hôtel . . . hard to beat, even in Paris." Most impressive to him was the way New Yorkers strove to make their southern guests feel at home, serving delectable versions of their regional drinks and foods. "For a good mint julep, cherry cobbler or anything else in that line," he asserted, one could not "fail to be well pleased at the bar of the Astor House, St. Nicholas, or Metropolitan Hotels."[45]

Two of the hotels Oxley mentions in his letter, the St. Nicholas and the Metropolitan, were manifestations of the rapid progression of luxury hotels north up Broadway during the 1840s and 1850s. The St. Nicholas was situated fourteen blocks beyond the Astor House near the newly built and equally luxurious Metropolitan. And these new high-priced hotels were being filled by a rising tide of southern visitors as rapidly as they were finished and made ready for occupancy. Arriving in the city at about the same time as her friend and fellow Tennessean Stewart Oxley, Sue Henry was not an atypical traveler when she wrote to her mother that she had encountered "great difficulty" obtaining a room in one of these popular new Broadway establishments, although she had "telegraphed a week beforehand." New York, she complained, was absolutely "overflowing" with visitors; and she had consequently been forced to settle for the Clarendon, located beyond Greenwich Village on 5th Avenue and 23rd Street at Union Square and well north of her preferred Broadway choices. Though the Clarendon, famous for its capacious bathtubs, was as luxurious an accommodation as the more venerable Astor House, Sue found the location a bit disappointing. She rather forlornly observed that it was situated "about a mile and a half from the St. Nicholas and Metropolitan" in a new section of Manhattan where "not much [was] to be seen."[46]

Sue Henry described with a hint of envy one of her friends who, upon returning home from a voyage to Europe, had been fortunate enough to obtain a room at the more centrally located Metropolitan. There, she wistfully observed, he had "met with a great many friends from Tennessee," including mutual friend Stuart Oxley. Henry's expectations were perhaps a bit too exacting. By the 1850s antebellum New York closely resembled its twenty-first-century incarnation in boasting many comfortable and even sumptuous hotels that were spread over the broad urban expanse of Manhattan. Earlier in the summer of 1853 Georgian Sarah Gayle Crawford had been perfectly contented to lodge downtown in the venerable Astor House, and she had found it, like the luxury hotels situated further north, "unusually crowded." Nevertheless, she had been delighted to discover the entire world on display in this by-now hallowed Manhattan establishment, including numerous "strangers from the South and West."[47]

Once southern tourists had checked themselves into their four-star accommodations, they set out to do what wealthy southerners of the early decades of the nineteenth century had done and what wealthy southerners of today continue to do: they went shopping. As we have seen, even a parsimonious southern nationalist like Clement Clay had not been able to resist completely the city's consumer offerings, descending enthusiastically upon Gotham's bookstores in search of bargain legal tomes. And more free-spending southern ladies like Sue Henry were drawn ineluctably to the fashionable women's apparel shops of Broadway. Henry wrote her mother that as soon as arriving in Manhattan she had gone shopping and purchased "a little [short cloak] and gave thirty-five dollars for it." She found the "beautifully embroidered" item irresistible, though she was afraid that her mother would "think it too small."[48] Having spent the modern equivalent of around a thousand dollars on her cloak, Sue had every reason to hope that her mother approved of its size.

Southern belles like Sue Henry often made purchases not only for themselves but for friends and family members back home who had not been fortunate enough to make the big trip north to Gotham. One Charleston lady acknowledged her mother's "long letter of commissions" and assured her that she had gone straight to work to fill her requests. These had included three "very pretty white . . . tassels at sixty-three cents apiece," a "set of pretty linens," a "steam engine that winds up," and two other "pretty toys." All these delightful purchases had been made for a total of slightly more than six dollars. This young lady was an enthusiastic shopper, but she always kept her eye on the price tag. She had seen, she wrote, "fan-parasols of all colors and prices," ranging from "a very pretty purple one, with spangles and a white handle" priced at five and a half dollars to an "ugly" dark blue one that sold for two and a half dollars. Though assiduous in filling her mother's requests, this daughter's letter suggests that she was at least as intent on fulfilling her own fashion needs. She reminded her mother that a bill she had sent home earlier had been "for the ball dress" that she had had made for her while in the city and for "the alteration" of her "French silk gown." She was also having a bonnet made that was "rough and ready . . . trimmed with scarlet and black velvet and scarlet and black owl's feathers." She was confident that when her bonnet was finished it would be "very becoming and very nice for the present," though "of course" it would "not do for a best bonnet." Nonetheless the new hat would suit her very well in New York as it was "very fashionable to go to shows and to shop in."[49]

Even the most self-disciplined of southern tourists sometimes acknowledged that the allure of shopping in New York City was irresistible. In the nineteenth century, just as today, parents and grandparents were often surprised to discover that they were succumbing to the overpowering urge to spend, if not for themselves, then for their offspring. Sarah Gayle Crawford was not embarrassed to admit that she enjoyed window-shopping "a good deal" on Broadway, though she was rarely tempted to walk inside and make an actual purchase. The only wares that seriously and repeatedly enticed her were those showcased in the window displays of that avenue's numerous toy shops. "Then," she confessed, "I want everything for the children."[50] The toy shops of nineteenth-century Broadway have today been supplanted by grand midtown emporiums like Toys "R" Us and American Girl, but Crawford's simple expression of a nineteenth-century mother's temptation to buy "for the children" is one with which most twenty-first-century parents would easily identify.

———————————

Southerners were by no means complete materialists when it came to enjoying Gotham's wide array of offerings. From the very beginning of their annual summer pilgrimages many of them had availed themselves fully of the city's cultural opportunities. In 1818 Ann Wagner had extended her stay in Gotham so that she could attend more opera performances. And in 1828 William Elliott had liberally attended plays, concerts, and dance recitals. He wrote to his wife of having savored the "admirable" performance of Junius Booth in "Richard Third," and told her that he had "heard 'Miss Cramer' the new English singer warble her fine notes." "Last but not least," he had seen "Madame Vestris execute her wonderful dances." Lucia Elizabeth Vestris was a famous English actress and opera singer of the day who had made use of her beautiful legs to branch out into dancing. Even as early as 1828 New York had begun attracting the stars of the English theater and concert stage like Madame Vestris, and Elliott had been eager to see her. He had not been disappointed. "She throws all other dancers completely in the shade," he raved to his wife. "There is such finish in her steps, and such grace not only in the mere dancing, but in the walk, the attitude, and the play of her limbs."[51]

Twenty-five years later John Stewart Oxley expressed the same enthusiasm of cultivated visitors from below the Mason-Dixon when he wrote home describing with delight the excitement of being "amidst all the noise and bustle of omnibuses and carriages" and of having as fine a "choice of stores for everything you can possibly want, or fancy you want." Indeed, it was just such bustle and variety that made him feel as if he were in "old London." But Oxley, like other urbane southern travelers, was interested in more than admiring the contents of shop windows. Like Elliott before him he consumed a healthy portion of New York's artistic fare, and just as in London he was able to savor both operatic and dramatic performances. Soon after arriving in Manhattan, he had gone to the opera to see Gaetano Donizetti's "La Favorita," where, mixing culture with social concourse, he had met "many acquaintances, mostly from New Orleans, and among them two very pretty Creole girls with whom I came up the Mississippi in the [steamboat] Eclipse."[52]

Oxley believed that in the area of theater and music New York City was rapidly closing its cultural gap with London. Gotham's musical venues, he observed, were being rapidly augmented by auditoriums such as "Franconi's Hippodrome, well known both in Paris and in London." This massive hall had been fashioned by extensively remodeling the Harlem Railroad Depot at 26th Street and Madison Avenue, and frequently playing in new auditoriums such as the Hippodrome were performers who came straight from London. "Above all to remind one of Drury Lane" the Tennessee correspondent was pleased to report home that Gotham audiences were being regaled with "Jullien's concerts," advertised on Broadway by "flaming red placards." The year before Oxley enthusiastically reported his presence in New York Louis-Antoine Jullien, celebrated

Parisian conductor and composer of band music, had been in London, where his enormously popular orchestra had performed both opera and promenade concerts. Now he had arrived in New York, and the cultivated Tennessean lavishly described him in his letter "elaborately got up in white waistcoat, embroidered shirt front, white tie, and hair curled within an inch of his life." At almost the same moment he was providing this richly detailed portrait, his friend Sue Henry was writing to her mother about having heard Jullien's concert, judging it "without exception the best organized band I ever heard."[53]

Some southern visitors considered Gotham's musical culture to be not merely a pleasant addition to their activities in the city but the primary purpose of their journey. One of these cultural tourists was Virginia Clay-Clopton. Although she was the wife of Clement Clay, the Alabama lawyer and loyal southerner who so hated spending his money in New York, she did not share her husband's dim view of the city. Indeed, she was strongly attracted to its musical and theater culture, especially after Clay was sent to Washington to represent Alabama in the U.S. Senate in 1853. She enjoyed well enough her share of dinners, dances, and receptions in Washington, but to escape this sometimes tedious social round as well as the capital's dearth of quality musical concerts, she apparently was able to entice her husband, and "a few congenial friends" to travel numerous times to New York in the 1850s. There they "were enabled to hear" musical performances by major artists such as the celebrated British operatic soprano Euphrosyne Parepa-Rosa.[54]

Clay-Clopton and her friends were drawn to Gotham not primarily by its shops but by dramatic productions such as Julia Dean's *Ingomar*. Dean was one of the most renowned and popular American actresses of the mid-nineteenth century. But Broadway of the 1850s had begun to showcase celebrated English thespians as well. Clay-Clopton considered herself fortunate to have seen acclaimed English actress "Agnes Robertson, who set the town wild in the 'Siege of Sebastopol.'" The most sublime of Virginia Clay-Clopton's New York cultural experiences occurred in September of 1850, just months after her husband had written home to his brother describing the disgusting spectacle of hordes of southern tourists squandering their money in Gotham. With Clement Claiborne Clay sitting next to her—one can only hope in a better mood—she was privileged to hear opera sensation Jenny Lind, "the incomparable Swede, whose concerts at Castle Garden were such epoch-making events to music lovers in America."[55]

Gotham impresario and huckster supreme P. T. Barnum had orchestrated Lind's press campaign and her triumphant arrival from Europe at the Canal Street dock complete with twenty corps of firemen and triumphal arches on Broadway. This remarkable entrance had so galvanized New Yorkers that Barnum himself boasted that Lind "would have been adored if she had had the voice of a crow." Jenny Lind assuredly did not have the voice of a crow. For Virginia Clay-Clopton it was a marvelous vocal instrument, and it assured that no one would carry "for a longer time" than she "a clearer remembrance of that triumphant evening." Some had estimated the attendance at Castle Garden that evening at 10,000. Clay-Clopton only knew that "seats and aisles in the great hall were densely packed, and gentlemen in evening dress came with campstools under their arms, in the hope of finding an opportunity to place them, during a lull in the program, where they might rest for a moment." Lind had completed her performance with a rendering of the sentimental ballad "Home! Sweet Home!" The "beauty of her marvelous art" far surpassed for Clay-Clopton any "amusement . . . her broken English might have aroused," and as she sang "Mid bleasures and balaces" men and women "wept freely and unashamed."[56]

Castle Garden, the capacious and comparatively venerable auditorium in which Virginia Clay-Clopton heard Jenny Lind sing, sat in New York harbor near the foot of Battery Park and was linked to land by a wooden bridge. Formerly fortified and known as Castle Clinton, it had been refurbished as a theater in 1826. For nearly thirty years it would serve as a prime venue for musical performances, and southerners such as Agnes Tinsley and Elizabeth Ruffin in the 1820s and Virginia Clay-Clopton in the 1850s would cross its footbridge and pass through its doors. Mrs. Clay-Clopton would enjoy the aesthetic experience. Others would have a less enthusiastic response. Three years after Lind's famous concerts Sarah Gayle Crawford attended an opera at the Castle. But unlike Clay-Clopton she admitted in her diary that she had "never fancied the opera." It seemed to her that one paid "dearly for an occasional strain of sweet music," having to "sit for hours hearing that which" one did "not enjoy."[57]

Lest one judge Crawford a complete philistine it is incumbent to note that her lack of enthusiasm for opera was balanced by her decided enthusiasm for painting. Though her response to the Castle Garden opera performance might suggest a narrow provincialism, other diary entries reveal her to be a more open and eager tourist. In one passage she remarks that she and two female companions felt "quite independent" enough to venture out alone and ride "with confidence in the omnibuses." One of these excursions had climaxed with a pleasurable visit to Dusseldorf Academy. Here she had been most favorably impressed with the paintings, especially "Hildebrandt's 'King Lear.'" Crawford's visit to the Dusseldorf Gallery suggests the extent to which art markets were expanding in New York. By the 1850s so much individual wealth had accumulated in the city that art dealers in nineteenth-century European art centers like Dusseldorf were establishing branch offices to promote the sale of native painters like Theodor Hildebrandt, and American dealerships were growing more plentiful as well. In the two decades before the Civil War there were an abundance of galleries for wealthy southerners to visit and plenty of paintings, both European and American, for them to appreciate and consider purchasing. In 1857, four years after Crawford had admired *King Lear,* southern art enthusiasts would be among the thousands who daily crowded into a Broadway showroom to view Edwin Church's massive and imposing *Niagara.*[58]

New York City's impressive offerings of music, theater, and art certainly delighted cultivated southerners. But the close commercial ties between the South's cotton aristocracy and Gotham's mercantile elite guaranteed that social ties between the city and the antebellum South would be correspondingly intimate. Sue Henry took pleasure in attending opera and concerts during her visit, but she also had a delightful entrée into private dances and parties that many contemporary southern visitors can only envy. Sue wrote to her mother that she had enjoyed "a hop at the Metropolitan night before last. Mrs. Morgan invited me, and we had a rare time of it with some young officers who came over from Governor's Island one supposes." One of these young men had been "very tall and fine looking." He had hailed "from Maine" and "graduated at West Point." Sue confessed to her mother that she had been "*mightily taken*" with him. This Yankee Lochinvar had given the Tennessee belle "a brass button," and he had promptly called on her the next morning. Conversation between the two had been facilitated by the discovery that one of Sue's good friends had attended West Point while the Maine cadet had also been enrolled there.[59]

Sue Henry's letter alludes to the close social ties that bound New York and the South into the 1850s. "Mrs. Morgan" was a New Yorker whose high social pedigree is suggested by her participation in a private dancing party at one of the city's most prestigious and elegant hotels.

One can also reasonably hypothesize that the connection between her and the plantation-owning Henry family was one based in some way on the cotton trade. As we have seen in chapter 1, wealthy southern planters and merchants were commonly acquainted with wealthy New York merchant and banking families in a personal as well as a professional way. And both social sets not uncommonly sent their sons to the same schools where they could associate with the sons of other gentlemen—schools like West Point. Sue Henry's missive provides vivid evidence for historians like Ira Berlin and Leslie Harris, who argue that New York remained on the eve of the Civil War practically "an outpost of Southern culture."[60]

No matter what their major interests might be, in the decade preceding the Civil War nearly all southern visitors to New York made their way to two of the city's not-to-be-missed attractions—P. T. Barnum's American Museum and the Exhibition of the Industry of All Nations, more popularly known as the Chrystal Palace Exhibition. Barnum's museum was the older of these touristic shrines, established in 1841 on lower Broadway near city hall and the Astor House. The founder's purpose was "to make the Museum the town wonder and town talk," and he succeeded probably beyond his wildest dreams. For nearly twenty-five years, thanks in part to the brilliance of Barnum's promotional ads, posters, flags, and banners, it would reign as "the boast of city guidebooks." Year after year tourists flocked to his museum to see exhibitions of "jugglers and ventriloquists . . . automata and living statuary, gypsies and giants, dwarfs and dioramas, Punch and Judy shows, models of Niagara Falls, and real live American Indians.[61]

In the summer of 1853 Mississippian James Harrison wrote home describing the marvels that made Barnum's Museum a must-see New York experience. Among the "multitudinous wonders of the place" Harrison had viewed "not only anacondas and boa constrictors but a *bearded woman* with an immense fan of whiskers as large as [his friend] Allen's and blacker by far." Perhaps even more amazing was the sight of this strange woman's child "six months old with *a beard on*" and a husband who stood loyally "by the side of his 'bonnie bride.'" In this fantastic tableau the bearded wife sat reading a book "with the utmost *naiveté* while her husband stood by her "with a smirk on his countenance which would seem to signify, 'now she's something, ain't she stranger.'" The bearded lady who so amazed Harrison in 1853 was the latest in a line of human freaks, the central attraction around which Barnum chose to arrange his varied exhibitions. It rivaled but did not surpass his initial curiosity, "a two-foot, one-inch midget named Charles Stratton, better known as General Tom Thumb."[62]

Sarah Gayle Crawford and Sue Henry were visiting the city at about the same time as James Harrison, and they too thoroughly enjoyed viewing Barnum's curiosities. By staying downtown at the Astor House Crawford had placed herself practically across the street from the American Museum, and she visited it almost immediately after she arrived in New York. There she was wonderfully entertained by a performance of "dogs and goats, and monkeys." Like Harrison she considered viewing the bearded lady with husband and child an essential touristic experience. Unlike Harrison, however, she seems to have been as interested in the husband as in his bearded wife, judging him to be surprisingly "good looking." Later in the fall Sue Henry would also find herself at Barnum's being "highly delighted" by the performance of "some miraculous feats, such as cutting a man in two, the head walking off in one direction and body in another."[63]

Twelve years after the opening of the American Museum its supremacy as the city's top tourist destination would be challenged by the opening of the Chrystal Palace Exhibition in the summer of 1853. Inspired by London's enormously popular 1851 Chrystal Palace Great Exhibition of the Works of Industry of All Nations, ambitious New Yorkers determined to create a rival palace in Manhattan. With amazing rapidity, they constructed their own iron- and glass-domed structure on the outskirts of the fast-expanding metropolis along Sixth Avenue and between 40th and 42nd Streets, the site of present-day Bryant Park. For over five years, until its fiery demise in the fall of 1858, large crowds roamed its halls and admired the products of a new era of science and technology. They saw modern "miracles of the age, great and small." They were introduced to products as varied as gas lights, guns, carriages, scientific and agricultural implements, telegraphing equipment, and fire engines. And above all they were amazed by machinery—"machinery to pump water, sew, print, finish wood, refine sugar, set type, make ice cream, and wash gold."[64]

On July 15, 1853, just one day after the official Chrystal Palace opening, James Harrison was able to gain an advance look at what he called "the most beautiful building on this side of the Atlantic." Sheathed in translucent glass he marveled that from the outside one could see "no iron about it at all." Inside Harrison proclaimed it to be "more enchanting still," with "gilding and painted and stained glass" shown to even greater advantage. Throughout the halls of the palace the enthralled Mississippian admired "fine specimens of painting and statuary," a rich variety of mechanical arts, and a wonderful and dazzling presentation of "articles of *silver ware*." Even southerners like Stuart Oxley whose schedules were brimful with activities found time to see the show. Though his visit was of less than an hour's duration he pronounced himself "*very favorably* impressed with the arrangement and general appearance of the articles exhibited." One visit was not enough for Sarah Gayle Crawford. Being particularly interested in objects of art she found it imperative to enter the Chrystal Palace not once but three times. On each occasion she judged the exhibition to be a "grand spectacle." Of all the "enchanting" statuary she viewed on her three inspections none was more splendid in her estimation than the bronze figure of the "Amazon." This figure, created by nineteenth-century German sculptor August Edward Kiss, depicted an amazon on horseback being attacked by a ferocious tiger. It was a smaller zinc copy of what the exhibition catalog described as "the colossal bronze original which adorns the entrance of the Royal Museum at Berlin." As impressed as Crawford was with Kiss's craftsmanship, she was equally "astounded" by Milanese sculpture Giuseppe Croff's representation of a veiled face on marble. "The appearance of the veil," she thought, was little short of miraculous, "transparent—but not concealing the perfection of feature at all."[65]

By the fall of 1853 publications like the *Southern Literary Messenger* were dispatching correspondents to New York to describe and evaluate the city's visually stunning new exhibition. For the *Messenger*'s female reporter, identified as "Cecilia," the experience was a nearly overwhelming one. "What a wilderness of objects! Statues and statuettes, silks and satin, china and glass, furniture of all descriptions, and for all uses. What bright colors! What never ending glitter!" Indeed, "Cecilia" was as bewildered by the crowds flooding the Chrystal Palace as she was by the exhibit itself. "What crowds of people! What questions they ask, and how strange their criticisms." Amid this rather disconcerting variety of objects and opinions where might the more conservatively trained eye of a more modestly cultivated southern viewer find a place to rest? For "Cecilia" there was no answer to this question, but she could draw at least one definite conclusion from her visit to the exhibition. The perplexing array within the Chrystal Palace, she declared, in some fundamental way "must characterize New York."[66]

If "Cecilia's" *Messenger* review suggests the less enthusiastic and more conservative and provincial response to the dizzying variety of Gotham's Chrystal Palace, Major Alfred Mordecai's enthusiasm for the exhibition places him in the camp of more cosmopolitan southern visitors like Ann Wagner, William Elliott, Paul Hamilton Hayne, Stuart Oxley, and James Harrison. West Point educated and a member of a distinguished Jewish family prominent in North Carolina and Virginia, he wrote in November of 1853 to his brother Samuel in Richmond urging him to make haste to visit New York. If he did decide to come, Alfred assured his brother that he would be as gratified to see the Chrystal Palace Exhibition as he himself had been. The show did indeed require "exercise" on the part of those taking it in. He had arrived at ten in the morning and "stayed until 9 p.m., without sitting down the whole time, except for a moment to try an Austrian Chair." But there were wonderful rewards for the discerning visitor willing to take his time. Mordecai recommended a visit of at least three full days. If that prescription seemed too daunting, he assured Samuel that there were plenty of seats scattered about the Chrystal Palace. And "time spent in resting the limbs" was "by no means lost; for the general 'coup d'oeil' which you enjoy at such times is not the least pleasing part of the visit."[67]

Less than a week later sister Ellen Mordecai joined Alfred in imploring their brother not to delay seeing the Chrystal Palace. Arguing against Samuel's reluctance to spend money on such a trip, she reminded him that it would give him a practical opportunity to have "a good merchant talk" with his "business associates" in the city. What's more the exhibition ticket that Alfred had passed on to her when he had left Manhattan would "admit us both—so really my dear brother your only expenses would be travelling." As for travelling costs, Ellen's fare "by land" from Washington had cost her only "$13 and some cents." Though a "baggage master" had taken care of her trunk, she reminded Samuel that he "would probably only have your bag" and would thus "have no expense of baggage transportation." And why did Ellen feel that Samuel should rush to the exhibit? It was "urgent," she wrote, for her brother "to come before the 1st of December" because she wanted him "to see the Palace before anything [was] removed."[68]

Political events of the 1850s in America would be played out against the backdrop of increasingly bitter sectional confrontations, from furious debates over the enforcement of the Fugitive Slave Act to massacres in bloody Kansas and John Brown's abortive attack on the federal arsenal at Harper's Ferry. Yet throughout this politically volatile and contentious decade large crowds of southerners would continue to stream north to Gotham to enjoy themselves each season, even though they were unpleasantly and rather too frequently surprised by the heat of a northern summer. James Harrison thought that no Yankee should be allowed to complain about southern weather. During the August he was visiting the city "*hundreds*" of pedestrians and an even larger number of horses had been "*struck down* within the last few days" on the city's streets by what he termed the "*coup de soleil.*"[69]

But hot as it was in New York that late summer, Harrison nonetheless discovered it teeming with fellow Mississippians. Indeed, he found himself to "have alighted upon" practically the entire population of his hometown of Columbus. The list of Mississippi visitors he presents in his letter of August 15, 1853, seems to read like the social register of his native hamlet: "Miss Tripp . . . Betty Butler and Mrs. Fontaine, Martha Banks, Cousin Sally and family, Miss Belle Gates, Babe Gilmer and Sally Pickett, Mr. Cummins and Leo Gilmer, Cozart, Humphreys, John Witherspoon, Allen Randle, Luke and Henry Whitfield, Moore, Bennoit, Blair, Lumpkin, Otley, Johnson, Sherman, Young Butler, Jake Abbott, Knapp, Mr. Shepard . . . and young cousin Hobson, Cousin Albina's brother, etc. etc." Having recorded such an amazingly long list of fellow southern sojourners, Harrison's concluding and rather dry observation that there were at the time of his visit to New York City "acquaintances on hand" strikes one as a model of understatement.[70]

In September of 1859—six years after Harrison's sojourn and only a month before John Brown's raid on Harper's Ferry galvanized the nation and helped turn sectional divisions over slavery into an unbridgeable chasm—seventeen-year-old Kate Carney of Murfreesboro, Tennessee, was in New York with her father, mother, and sister, still enjoying the city as southern tourists had for the past four decades. Like southerners before them, the Carneys were delighted to find numerous visitors from Tennessee in their Fifth Avenue hotel, but not surprisingly they eventually opted for more centrally located quarters at the La Farge Hotel on Broadway. From the La Farge they were better able to stroll down Gotham's most famous street and to visit Barnum's Museum.

As southerners had before them, they enjoyed shopping at Broadway emporiums such as "Steward's fine silk house," and they admired the offerings of "a large store where they sold pictures, where there were many pretty ones." Like Sue Henry had been six years earlier, Kate was drawn to the city's shops. She purchased "all [she] desired" at a store "where trimmings were sold," and she was excited and delighted when her father bought for her "a handsome brown silk dress and a cloak." But like Sarah Gayle Crawford and Virginia Clay-Clopton, Carney sampled Gotham's cultural offerings as well as its shopping. She too admired paintings at the Dusseldorf Gallery, and she attended and was "very much" impressed by performances at the theater operated by Laura Keene, a famous actress and manager active on both the London and New York stage.[71]

If Kate Carney or her family amid all this activity were disturbed in New York by tensions related to the currently raging debate over slavery, she did not mention it. Indeed, less than two years before the outbreak of the Civil War the young Tennessee belle seems to have found Gotham a thoroughly comfortable place to visit. The La Farge Hotel was for her a particularly inviting place to stay, for it made southern guests feel right at home by offering "colored waiters in the dining room." And after returning from a brief foray to Boston the Carney's judged their accommodations at the Metropolitan Hotel to be even more suitable. Kate observed that southern gentlemen like her father preferred the Metropolitan "so much, on account of having colored waiters in the dining room, but white chambermaids." There is little in her enthusiastic accounts of her visit to suggest that even on the verge of civil war southerners found New York darkened by an oppressive abolitionist and anti-southern atmosphere.[72]

By 1860 one can only be struck by the extraordinary discrepancy between the attacks on New York City's perfidious and hypocritical waffling on the issue of slavery coming from southern politicians and polemical journalists and the enthusiastic reports of the many pleasures of the city coming from southern tourists and travel writers. Never had the South's attitude toward Gotham been more schizophrenic than on the eve of the Civil War. One month before the election of Abraham Lincoln would precipitate the secession of the Confederate states the *Southern Literary Messenger* regaled its readers with the itinerary for a lengthy and delightful trip, beginning in early August in interior Pennsylvania and New York state and proceeding through Niagara Falls to Toronto and Montreal.

The climax of this wonderful tour would be New York City. The *Messenger* travel writer advised his readers to "aim to spend the whole of September in the North, so as to reach New York while the Opera is in season, and to return home about the 10th of October, when cold or at least cool weather will have set in. Make the tour as we have advised, come back and thank us for the six happiest weeks of your life."[73] The southern traveler, had he faithfully followed the magazine's guidelines, would have returned to the South just in time to enjoy a balmy southern fall. Less than a month later, however, he would have been sharply confronted by the election of the despised abolitionist Abraham Lincoln to the White House. After this there would be no more delightful visits by southerners to New York City.

THREE

EARLY FICTIONAL APPRAISALS OF NEW YORK CITY

AS WE HAVE SEEN in the opening chapters, antebellum southerners who traveled to New York City for business or pleasure expressed varied, complex, and often contradictory attitudes toward the growing metropolis in their travel diaries and in letters home. These same convoluted attitudes appear in the works of antebellum southern authors who used New York as a setting or subject for their published essays and novels. Like their fellow-southern visitors, some writers loved Gotham, some hated it, and others seemed to have loved and hated it by turns. But adore the city or loath it, during the first half of the nineteenth century Manhattan exercised a cultural hegemony over the South nearly as complete as its economic dominance of the region's cotton trade.

Southern writers who sought the widest possible audiences for their poems, essays, and novels pragmatically recognized the value of having their works published in Gotham. The more prominent and ambitious a writer hailing from below the Mason-Dixon, the more likely he was to send his manuscripts north for publication. Popular writers of historical and plantation romances such as Virginian John Esten Cooke and South Carolinian William Gilmore Simms published nearly all their works in New York. Thus, the region's writers frequently found themselves joining the northern migration of planters, bankers, and lawyers to the commercial and cultural colossus on the Hudson. This literary exodus to the North included popular and relatively well-known southern writers like Simms and Cooke. But we have seen that even more provincial authors like Albert James Pickett deemed it necessary to make the long and arduous journey to Manhattan in hopes of securing a publisher. In New York southern writers, both well-known and obscure, could cultivate numerous publishers and critics and negotiate with the publishing houses of a metropolis that, in the words of Edwin Burrows and Mike Wallace, was rapidly establishing itself in the 1840s and 1850s as "the nation's information center, a fountain from which news and novels, stock quotes and lithographs flowed in ceaseless profusion."[1] It was, indeed, Gotham's superior access to information rather than its proximity to the South's cotton plantations or to England and France's textile mills that had helped it achieve preeminence in America's cotton market. English broker William Rathbone spoke from extensive experience when in 1849 he correctly predicted that New York City was destined to maintain and expand its dominance not only of the nation's cotton trade but of all its trade. "Within 10 days sail from England and within an hour of information [by the newly invented telegraph] and communication with New Orleans, St. Louis, Cincinnati, Charleston," he observed, the city was "in possession of more information of importance than at any other point."[2] Thanks to its growing power as an information hub Gotham did not need to be near the South's cotton fields. The South's cotton would come to New York. And thanks to the increasing efficiency of its presses and to the growing influence of its magazines, newspapers, and publishing houses, the South's literature, like its cotton, would also find its way to Gotham.

While southern writers recognized the value of cultivating New York's publishers and critics, most of them found no need to fictionally cultivate Gotham, to engage the city as a subject or to use it as a setting. Why would they have wanted to write about New York when nearly all of them were focused on creating idealized fictional southern landscapes populated by lordly plantation aristocrats, delicate, refined, and beautiful southern belles, and loyal and contented Black slaves? These rose-colored fictions were as popular with American readers as they were profitable for New York publishers, and as abolitionist agitation gradually but inexorably increased above the Mason-Dixon Line during the 1840s and 1850s romantic plantation novels served the pragmatic function of fictionally defending slavery and the plantation system as essentially benign, humane, and paternalistic institutions—manifestations of a high-toned and brilliantly cultivated agrarian society.

In the opening decades of the nineteenth century this romantic fiction had issued primarily from the pens of writers closely associated with tidewater Virginia. Novels such as George Tucker's *The Valley of Shenandoah* (1824) and John Pendleton Kennedy's *Swallow Barn* (1832) had given early romantic expression to an aristocratic plantation ethos that had first been nurtured in tidewater Virginia in the eighteenth century. Later novels by Virginia writers such as William Alexander Caruthers (*The Cavaliers of Virginia*, 1834) and John Esten Cooke (*Henry St. John, Gentleman*, 1859) further refined this fictional vision of the plantation and apotheosized even more completely the planter aristocrats who presided over it. By the 1850s this evocative romantic plantation landscape had been transplanted from the Atlantic tidewater to the more recently established plantations of the lower and interior South in novels by writers such as Caroline Lee Hentz (*The Planter's Northern Bride*, 1854) and Joseph Holt Ingraham (*The Sunny South*, 1860).[3]

Yet even though the antebellum southern writer's fictional horizons were usually limited by a provincial urge to defend and glorify plantation society, the South's scripters were occasionally willing to turn their attentions northward, and New York sometimes found itself the setting or the subject of a southern essay or novel. Writers who fictionally engaged Gotham were sometimes tourists like Georgian William Tappan Thompson or South Carolinian William M. Bobo, who after visiting the city found it interesting enough to use as a subject or a setting for their narratives. Others like Virginians William Alexander Caruthers and Edgar Allan Poe chose for professional reasons to reside in Manhattan for significant periods of time. Like the tourists who ascended annually during the antebellum period, all these writers exhibited complex feelings about the rapidly growing metropolis, viewing it now with wonder and enthusiasm, now with irritation and unease. By the politically contentious 1850s as North and South careened toward civil war, wonder was being rapidly supplanted in southern writing by outright and venomous hostility toward Gotham. By contrast, southern authors of the decades of the 1830s and 1840s, such as Caruthers, Poe, and Thompson, represented an earlier generation who were able to approach Manhattan in their writing with both considerable interest and a relatively open-minded tone.

Probably because he was an actual resident of the city for more than five years, William Alexander Caruthers (1802–46) assumed a more moderate and less hostile attitude toward New York than those southern writers who would train their focus on it in the 1850s. Having received a medical degree from the University of Pennsylvania, the young Shenandoah Valley physician was prompted by bankruptcy in 1829 to venture north to reestablish his practice. Caruthers's decision to try his fortunes in Gotham seems to have been dictated partially by his ambition to be a writer. As a young doctor who harbored ambitions of being a professional writer, he was aware of the value of Gotham's cultural currency and of the difficulty of a southerner's obtaining it. "There is evidently a current in American Literature," he ironically observed, "the fountainhead of which lies north of the Potomac, and in which a southern is compelled to navigate up the stream if he jumps in too far south." Caruthers had no intention of entering the cultural current too far south, and his rather bold professional move to America's most rapidly growing city was at least partially vindicated. Though he never became an imminent or wealthy physician in Manhattan, by the time he left it in 1835 he had transformed himself into a successful novelist. *The Kentuckian in New-York* (1834) and *The Cavaliers of Virginia* (1834) were both published by the highly regarded Manhattan house of Harper and were so widely reviewed that, in the words of one unfavorably inclined Boston critic, the author's name had come to be "liberally plastered by every McGrawler (second-rate editor), from Maine to Mexico."[4]

The Kentuckian in New York is an epistolary novel and, unlike Caruthers's later plantation fiction, it does not bear the strong impress of Walter Scott's historical romances. Through a series of letters and in rather disjointed narrative fashion the reader follows the traveling experiences of three students at the University of Virginia—two young South Carolinians who are traveling north from the Old Dominion to New York City and a fellow classmate with the impeccably Virginian name of Beverley Randolph. While Randolph's friends are heading above the Mason-Dixon, he is concurrently journeying south through the Carolinas. During their travels all three young men conveniently find time to court and fall in love with properly well-bred young ladies. The South Carolinians, Augustus Lamar and Victor Chevillere, are joined along their journey by a fellow traveler named Montgomery Damon, a backwoods Kentuckian full of colorful if not always grammatical speech. This character is obviously modeled on Davy Crockett, who had achieved the status of a well-known political and literary celebrity in the East at the time Caruthers was writing his novel. The author's use of a vivid and verbally rambunctious frontier character was probably intended to coast on the wave of Crockett's current popularity and jazz up his otherwise rather staid and tepid romantic plot.

What may interest contemporary readers of Caruthers's narrative today is neither the unremarkable adventures of its conventionally rendered young southern gentlemen nor the novel's homage to the Davy Crockett frontier character type. It is rather the frank discussion of the institution of slavery contained within the narrative and the plea for sectional harmony that Caruthers incorporates into his plot when he moves it north. Uniquely among antebellum southern romances *The Kentuckian in New York* exhibits the honesty and authorial courage to question the wisdom of the South's peculiar institution and to assert the fundamentally American characteristics that firmly bind southerners and northerners. The book's surprisingly searching analysis of slavery is conducted in the letters that Beverley Randolph writes from the Carolinas to his friends traveling to New York. As he journeys south, he is struck by the "immense chasm from the rich to the abject poor" that is much more oppressively obvious than in his native Old Dominion and that he believes is a product of the ubiquitous and culturally deadening dominance of chattel slavery.[5]

In Virginia, Randolph notes, social gradations among the Old Dominion's white inhabitants are less pronounced and more "regular" (1:76). By contrast in the Carolinas the middle class of yeoman farmers, men who constitute "the very happiest, most useful, and most industrious class of a well-regulated community," is relatively small. The yeoman's place is "filled up by negroes; in consequence of which, your aristocrats are more aristocratic, and your poor still poorer" (1:76–77). The young Virginian bluntly asserts that slavery is an "incubus upon" (1:77) the region's prosperity and culture. And its baleful effects can be seen as one journeys through a countryside that becomes "more miserable" the "more deeply" it is penetrated (I:78). It is not, he writes to his South Carolina friends, that the region lacks "splendid mansions, and magnificent cotton-fields varied with flowers, rich and tropical gardens." But despite the occasional opulence that one encounters, social "seeds of decay" are all too apparent to a visitor, scattered about a rural landscape where "energy—enterprise—national pride—industry—economy—amusements—gayety—and above all, intelligence, should grow, namely, with your yeomanry" (1:78). Randolph ironically notes that in the Carolinas slavery seems to have blighted even slave-owning whites; for, as he observes to his friends in one missive, "to tell you the plain truth, many of your little slaveholders are miserably poor and ignorant" (1:119). Only in western North Carolina does he discover widespread "happiness," "prosperity," and "substantial wealth" in the close-knit communities of "simple and primitive Moravians" (1:80). For Randolph the explanation of this paradox is simple. "There are no slaves in this little nation, and labour is no disgrace" (1:81).

As Caruthers has conceived him, Beverley Randolph is the refined product of a tidewater Virginia plantation culture that imagines itself as having created a more venerable, softer, and civilized form of slavery than states to the south and west. He is intellectually and emotionally tied to the great tidewater Virginians who have come before him—planter-aristocrats such as George Washington and Thomas Jefferson. Like Washington, who recognized the humanity of the slaves he owned and freed them upon his death, Beverley Randolph possesses the Virginia aristocrat's sense of noblesse oblige. And he displays in his letters the well-bred and well-educated Tidewater gentleman's sophisticated and flexible intellect, one that allows him to ponder, like Jefferson did in his *Notes on the State of Virginia* (1783), the darker implications of the institution of slavery upon which the South's plantation system has been built. He clearly considers slavery in the lower South to be much harsher and less humane than the Old Dominion model, and he delivers on the planters of the Carolinas a remarkably severe and unvarnished judgment:

> With us slavery is tolerable, and has something soothing about it to the heart of the philanthropist; the slaves are more in the condition of tenants to their landlords—they are viewed more as rational creatures, and with more kindly feelings; each planter owning a smaller number than the planters generally do here, of course the direct knowledge of, and intercourse between each other is greater. Every slave in Virginia knows, even if he does not love, his master; and his master knows him, and generally respects him according to his deserts. *Here* slavery is intolerable; a single individual owning a hundred or more, and often not knowing them when he sees them. If they sicken and die, he knows it not, except through the report of those wretched mercenaries, the overseers (1:115).

Though Randolph insists that tidewater slavery is more benign in practice than slavery in the lower South, he recognizes that this labor system is everywhere in the South a social and political anachronism that contributes to the poverty of the mass of white workers, and he believes that the days of the South's peculiar institution are and should be numbered. He somewhat defensively protests to his friends that he is "no *abolitionist,* in the incendiary meaning of the term." Indeed, he would "boldly deny" to any Yankee moral crusader that he opposes slavery. Yet he frankly confesses in his letter to his South Carolina friends that he is at heart one of that despised party. Like Hinton Rowan Helper—who twenty-three years later in his *Impending Crisis of the South* (1857) would express very similar opinions on the inutility of slavery—Randolph's abolitionism is a southern variant with its own regional inflections. "If I am, therefore, an abolitionist," he writes, "it is not for conscience-sake, but from policy and patriotism" (1:77). And what reasonable and pragmatic southerner would not wish for the end of slavery? "We can never rival those northern people," he concludes, "until we assume the modern tactics in this provincial warfare; that is, throw aside all useless baggage, and concentrate our energies upon a single point at a time" (1:77). Alone among antebellum southern fictional characters, Caruthers's Beverley Randolph provocatively places chattel slavery at the top of his region's pile of useless ideological baggage.

Appearing in 1834, *The Kentuckian in New York* was the last fictional expression of a more tolerant early-nineteenth-century tidewater southern mind, one that could entertain objections to the South's system of chattel slavery and that did not consider a united and uncritical acceptance of slavery de rigueur for a southern writer. It was also unique among southern novels of the period in making a strong claim for a common national identity, and it subsumed the regional depictions of Yankee and southerner by emphasizing the common traits that underlay and united these regional stereotypes and made them variant expressions of a more encompassing American national character. Ironically and no doubt quite deliberately the nationalist Caruthers chose as his fictional spokesman for American unity was South Carolinian Victor Chevillere, native of a state known for its fierce and militant defense of state's rights and regional identity, a state that just two years prior to the publication of *The Kentuckian in New York* had issued its Ordinance of Nullification against federal tariffs imposed by the Andrew Jackson administration.

Chevillere makes a forceful case for national unity in two scenes. The first occurs in Harper's Ferry as the two young Carolinians are about to set off on their journey to New York. At a local hostelry his friend Lamar observes a young traveler demanding immediate attention from the staff. This unpleasantly brusque personage strikes him immediately as a member of that class of "inexperienced gentlemen" who "assume airs and graces which are merely put on as a travelling dress" (1:10). So confident is Lamar in the superiority of his own southern breeding that he quickly moves to his next judgment: "I would bet my horse . . . that fellow is a Yankee . . ." (1:12). Chevillere proves that he is more socially poised and less provincial than his proud friend when he immediately delivers a gentle reproof. "He may be a Yankee," he observes, "but you have travelled too much and reflected too long upon the nature of man, to ascribe everything disgusting to a Yankee origin" (1:12). Personal obnoxiousness, he reflects, is not the exclusive province of a single region, and the "puppyism of Charleston and that of Boston are only different shades of the same character" (1:13). Chevillere understands that snap judgments like his friend Lamar's based on negative regional stereotypes are particularly destructive to a young and far-flung country striving to establish a common national identity. He concludes that "the mutual jealousy of the North and South is a decided evidence of littleness in both regions, and ample cause for shame to the educated gentlemen of all parties of this happy country" (1:13).

Further on in his novel Caruthers gives his South Carolina nationalist a second occasion to promulgate harmony among the United States of America. Having received a letter from his friend Randolph in which he has casually observed that he "hates Yankees," Chevillere reminds him that in London or Paris he too would be considered a Yankee. "The national denomination we have abroad, is 'the nation of Yankees,' or the 'universal Yankee nation.' 'Tis galling to our southern pride, I grant you" (1:71). Yet he humorously assures Randolph that southerners really have no recourse to this outrage: "We must brook it until we can outdo them, in literature at least" (1:71). To the dismissive southern jibe that Yankees are nothing more than petty sellers of "wooden nutmegs," Chevillere demands that Randolph show him "where the country is, where the population is growing dense—where means of living are scarce—land high—trades overstocked—professions run down—and manufactures injured by foreign competition, in which the little arts of trade . . . do not also flourish" (1:71-72). As to the aristocratic Virginian's disdain for "canting and sniveling" Yankee Puritanism, Chevillere poses this query: "Tell me, liberal sir, if you have not, in the very bosom of your great valley, as genuine Presbyterians and Roundheads as ever graced the Rump Parliament or sung a psalm on horseback. And to give the devil his due, these same Presbyterians are no bad citizens of a popular government" (1:72). Having no doubt been stung by Randolph's critical description of a South Carolina landscape overpopulated by slaves and largely denuded of self-reliant and enterprising yeomen, it must give Chevillere pleasure to remind his Virginia friend of the native Presbyterian Puritans who lived and thrived among the Old Dominion's celebrated Cavaliers, particularly in the Shenandoah Valley.

Having established Victor Chevillere in the distinctly atypical role of South Carolina nationalist, Caruthers can move him and his friend Lamar along the road to New York City, the place that was beginning to epitomize the growth, energy, and enterprise of the new nation. To give the New York section of his novel a zest and vitality reflective of its setting, he obviously saw the need of introducing an additional character, one whose language and behavior were not molded in the polished and refined cavalier image of his young southerners. Using the popular western hero Davy Crockett as his inspiration he introduced Kentuckian Montgomery Damon, a ring-tailed roarer whose colorful and demotic frontier English would please readers, Caruthers judged, the way Crockett's own travel accounts were pleasing them in the 1830s. On the Baltimore turnpike the two young Carolinians meet and adopt as a travelling companion the tall, well-built Kentuckian, a "bold, talkative, and exceedingly democratic" fellow who entertains his new friends with conversation "full of quaint, rude, and wild humour" (1:19). Damon despises federalists, or "Tories" as he terms them, as much as he hates "bloody Injuns"; and he is not surprisingly a Jacksonian Democrat and "a devoted follower of Old Hickory" (1:20). Despite the outlandish opinions and the verbal extravagance of the frontiersman, Chevillere professes to entertain "a serious respect for Damon and his unsophisticated honesty, degenerating, as it sometimes does, into prejudices and ludicrous fancies" (1:40). And he finds it easy to include the Kentuckian in his traveling party.

Montgomery Damon's incorporation into Caruthers's New York City narrative demonstrates that the writer was aware of the newly developing school of southwest humor writing issuing from the semi-frontier regions of the interior South, a genre that during the 1830s was fast gaining popularity among American readers. By adding his frontier character to the narrative, he sought consciously to employ this new style of southern backwoods humor to enhance the appeal of his otherwise conventional romantic novel. Southwest humor writing of the 1830s, 1840s, and 1850s that featured characters like Montgomery Damon improbably coexisted during these same decades alongside highly idealized southern plantation fiction. But while romancers like John Esten Cooke, Caroline Lee Hentz, and—in all his other novels—Carruthers himself fashioned slave-cultivated demesnes ruled over by idealized aristocratic planters, other writers of the backwoods South, such as Davy Crockett, Johnson Jones Hooper, Augustus Baldwin Longstreet, Hardin Taliaferro, and William Tappan Thompson chose to portray the varied life of the region's rustic yeomen—from hunts, dances, and camp meetings to drinking bouts, gambling quarrels, and outrageous frontier pranks. Most significantly these writers opted to render the life of the southwest frontier in the fresh and metaphorically vivid language of their yeoman characters. In *The Kentuckian in New York* Carruthers became the only southern romance writer of the antebellum period to breach in his fiction the literary cordon sanitaire that separated supposedly more refined southern plantation writers from the earthy and deliberately unromantic writing of their southwest humor–writing kinsmen.

There was some risk attached to Carruthers's introduction of Montgomery Damon into his novel. For as popular as such characters were with ordinary readers, such exuberant voices celebrating the earthy and bawdy life of southern plain folk were never judged by the American literary establishment to be proper accoutrements to seriously belletristic novels. The primary outlet for the tales of these humorous frontier types—in addition to newspapers like the New Orleans *Picayune* and the St. Louis *Reveille*—was a New York weekly edited by William T. Porter called the *Spirit of the Times* (1831–61). This periodical styled itself as a "Chronicle of the Turf, Agriculture, Field Sports, Literature, and the Stage." Providing a quirky mix of the contents of magazines as varied as today's *Field and Stream* and *Esquire,* the *Spirit of the Times* was characterized through all its varied contributions by "a racy masculine flavor."[6] Carruthers no doubt read the magazine during the years he was living in Manhattan. The dominant influence of this New York sporting magazine on southwest humor writing confirms that, whether racy or refined, antebellum southern writing usually found its way to Gotham in order to reach the widest possible audience.

Southwest humor writing was able to coexist comfortably with plantation fiction of the period because it commonly adopted specific literary conventions that contained and ultimately bound its disorderly yeoman vitality and confirmed the essentially aristocratic foundation upon which southern society—even the crude society of the interior South—was assumed to be established. The most important of these conventions was the framework narrator. Unlike the unsophisticated frontier characters who usually related the humorous dialect tales in first-person point of view, the framework speaker was conventionally well bred and well spoken. Lest the hairy-chested reader of southwest humor be inclined to forget—amid the riot of colorful southern dialect and violent, bawdy, and burlesque action—that the South was after all governed by fundamentally aristocratic principles, these readers could expect that a suitably genteel framework narrator would insert himself at the conclusion of the story. He could be relied upon to control the point of view and remind the reading audience of who was ultimately in fictional command.

Writers of southwest humor were just as concerned as writers of plantation fiction that northern readers recognize them as gentlemen. Therefore, they usually adopted the detached authorial perspective of a framework narrator who spoke at the beginning and end of the story in the measured tones of the southern aristocrat, highlighting the contrast between that aristocrat's formal style and the colorful but crude dialect of the central story's more humble characters. "The Southwest humorist wanted to laugh at the earthy life around him and to enjoy it," Hennig Cohen writes, "but he did not want to be identified with it. Like the romantics, he recognized the existence of the more humble aspects of life, but he had no desire to cast his lot with the yokels."[7]

Caruthers adheres closely to the framework narrative convention of southwest humor writing, and he adopts that tradition's customary tone toward his Kentucky frontiersman, a subtle mixture of admiration and amused condescension. In *The Kentuckian in New York* the author utilizes Chevillere just as southwest humor writers employ their framework narrators to render the mixed judgment of a southern aristocrat on Caruthers's yeoman character creation. During his journey to New York Chevillere gradually develops a "serious respect" for Damon's receptive and democratic attitudes, his lack of pretention, and his "unsophisticated honesty." At the same time the well-bred Carolinian can only feel superior to a man who exhibits along with his colorful but bad English grammar, ignorant "prejudices, and ludicrous fancies" (1:40). Caruthers maintains this ambivalent tone to his novel's end. There Chevillere admits that his acquaintance with the frontier yeoman "was doubtless commenced in the waywardness of our old college mischief, but it has ended in our respecting Damon for his good qualities and looking upon his foibles rather as sources of amusement than as unpardonable faults" (2:108). From the beginning to the end of this narrative there is no separating of Damon's "foibles" from his more dignified character traits.

There is no doubt that Montgomery Damon gives the New York sections of Caruthers's novel a genuine narrative kick that could not be provided by his more restrained Carolina aristocrats. The humor is much akin to that of Davy Crockett's *Tour to the North and Down East* that was entertaining the nation's readers at almost the same time as Caruthers's novel. Both books generate considerable fun by playing off the contrast between frontier naiveté and big city sophistication. The description of Damon's visit to the opera provides an excellent illustration of how this humorous contrast works. At the performance the Kentuckian marvels at the conductor, "that feller that sets at the top of the mob, on the high chair in the middle," and he is amazed at "how he looks at that book before him, as if that stuff could be put down there in black and white." "It *is* all down there, Damon," Chevillere tells him. But the frontiersman remains incredulous. "Come, come, now, strangers, you have stuffed me enough! I can't swallow that exactly neither! All the lawyers in Philadelphia couldn't write down half the wriggle-ma-rees one of the chaps has made since I set here" (1:222)! Damon also remains heartily skeptical of the beauties of classical melodies. When Lamar reminds the Kentuckian that he is listening to "fine Italian music," he responds rather less enthusiastically, "there's 'four-and-twenty fiddlers' sure enough! But I rather suspicion that it would puzzle some of our Kentuck gals to dance a reel to that music" (1:217). New York's theater leaves Damon similarly unimpressed. "'The theater!'" he exclaims. "Would you put this clamjamfry against a deer drive, or a fox-chase, or a 'coon hunt? Why, I wish I may be perlequed through a saw-mill, if I wouldn't rather go to a country-wedding, any day, than come to this place. Why, here it's all make-believe; it's all sham; but out in old Kentuck we *have* the *real* things which you *pretend* here; like we do scarecrows to a corn-field" (2:108).

Perhaps because both Montgomery Damon and his creator were Jacksonian Democrats and not Whigs like Davy Crockett, Caruthers's Kentuckian renders a distinctly more favorable judgment on Gotham than Crockett does in his *Tour to the North and Down East*. He may not be swept away by the splendors of New York opera and theater, but in a general sense he likes the city. And he responds to it positively because of the democratic and egalitarian nature of its culture, the same disorderly free-for-all culture that seemed to repel Crockett. Indeed, he bestows on Manhattan what for him is the supreme compliment. It is, he proclaims, "a real Kentuck of a place, a man can do here what he likes; they don't look at the cut of a feller's coat, but at the cut of his jib. I could wear my coat upside down here . . . and nobody has time to turn round and look at me" (1:190). Damon could never be content living in New York. As he asserts, he doesn't "like to be crowded,—living or dead." And when he reaches the longed-for "open forest ranges" of his native state he rather expects that he will "snort like a wild beast, when he first snuffs a stranger" (2:107). Yet he returns home believing that common cords of democracy and opportunity tie Kentucky to New York City, and in his own homely way he serves just as effectively as the aristocratic Chevillere as a spokesman for national unity.

Damon's uninformed, naïve, yet often remarkably discerning response to Gotham, like the framework narratives of southwest fiction, is contained within the more cultivated and highly articulated observations of his friend Chevillere. Not surprisingly, the high-born South Carolinian is more adept than his Kentucky friend at intuiting the differences in the structuring of social gradations in New York and the South. Among Gotham's upper mercantile class, he detects a "kindred aristocratic feeling" that facilitates his discourse with them. But he also realizes that those on top of Manhattan's social pyramid have a more complicated task than the South's plantation aristocracy in separating themselves from those beneath them. "It is necessary here," he observes, "to have many more bulwarks between this class and those below them than is needful with us; as there is here a regular gradation in the divisions of society. The end of one and the beginning of the next are so merged, that it would be impossible to separate them without these barriers." The barriers, he believes, are subtle. "They consist in little formalities,—rigid adherence to fashion in its higher flights,—exhibition of European and Oriental luxuries, et cetera" (1:203). Chevillere does not suggest that the South's social structure is better or more reasonably composed than New York's. Instead, he observes sharply and impartially that Gotham's social structure is marked by finer, more subtle, more numerous, and perhaps more vexing class gradations.

In his own way Chevillere is as open-minded and as favorably inclined toward New York as Damon. Unlike his Kentucky friend he surrenders

himself to the city's opera and theater, and he is impressed with its vibrant and robust commercial life. Southerners who condemned the city
for its fanatical worship of mammon would not find the highly bred Carolinian among their party. For he was convinced that "trade" was not
"the only thing" that flourished on the Hudson. "The arts of polished and
refined life, refined literature, and the profounder studies of the school-
men," he assured his reader, "all [had] their distinguished votaries" in
Manhattan (1:181).

Despite his enthusiasm for Gotham's commerce and culture, Chevillere was by no means blind to New York's darker aspects. Like southerners both before and after him, he decried the extreme and brutal
contrasts between great wealth and dire poverty to be found all too frequently on display. Embarking on a trip to the Five Points slum during
an epidemic, he encountered several "heart-rending scenes." A humane
southerner could only be shocked to be told of "parents just landed from
Europe, who die and leave little children wandering about the streets,
without any one to know or care for them." And who would believe that
in a place of such massive fortunes one might unknowingly walk past
tenement houses in which dead bodies lay "by twos and threes and sixes;
no one caring or knowing of them, until the corporation officials come
round, and then they are dragged out into the middle of the floor and
thrown into pine coffins, clothes and all—unknown oftentimes, even by
name" (2:29). Chevalier's graphic account of death undoubtedly reflected
Dr. Caruthers' own professional experiences during New York's cholera
epidemic of 1832 that during the summer of the year raged through the
city, prompting roughly half of its citizens to flee and taking the lives
of over 3,500 New Yorkers who would not or could not afford to leave.[8]

The novel's description of a Manhattan slum epidemic might easily
have confirmed the prejudices of the most virulent of the South's Gotham haters. But other than this one scene, there is little in Caruthers's
narrative to comfort these southern naysayers. The novelist had chosen
to live in the city for nearly five years, and this novel indicates that,
concerning this choice, he had little to regret and much to be thankful
for. New York had given him the opportunity to establish his writing
career on a national level. What's more, his sojourn in Gotham seemed
to have strengthened his sense of national unity and fortified his conviction that, if the United States was to have a dominant metropolis,
that metropolis would be New York City. Chevillere, rather than Montgomery Damon, served as a more eloquent spokesman for the writer's

nationalistic themes. "Every southern," the Carolina aristocrat believed, "should visit New-York. It would allay provincial prejudices and calm his excitement against his northern countrymen. The people here are warm-hearted, generous, and enthusiastic, in a degree scarcely inferior to our own southerns. The multitude move as one man, in all public-spirited, benevolent, or charitable measures." By the end of his visit Chevillere believes that he has attained an understanding of why New Yorkers are so commonly and remarkably "above local prejudices." The city's catho-licity, he intuits, is a product of its civic self-confidence. Unlike so many southerners, Gothamites can afford to be broad-minded because they truly consider their hometown "as the commercial metropolis of the Union and all the people of the land as their customers, friends, patrons, and countrymen" (1:181). In passages such as these Caruthers employs Chevillere to make a singular and heartfelt case both for national unity and for New York City as the dynamic epitome of that unity. No southern writer who followed him would speak so strongly for the new American nation and for New York's positive and primary role in that Union as Caruthers did in *The Kentuckian in New York*.

In April 1844, roughly a decade after William Alexander Caruthers ended his five-year residence in New York, another Virginia writer made the decision to move to the city in pursuit of literary fame. The writer was Edgar Allan Poe, and the move was his second attempt to establish a literary beachhead in Gotham, a brief 1837 stay having met with pro-fessional disappointment. Accompanied by his frail young wife and his mother-in-law, this second nearly five-year sojourn proved to be more sanguine for his publishing career, and less than a year after his arrival it resulted in the issuing by New York publisher Wiley and Putnam of both his collected *Tales* and his *Poems*. Poe's biographer, Arthur Hobson Quinn, speculates that the writer was drawn as much by the intoxicating "atmosphere of the growing metropolis" as by the prospect of improving his publishing opportunities. Unlike William Alexander Caruthers, his ambition was to achieve worldwide, not just national, literary renown, and in the 1840s there was no city in American better positioned to attract the attention of Europe's literati than Gotham. By the time he moved on to his native Richmond in 1849 he had written and published in New York's *Evening Mirror* his most famous poem, "The Raven," and he had begun to attract an audience in Europe, especially in France. In his five years in the city he would discover, in the words of Quinn, "both the readiness of New York to treat a visitor with open arms if he has wares to sell, and equal willingness to close its doors to the aspirant who remains to storm the citadel."[9]

Edwin Burrows and Mike Wallace have accurately and pithily observed that Poe "was no fan of cities."[10] Indeed, if he was destined to live in an urban locale it seems overall that he would have preferred residing in the City of Brotherly Love, where he had resided for six years before moving to New York. In one of a series of letters written to a small Pennsylvania newspaper called *The Columbia Spy* just after arriving in Gotham in the spring of 1844, Poe drolly commented that visitors to Manhattan were "apt to speak of the great length of Broadway. It is no doubt a long street," he sniffed, "but we have many much longer in Philadelphia." Despite the quantities of fresh water made available by the newly constructed Croton waterworks, Poe found the long and broad New York avenues "insufferably dirty." Though certain areas of Manhattan like Bond Street and Waverly Place in the "more retired and more fashionable quarters" of Greenwich Village might "surpass in purity the cleanest districts of Philadelphia," on point of general cleanliness he found there to be "no comparison between the two cities." Of course, Poe might well have been trying to curry the favor of his Pennsylvania readers, but he also seems to have found the noise and dirt of New York's streets to be genuinely and profoundly unpleasant. Disagreeable "street-cries" were surpassed by even more disagreeable noises generated by the "immense charcoal-wagons" that infested the city's "most frequented thoroughfares, and [gave] forth a din which I can liken to nothing earthly." And heightening the offense to the ears were the "unmeaning round stones" with which New Yorkers seemed perfectly satisfied to pave their streets, stones that proved to be nothing more than "ingenious contrivance[s] for driving men mad through sheer noise."[11]

Like fellow Virginian Thomas Jefferson, Poe tended to associate cities such as New York with crass commercialism, unbridled materialism, poverty, and crime. But luckily for him the northern expanses of Manhattan Island remained during the 1840s relatively bucolic. He quickly removed his family from dirty and expensive quarters on Greenwich Street to a two-hundred-acre farm owned by the Brennan family five miles outside town off the Bloomingdale Road near present-day West 84th Street. It was from this farm that he roamed "far and wide over this island of Mannahatta" and penned some of the most interesting and evocative descriptions we have of mid-nineteenth-century New York. At the time of Poe's residence scattered forests remained in what we now know as the Upper West Side, and the writer observed that "some portions of [the island's] interior [retained] a certain air of rocky sterility which may impress some imaginations as simply *dreary*." To Poe, however, such tracts conveyed a sense of "the sublime." And his admiring description of Upper Manhattan Island recalls the wonder of fellow Virginian St. George Tucker when he gazed upon the same scene from Washington Heights roughly sixty years earlier. Poe believed the eastern or "Sound" face of this relatively undeveloped section contained "the most picturesque sites for villas to be found within the limits of Christendom." So entranced was he by Manhattan's upper shore that he "procured" a "light skiff" with oars and made his way "around Black-well's Island [present-day Roosevelt Island], on a voyage of discovery and exploration." Here, where the apartment buildings of the Upper East Side and Yorkville now stand, Poe delighted in viewing the "particularly picturesque" houses that lay scattered along the banks of the East River, dwellings that were "without exception, *frame*, and antique."[12]

Even amid these rapturous descriptions of upper Manhattan, however, Poe exhibited the romantic writer's sense of mutability and decay brought about by the ravages of time, a mutability that was nowhere more disturbingly evident in nineteenth-century America than in New York City. The charmingly antique wooden houses evidenced for the writer not so much a venerable endurance in the face of change as the brutal reality that "nothing very modern [had] been attempted" in the area for years, "a necessary result of the sub-division of the whole island into streets and town-lots." As Poe sadly observed in another of his letters, these "magnificent places were doomed. The spirit of Improvement has withered them with its acrid breath. Streets are already 'mapped' through them." With acute prescience he realized that it was impossible to "look on the magnificent cliffs and stately trees" of Manhattan Island "without a sigh for their inevitable doom—inevitable and swift. In twenty years, or thirty at farthest, we shall see here nothing more romantic than shipping, warehouses, and wharves." In another of his letters he again foresaw the calamitous advance of a future New York City with this grim description: "Every noble cliff will be a pier, and the whole island will be densely desecrated by buildings of brick, with portentous *facades* of brown-stone, or brown-*stonn*, as the Gothamites have it."[13]

If Poe found New York a less-than-pleasant place to live, he judged Brooklyn, its rapidly expanding sister city on the opposite bank of the East River, to be even less appealing. In fact, he declared that he had known "few towns which inspire me with so great disgust and contempt." Despite its salubrious situation on the shores of the most beautiful harbor "in the northern hemisphere," New Yorkers had poured across the river on two-cent ferries and swiftly "disfigured" Brooklyn with their "atrocious *pagodas,* or what not—for it is indeed difficult to find a name for them." Some residences, he conceded, had been built with "tolerable" taste; but the majority . . . [were] several steps beyond the preposterous." Poe judged the architectural pretensions of this new city to be ridiculous. For what, he asked, could "be more sillily and pitiably absurd than palaces of painted white pine, fifteen feet by twenty. . . . You see nowhere a cottage—everywhere a temple which . . . might have been tasteful had it not been Gothamite—a square box, with Doric or Corinthian pillars, supporting a frieze of unseasoned timber, roughly planed, and daubed with, at best, a couple of coats of whitey-brown paint."[14]

Poe's letters to *The Columbia Spy* suggest that he was as disenchanted with New York's municipal governance as he was with the banal and pretentious architectural taste of its bourgeois inhabitants. He noted that with each change in Gotham's administration there inevitably came a period in which lame duck office holders abandoned all pretense of serving the public in pursuit of their own private gain. Soon after his arrival in the spring, he complained, "entire districts" of the city had languished in darkness, "the lamp-lighting functionaries flatly refusing to light up; preferring to appropriate the oil to their own private and personal emolument, and thus have a penny in pocket, with which to console themselves for that dismissal which is inevitable." Major thoroughfares "thronged" with traffic and pedestrians had remained dark for weeks. Poe asserted that when one questioned native New Yorkers about whether these civic scoundrels could be punished for their malfeasance, their reply was "invariably—'oh, no—to be sure not—the thing is expected, and will only be laughed at as an excellent practical joke. The comers-in to office will be in too high glee to be severe, and as for the turned-out, it is no longer any business of theirs."[15]

Despite Poe's numerous complaints about New York in his letters to *The Columbia Spy,* certain aspects of the city's life did impress him. He was, for example, very aware of and intrigued by Gotham's transformation in the 1840s into America's richest urban area, one that was also swiftly assuming its position among the most opulent cities in the world. By the time of his arrival Gotham boasted a super-rich class of mercantile and commercial titans, and these men and their families could afford to buy the most expensive luxury items that Europe could produce. Among those retailers hastening to supply the needs of Manhattan's newly minted plutocrats were two New Englanders, Charles L. Tiffany and John P. Young. Having opened a stationary and dry-goods shop on Broadway in 1837, Tiffany and Young had by 1844 skillfully transitioned to luxury goods imported from Europe and around the world. Poe devoted a significant portion of one of his letters to the *Spy* describing the "great raree-show of Messieurs Tiffany, Young, and Ellis, Broadway, at the corner of Warren."[16]

The newly arrived southern writer regaled his rural Pennsylvania readers with a description of a store whose warehouses were "beyond doubt, the most richly filled of any in America; forming one immense *knicknackatory* of *virtu*." Though Poe's phrasing suggests a distinct superciliousness of authorial tone, the detailed catalog of *objects d'art* that he included for his readers leaves little doubt that he considered the items he cataloged to be of uniformly high quality. The detailed list included "a beautiful assortment of Swiss osier-work; chess-man—some sets costing five hundred dollars; paintings on rice-paper, in books and sheets; tile for fencing ornamental grounds; fine old bronzes and curiosities from the ancient temples . . . solid carved ebony and 'land-scape-marble' chairs, tables, sofas." Like many of his southern contemporaries who were visiting the city, Poe was amazed by the wares on display in this New World metropolis. He would probably have been even more amazed had he known that four years later Tiffany would purchase the personal jewels of Maria Amalia, wife of the recently deposed French King Louis Philippe, put them on display in his store, and win for himself the commercial title "King of Diamonds."[17]

Addressing his descriptive letters to a small audience in rural Pennsylvania, Poe must have considered his work far enough removed from the eyes of New York readers to avoid raising their ire. The deprecating and even scathing tone of many of his observations about Gotham does suggest, however, the tendency toward authorial indiscretion and vituperative language that would ultimately prove his undoing. Initially he basked in the huge success and popularity that the publication of "The Raven" brought to him in January of 1845. Immediately after this signal publishing event New Yorker Charles Briggs took Poe on as his junior partner when he established the *Broadway Journal,* a magazine that was to be devoted to celebrating the city's increasingly vibrant cultural life. Befitting the open and flexible temper of Gotham's cultural elite, he was also admitted into Manhattan's literary salons. Prominent among these gatherings was Anne Charlotte Lynch's Saturday "conversaziones," where Poe could freely intermingle with literary lions such as Washington Irving and William Cullen Bryant. But Edgar Allan Poe's days in Gotham's cultural sun would be numbered. By January of 1846 the *Broadway Journal* had collapsed, plunging him into debt. And to make matters worse he entered a feud with Lewis Gaylord Clark, the editor of the venerable *Knickerbocker* magazine and a close friend of both Irving and Bryant. Poe would successfully sue Clark for libel, but legal success would result in his professional undoing. The doors that had been opened to him in 1845 were firmly shut in 1846 as New York's cultural community rallied to support Clark, a pillar of the city's literary establishment.[18] Poe's five minutes in the city's celebrity spotlight were over. To complete his misery his beloved child bride, Virginia, would die of tuberculosis in Fordham in January of 1847.

By 1849 Edgar Allan Poe would be ready to say goodbye to New York City. In July of that year, he returned to his native Richmond, Virginia, to renew a courtship with an old friend, a socially prominent widow named Sarah Elmira Royster Shelton. But before he left Manhattan, he exacted a small measure of literary revenge on the place that had liberally opened and then slammed shut the door to literary fame. In February he published in a rather minor magazine called *Flag of Our Nation* a science fiction tale entitled "Mellonta Tauta," the action of which is set a thousand years into the future. The narrator of this story, who calls himself Pundita, is a passenger on a huge balloon named the "Skylark" traveling above the world at the impressive speed of over 100 miles an hour. Despite the balloon's velocity, Pundita finds the trip boring, being inconveniently cooped up on the aircraft, like passengers today on a commercial flight to Europe or Asia, with "some one or two hundred of the canaille [common people]." As they fly over "Kanadow," the home of the ancient "Amriccans" who were Pundita's "immediate progenitors," the narrator and a friend named Pundit relieve their boredom by fashioning a wildly inaccurate account of the American civilization that once flourished below them.[19] In Pundita's description of the ancient city of Manhattan Poe fabricates a brief but devilish lampoon of the city that had so thwarted his ambitions.

Now wholly a part of "the Emperor's Garden," the nine-mile-long island that Pundit and Pundita see below them "was, about eight hundred years ago, densely packed with houses, some of them twenty stories high; land (for some most unaccountable reason) being considered as especially precious just in this vicinity." Because Manhattan was destroyed by a massive earthquake in 2050, it has been difficult for even the "most indefatigable of our antiquarians" to obtain "sufficient data . . . wherewith to build up even the ghost of a theory concerning the manners, customs . . . of the aboriginal inhabitants." The best that Pundita can report about them is that "they were a portion of the Knickerbocker tribe of savages infesting the continent at its first discovery by Recorder Rider, a knight of the Golden Fleece." Manhattanites, Pundita conjectures, were "by no means uncivilized" and were "acute in many respects." Yet they were "oddly afflicted with monomania for building what, in the ancient Amriccan, was denominated 'churches'—a kind of pagoda instituted for the worship of two idols that went by the names of Wealth and Fashion." The ancient city's women were also odd, "deformed by a natural protuberance of the region just below the small of the back—although, most unaccountably, this deformity was looked upon altogether in the light of a beauty. One or two pictures of these singular women have, in fact, been miraculously preserved. They look very odd, *very*—like something between a turkey-cock and a dromedary."[20]

Edgar Allan Poe viewed New York City with a jaundiced writer's eye, and if his published descriptions of it are any indication, familiarity did not lessen his contempt for many aspects of its culture. He flayed it for its noise and dirt, its municipal corruption, its banal architectural taste, and its fundamental materialism and superficiality. Possessed of a romantic aesthetic, he was not interested in and consequently he was largely blind to the cultural and commercial dynamism that was transforming the metropolis into the largest and most quintessentially American of our nation's cities. Lacking fellow Virginian William Alexander Caruthers's nationalistic vision, he could not appreciate New York's central role in the life of the new nation. Poe's romantic sensibility, however, did endow him with an intense and vivid apprehension of what was being lost and destroyed in the wake of Gotham's extraordinary expansion up Manhattan Island. What the poet imagined was not the city as a symbol of the new Republic's triumphant future, but the city as an emblem of the dehumanization and destruction that accompanies rapid material progress. What he elegized in his letters was the disappearance of the place he preferred to call "Manahatta." Poe's valediction to the unspoiled landscape of Manhattan Island would be wistfully echoed approximately seventy-five years later by another great American writer, who would also yearn for an "old island here that flowered once for Dutch sailor's eyes—a fresh, green breast of the new world." Though Poe was no more a native New Yorker than Scott Fitzgerald, he possessed an elegiac sense of Gotham's savagely erased past that would tally suggestively in the future, not only with Fitzgerald, but also with the melancholic tone of New York's great nineteenth-century wordsmiths, Herman Melville and Henry James.

———————

Walking the streets of New York in the mid-1840s it is just possible that Edgar Allan Poe unknowingly walked past a Georgia writer named William Tappan Thompson, for Thompson visited Gotham during the middle of that decade, and he subsequently transferred his New York experiences to his popular fictional creation, Major Joseph Jones, one of the most original and appealing characters in southwest humor writing. Like quite a few other prominent southern writers of the antebellum period—Joseph Holt Ingraham and Caroline Lee Hentz, to name two—Thompson was not a native-born southerner. He grew up in Ohio, but he moved to the South as a young man. And like most of the South's northern transplants he quickly and thoroughly assimilated himself into southern plantation society. He lived most of his life in Georgia, and that state was the setting for his humorous tales. His most famous character, Major Jones, was a planter and slave owner of modest origins whose vividly detailed romances, adventures, and travels were rendered in letters employing dialect spelling to convey the semiliterate language, the vivid metaphors, and the often outrageous and bawdy action of southern frontier writing. Thompson's first collection of letters, entitled *Major Jones's Courtship,* appeared in 1843. The popularity of his character resulted in several enlarged editions of this work, as well as new collections. *Major Jones's Courtship and Travels,* appearing in 1848, remains today especially notable for its arresting description of a visit taken by the title character to New York City in 1845.

At the opening of *Courtship and Travels* Major Jones has successfully wooed and married his sweetheart, Mary Stallins, and she has recently borne him a son. To celebrate his new life as a married man Jones has planned an ambitious itinerary that takes him and his new family by stagecoach, rail, steamboat, and ferry through Augusta, Charleston, Wilmington, Washington, Baltimore, Philadelphia, and, finally, to New York. His journey makes it abundantly clear that even after the advent of the railroad getting from the interior South to Gotham in the 1840s remained an arduous experience for the southern traveler requiring several forms of transportation. As Jones tells his correspondent, he has procured a "first-rate overseer to take care of the plantation" and his wife is "tickled to deth at the idee of seein New York." She plans on "getting a new bonnet rite from the French milliner; and the galls is all gwine to send for new frocks to be made in the very newest fashion." Jones's mother-in-law looks upon the trip as an outrageous folly. She would not "give a thrippence to see all the bominable Yankees in the world." To her mind Georgia has "as many fine plantations, and handsum towns . . . as many cataracks and sulfer springs . . . as she wants to see." Why risk "shiprack" or being blown apart by "some everlasting steamboat bustin its biler?" It's no wonder that southerners complain about "hard times," she grumbles, "when they go to the north every summer and spend all ther money in travelin and byin fineries."[21]

Major Jones ultimately decides that he should take the trip to Gotham alone. Considering the absolute chaos of his arrival into Manhattan by ferry from Jersey City the reader feels that he is probably better off having to fend only for himself. Amid hordes of arriving passengers and clamoring porters he must somehow manage to transfer his bags from the New Jersey train terminal to the Hudson River ferry. Jones is so confused by multiple competing demands for his luggage checks that he finds himself "deaf and dumb," not understanding "a word they sed." Finally, an "honest lookin Irishman" asks him politely if he can handle his bags. "Ther was," Jones observes, "sumthing like honest independence in the feller's face, and I gin him my checks, and in he went for my trunks." Returning with one of the trunks, the Irish porter asks him to stand by it while he retrieves the second. "I tuck my stand, and it was jest as much as I could do to keep the devils from carryin it off with me on top of it" (11, 109).

Nothing in Georgia has prepared Major Jones for New York's chaos. "Ther was sich a everlasting rumpus I couldn't hear myself think. The clerks was callin out the numbers—evrybody was runnin about and lookin after ther baggage, children was cryin, wimmin was callin for ther husbands to look out for ther bandboxes—hackmen and porters was hollerin and shoutin at the people and at one another—whips was stickin in your eyes evry way you turned—and trunks, and carpet bags and boxes was tumbling and rollin in every direction, rakin your shins and mashin your toes in spite of all you could do" (11,109). The bedlam of the Jersey side is replicated by the mayhem of Manhattan. The Irish porter leads Jones to his hack "what was standin in the middle of 'bout five hundred more hacks and drays, all mixed up with the bowsprits and yards of ships that was stickin out over the edge of the wharves and poking there ends almost into the winders of the stores." Asked which hotel he wants to go to, Jones requests that his porter to take him "whar the southern travel [stops]" (11, 110). He is subsequently driven to one of the hotels that specialized in accommodating southern travelers during the 1840s, the American Hotel, situated on Broadway directly across from City Hall.

The derangement of senses that Gotham brings to southerners like Major Jones accustomed to quieter rural living is epitomized in the writer's attempt to navigate the sidewalks of Broadway. Maintaining one's course, he concludes, is about as difficult as safely negotiating a small boat down the flood-swollen Savannah River. "A body must watch the currents and eddies, and foller 'em and keep up with 'em, if they don't want to git run over by the crowd or nocked off the sidewalk, to be ground into mince-meat by the everlasting ominybusses." And he quickly realizes that he should forget about following pedestrian rules. Trying to keep "to the right as the law directs," he finds himself "run over by the crowd of men and wimmin and children and n——s, what was all gwine as fast as if ther houses was afire." Like Edgar Allan Poe he must also suffer the racket generated by omnibuses clattering over the city's infamous round stone pavements, "whirlin along over the stones like one eternal train of railroad cars, makin a noise like heaven and yeath was cumin together." Jones finds the cacophonous combination of "carriages and hacks and market wagons and milk carts, rippin and tearin along in every direction—the drivers hollerin and poppin ther whips . . ." enough "to drive the very old Nick himself out of his senses" (2, 111).

Once he accommodates himself to Manhattan's infernal clamor Major Jones encounters both the city's low and its high life. Coming upon a poor beggar lady with a bundle in the street, he kindly gives her a dollar. She asks him to hold her bundle while she goes to a drug store to buy medicine. When after a long period of waiting she does not return, Jones investigates the bundle and finds a baby nestled among the rags. The policeman who subsequently relieves him of the infant assures him that such tricks of the poor are not uncommon in Gotham (11, 113–16). To experience a higher aspect of the city's culture a friend takes him to the Olympic Theater for the presentation of Gaetano Donizetti's comic opera "The Daughter of the Regiment," where "the house [is] packed like a barrel of pork, whar ther ain't room enuff left to git another foot or jowl, nor so much as an ear into the barrel, all except my fren's private box." Major Jones enjoys the opera well enough, but like Caruthers's Montgomery Damon he announces that he would like such performances "a good deal better if ther wasn't so much singin in 'em" (11,118–19).

Assessing New York's men and women toward the end of his visit, Jones finds both sexes inferior to their southern counterparts. In evaluating Gotham's male population, he refers to "Colonel Bill Skinner of Pineville," a "full-grown Georgian" now visiting the city and celebrated by its newspapers as the "Georgia giant." Thompson's narrator avers that Bill would be considered merely big back home in his native state. "Among us," he writes in the braggadocio manner of the southwest humorist, "he don't look more'n half so big as he does here, whar the average size of the men is much less than it is in our genial soil, whar men's bodys as well as ther harts git to be as large as ther Maker ever intended 'em to be" (11, 122). As for Gotham's fairer sex, there is no doubt that "so far as dressin is concerned, they beat Baltimore and Filladelfy all holler." But their comeliness is another matter. In truth Major Jones finds "the further North" he goes "the more fine clothes and the less handsum faces I see" (11, 123). And even the "prettiest blue eyes you meet" in New York "has a kind of a hard, cast-steel expression, so different from the soft, meltin looks of our modest, blue-eyed Georgia galls." No doubt, Jones concludes, living as a woman in a city like New York and confronting the "gaze of strangers" every day makes a lady "less bashful and shrinkin than our Southern galls is." Perhaps also northern education and habits "make 'em less feminine in the style of ther buty. But certain it is ther is the greatest difference in the world between them and the wimmin of the South, and in my opinion the advantage is all on the side of our Southern galls" (11, 124).

The response of Major Jones to New York City is roughly consonant with those of earlier fictional southern yeomen. Jones does hew a bit more closely to the negative tone of Davy Crockett than he does to the more enthusiastic response to the city expressed by William Alexander Caruthers's Montgomery Damon. Generally, however, William Tappan Thompson's narrative situates Gotham comfortably within the genial parameters of frontier humor. It spoofs the city, but it spoofs it in an essentially affable manner. Nonetheless there is one scene in the book in which the tone becomes darker and more bitter—a scene that suggests the widening gulf between New York and the antebellum South that was being created by ever-more-pronounced regional disagreement over the issue of slavery. The episode occurs early in the narrative, and it explains why Major Jones had determined that his wife could not accompany him to Gotham, despite her desire to see the city and procure a new bonnet.

The potential danger associated with southerners traveling to New York is explained to the Joneses by Mr. Montgomery, a family friend who has traveled north and presumably speaks from experience. Mary has informed him that she intends to make the journey with her slave Prissy, a "very careful nurse" who is "so devoted" to her newborn son that "she won't hardly let [Mary] touch him." Upon hearing of her intention Montgomery bursts into laughter. "Haint you got no better sense than to think of takin sich a valuable n—— as that with you, to have her fall into the hands of them infernal abolitionists." He is convinced that Jones could not keep his slave in the city for more than a day. "They'd have her out of yer hands quicker'n you could say Jack Robinson." But Mary protests, "Prissy wouldn't leave us on no account—she knows as well as anybody when she's well treated." According to Montgomery Mary's kindness to Prissy is immaterial. "They wouldn't ax her nothing about it. The fust thing you'd know she'd be gone, and then you mought as well look for a needle in a haystack, as to try to find a n—— in New York." Mary's mother asks if there is there no law against "n—— stealin." "Law!" exclaims Montgomery, "they've sold all ther n——s long ago, and got the money for 'em—so the law don't care whose n——s they steal" (11, 11–13).

Major Jones wonders whether to save his family trip a nurse cannot be found for the baby among the white serving classes of New York. But Mary indignantly refuses to consider this option. And her objections are evidently reasonable ones for a properly raised southern lady. "It may do well enuff for people what don't know the difference between n——s and white folks," she asserts, "but I could never bear to see a white gall toatin my child about, and waitin on me like a n——. It would hurt my conscience to keep anybody 'bout me in that condition, who was as white and as good as me." Her sentiments represent for the modern reader a stunning and grotesque blend of southern backwoods egalitarianism and southern backwoods racism. But no one engaged in this conversation finds anything grotesque or ironic about the opinions being expressed. Mary's mother agrees with her that "no Christian lady" could employ a white nurse; and Mr. Montgomery seconds her sentiment, shaking his head over the idea of northern people making "n——s gentlemen, and their own children servants." They all heartily endorse Mary's final surreal truism on the subject: "N——s is n——s, and white folks is white folks, and I couldn't bear to see neither of 'em out of ther proper places" (11, 12–14).

One would prefer to think that in this scene William Tappan Thompson is ironically distancing himself from the racism of his characters. But in truth it is hard to conclude exactly what kind of authorial tone is on display in this unsettling episode. Mary stays home, sending her husband on to New York alone. The author seems neither to approve nor to condemn her decision and the orthodox southern racial assumptions upon which that decision is based. One might argue that Thompson is implicitly allowing the opinions of his characters to condemn themselves. But one must also note that when the author briefly allows the enslaved Prissy a brief voice in the discussion, he takes care to assure that her words are loyally supportive of her white masters. "'Ki,'" she exclaims, "lookin like she was half scared out of her senses, 'den I aint gwine to no New York, for dem pison old bobolitionists for cotch me'" (11, 12). It is also hard to ignore the impression that the author shares a measure of Montgomery's bitterness toward Gotham when his character observes that, having divested themselves of their slaves, rapacious New Yorkers "don't care whose n——s they steal" (11, 13).

Whether William Tappan Thompson has or has not achieved a degree of ironic distance from his characters' racism, he has introduced into his narrative an element of serious conflict between Georgia and New York City. The testimony of Montgomery makes it abundantly clear that southerners were beginning to view their favorite emporium as a place rife with abolitionists where slave stealing was becoming a commonplace experience for vulnerable visiting slaveowners. Within a few years of the publication of *Major Jones's Courtship and Travels* southern writers would grow even more furious with the imagined depredations on and insults to southern tourists that the scene with Montgomery was intended to highlight. Southerners would demand that Gotham rigorously enforce the 1850 Fugitive Slave Act, and they would condemn with mounting vehemence what they considered the city's hypocrisy and its unreliability on the issue they considered paramount to the survival of their way of life—the preservation of the institution of slavery.

FOUR

BLOTTED FROM THE LIST OF CITIES

SOUTHERN WRITERS ASSAIL GOTHAM

IN 1852, FOUR YEARS after William Tappan Thompson's *Major Jones's Courtship and Travels,* William M. Bobo published in Charleston his *Glimpses of New-York City, by a South Carolinian,* the most detailed guidebook and the most fascinating consideration of Gotham's spirit and character to issue from the pen of an antebellum southern writer. In his book Bobo assumed the role of travel guide for his friend, "Colonel Hammond, of South Carolina."[1] This acquaintance was almost certainly James Henry Hammond. As we have seen in the opening chapter, Hammond was a fierce defender of slavery who would serve over a long political career as the Palmetto State's governor, serving also as its representative to Washington in both the House and the Senate. The survey of Gotham that Bobo detailed for Hammond and for his fellow Carolinians was comprehensive, with chapters focusing on areas of the city as varied as Brooklyn's Greenwood Cemetery, Wall Street, Third Avenue, and Five Points. The book described and rated hotels, restaurants, and shopping districts, and other sections contained evaluations of Gotham's cultural and commercial life. It also considered the nature of the city's people, especially the wide and—for the writer—disturbing spectrum of Gotham's social classes.

William Bobo's response to New York City generally reflected the divided views of earlier southern writers. Like those before him he was genuinely impressed by Manhattan's monuments and public works. Chief among these was the Croton Aqueduct, a huge bridge "of stone . . . about two hundred feet above the water and about a half mile long" that brought clean water from Westchester County reservoirs across the Harlem River to Manhattan and that testified to what Bobo termed "the indomitable perseverance and genius of the universal Yankee nation" (49). The writer was equally amazed by the industry of New Yorkers when he visited block upon block of docks lining the Hudson and East Rivers. Such imposing labors led him to prophesy that within a century the city would "surpass in its metropolitan splendor all the cities ancient and modern." This splendid future would be achieved thanks largely to the current generation of Gotham business magnates who had possessed the foresight and the entrepreneurial energy to establish multifarious and vital lines "of ships and steamers" and thus had made New York the dominant cotton trading center and "forever the chief commercial city of this continent" (79).

Though Bobo enthusiastically praised New York's civic and business dynamism, he responded more ambivalently to the banks and commercial exchanges of Wall Street, and he was both fascinated and repelled by what he termed the "miscellaneous" quality that characterized an area that was rapidly becoming the financial heart of the nation. What seems to have disturbed this high-born South Carolinian most about Wall Street were the blurred racial lines that the city's businessmen tolerated so matter-of-factly. "The Jew and the gentile meet here," he observed drolly; "priest and Levite congregate at the Post-Office." With such a large and promiscuously assembled congregation of mammon worshippers how could one possibly determine whether right and proper men were in control of the levers of investment? For Bobo New York was lamentably deficient in the social homogeneity most likely to reassure a southern gentleman venturing among Gotham's financial barons in the city's teeming financial district. One could stand in the same place "for hours on different days" to see if one "could recognize a single individual come twice" to that location (44). But one's vigil would almost certainly be in vain.

Bobo was bemused by Wall Street, and he was as revolted as many earlier southern tourists had been by the festering slums that affronted him along Chatham and Church Streets and West Broadway, only a few blocks away from its financial houses. Indeed, a short walk from

Gotham's magnificent city hall brought one to the Five Points area where, according to the writer, "poverty, sickness, filth, crime, and wretchedness" met the visitor "full in the face at every turn" (32). The essayist presented as a concrete example of the extreme destitution that a visitor commonly encountered in New York his description of a "haggard-eyed, squalid, and dirty" wretch who carried in her arms an "entirely naked and unwashed" infant delivered, she assured Bobo, only an hour before under a pile of nearby boards. When the gracious Carolinian offers to give her money, she is surprised. "The thought of asking for charity did not occur to her—that forlorn hope, she had tried too often unsuccessfully perhaps before this grand climax of her dreadful life" (32–33). The writer offers this scene as a personal experience, and there is no way to prove its inauthenticity. But one is bound to observe that the destitute woman-with-child tableau had become by the 1850s a favored narrative stereotype for southerners who chose to pillory Gotham's tolerance for extreme poverty. As we have seen earlier, William Tappan Thompson's Major Jones and South Carolina congressman John McQueen both described and professed to having experienced nearly identical and similarly wrenching encounters.

What differentiates William Bobo's attacks on New York's shocking poverty from earlier descriptions by southern writers such as Caruthers and Thompson is his pronounced tendency to use his criticism of Gotham as part of a spirited defense of both the institution of slavery and the southern way of life established upon it. By 1852, the year Bobo published his book, the overall failure of the Compromise of 1850 to soothe antislave agitation was widely acknowledged on both sides of the Mason-Dixon. The South felt itself more and more under attack, and it believed its culture to be the unfair object of increasingly virulent abolitionist onslaughts. What extreme proslave advocates and nascent southern nationalists now began to demand from Gotham's mercantile establishment was not moderate support for the maintenance of slavery but absolute support for slavery that included its future expansion into America's new territories. They insisted that a racially diverse and culturally and politically heterodox metropolis demonstrate something like the same homogeneity of opinion as the slave states had attained on the issue of slavery. If southern writers of the increasingly contentious 1850s like Bobo determined that New York was being insufficiently supportive of the South's peculiar institution, they felt perfectly free to savagely attack their inconstant ally's disingenuousness and hypocrisy.

One can see this new belligerence of tone in Bobo's treatment of what he considers the appalling poverty of so many of the city's inhabitants. Davy Crockett had earlier voiced humorous disapproval of the social promiscuity between white and black slum dwellers that pervaded Five Points. And not surprisingly the South Carolinian was discomfited by the sight of "Dutch and negroes" standing on the same omnibus platform, and he was similarly disgusted to encounter in the city "such a mixture of negroes and whites all on an equality" (126). But Bobo sees more in this casual mixing of races than just the weakening of social hierarchies and boundaries that extreme poverty produces. Unlike Crockett, he goes further to connect this disturbing racial amalgamation to specific southern discontents, such as the issue of fugitive slaves. Observing "gangs of lazy idling negroes" clustered on street corners, he "shrewdly suspect[s] that three-fifths are fugitives or the children of fugitives" (125).

In a similar manner his description of the encounter with the hag and the naked baby ultimately turns into a screed on the horrors of Gotham's wage slavery and on the damnable hypocrisy upon which its toleration rests. He reminds his readers later in his narrative that the plight of this unfortunate woman is scarcely different from that of thousands of Manhattan's sewing girls, grossly overworked and underpaid like so many other working women. How can a city condemn the evils of southern chattel slavery while at the same time tolerating and turning a blind eye to the ubiquitous misery of its own wage slaves? In Bobo's opinion such profound hypocrisy renders Gotham a thoroughly worthy object of divine judgment. "Oh, ye men of New York! You have a list of charges to answer to, which I fear you will not stand acquitted of, at the throne of god" (112).

Bobo repeatedly uses his criticism of the pervasiveness of New York poverty to affirm the superiority of the southern way of life over Gotham's. In Five Points alone, he contends, there are more cases of crime enacted "than the entire South put together." Likewise, there "is more poverty, prostitution, wretchedness, drunkenness . . . in this city, than the whole South." These observations lead him directly if somewhat illogically to a condemnation of abolitionism. "When the *Abolitionists* have cleaned their own skirts," he petulantly asserts, "let them then hold up their hands in holy terror at the slave-holder, and the enormity of his sins" (97). Bobo believes that there is a lesson to be gleaned from the presence of so many miserably poor people living, as he sarcastically observes, "within the corporate limits of this wealthy, law-abiding, and religious city" (34). The evils of slavery—if evils they be—are dwarfed by the poverty and human misery of a northern social system dominated by hypocritical abolitionists.

But it is not northern abolitionists alone who are wildly in error. What he sees in the slums of New York confirms the reactionary South Carolina gentleman's conviction that even the political precepts of one of the South's great founding fathers, Thomas Jefferson, are intellectually bankrupt. He casually dismisses the Sage of Monticello's principle that "all men are born free and equal" as a concept that is quite simply "absurd." What he sees in Five Points and on West Broadway strengthens his belief that "men are born helpless and dependent things, and are not free and equal, nor never can be either." With breathtakingly dismissive arrogance he labels the core principle of America's Declaration of Independence a mere "dogma." And he assures his readers that the notion that this belief "contained sense or patriotism has exploded long ago" (34–35).

William Bobo's anti-Gotham tirades suggest that within the space of the few years spanning the late 1840s and early 1850s something had begun to go haywire in the southern psyche. Davy Crockett, William Alexander Caruthers, and William Tappan Thompson had all been critical of New York to some degree, but none of them would have thought of using their critique as an opportunity for championing the reactionary defensiveness so proudly on display in the pages of *Glimpses of New York City*. Crockett and Thompson were racial conservatives and typical of their region. But neither would have considered defending slavery by trashing the principles of Jefferson's Declaration of Independence. And there is a startlingly wide gulf between Caruthers's thoughtful mid-1830s critique of the South's peculiar institution and Bobo's mid-1850s assertion of the superiority of the system of chattel slavery to New York's wage slavery. The fiercest southern champions of slavery were now defending and upholding slavery by embracing radical and profoundly antidemocratic principles that could do nothing but widen the gulf between the southern states and Gotham.

Bobo's condemnation of New York's hypocrisy extends to his assessment of the character of its inhabitants, one that he judges to be far inferior to that of noble and gracious southerners. "Here," he wryly observes, "the people worship that Trinity known as the goldeneagle, the silver dollar, and the copper cent, with an idolatry equaled only by a faithful follower of Mahomet." Unwilling to acknowledge that the buying and selling of human chattel and the employment of slave labor have anything to do with greed or with the devotion to Mammon, he blithely assures his readers that Gotham's money worship produces a mercenary spirit that is in "contradiction to that which exists in the South" (11). Unlike southerners, he pontificates, the "great object" of New Yorkers of all origins and classes "is *the penny,*" getting it and keeping it (138).

It scarcely comes as a surprise for the writer to learn that people so intent on acquiring money are interested in other people only in so far as they can prize money out of them. Bobo himself claims to have been introduced to a merchant who, while the writer expressed an interest in buying his wares, "was really burthensome with his attentions," inviting him and his wife to his house and taking them for carriage rides and to the theater. As soon as this fawning merchant received a check for "a pretty smart bill" this "'overly' polite friend took a seat with his back to me," Bobo observes, "put his feet against the stove, and commenced reading the morning paper." Though the author and his wife remained in New York for another month, the merchant "never troubled me again." He humorously remarks that he ran into the man two more times. The formerly solicitous merchant "nodded the first, but not the second time to me" (139).

His experience with the merchant confirms Bobo's conviction that New Yorkers, consumed by the prospect of material gain, are almost entirely lacking in the politesse that so distinguishes southern gentlemen. Gotham's manners, he opines, are founded on the determination "to admire nothing, care for nothing, [and] be startled by nothing"; thus Gothamites expend their greatest efforts "to emancipate themselves from all the punctilios of old-fashioned politeness" (140). To hear the narrator tell it "New York men . . . never introduce" friends or guests to others. In consequence a visitor at their parties and other social functions often feels like a "waif, an estray" (141–42). The writer contends that no one in Gotham "could be more indisposed to take the responsibility of presenting you than your own particular friend and companion." Indeed, at social functions a citizen of the city tends to treat his guest as if he were "an escaped convict from Sing Sing" (142). Of course, a more resolute visitor can persist and directly ask to be introduced. In that case according to Bobo the average New Yorker expresses surprise that you do not already know the man and proceeds to slide "away from you." In Manhattan's Darwinian social scene, the visitor who demands too much attention is "troublesome." In this citadel of commerce and social ambition, Bobo wryly determines, one is expected to survive by shaking his "own paw" (143).

Summarizing the character of Gotham's inhabitants, Bobo concludes that the population of Manhattan is composed of not one but three Yankee types. The first, the "New York Yankee," will "skin you and then kick the body out of the house because the hide was not worth more." The second, the "Connecticut Yankee," will fleece you "from principle." The third, the "Down Easter," possesses the most "soul," and for that reason, he will give you "at least half the worth of your money in amusing you while you're under [his] operation" (143). In the author's opinion none of these grasping New York types possess the "nobleness of spirit," the "warm-heartedness," or the "generosity of sentiment and feeling which pervades the soul of the Southerner" (145). Gotham's worship of mammon crushes the genteel temperament of its mercantile elite and smothers the instincts of noblesse oblige that so distinguish and elevate the South's planter aristocracy.

Despite Bobo's crude and broadly stereotypical treatment of the character of the city's residents, he possesses a genuine and sharp apprehension of the impersonal, anonymous, and disaffected nature of life in the rapidly growing metropolis. Earlier southern writers like William Carruthers had also been struck by this pervasive social anonymity, but they had seen it more positively as a reflection of the city's spirit of entrepreneurial energy and cultural heterogeneity and its attendant atmosphere of democratic leveling. In *The Kentuckian in New York* backwoodsman Montgomery Damon had jauntily observed that while visiting Manhattan he could have worn his coat "upside down" and nobody would have had the time to turn around and look at him. Yet the Kentuckian had been quite comfortable visiting a place where residents ignored the "cut of a feller's coat" and focused more practically on his character, what Damon terms "the cut of his jib" (190).

Quite unlike Caruthers's 1830s backwoods protagonist, William Bobo was both a more aristocratic and more profoundly parochial southern product of the polarizing 1850s, unsettled and even repelled by the same depersonalized atmosphere that a character like Damon had found to be so liberating. "I know men," the author wrote in a tone of amazed disbelief, "who have done business ten years in the same storeroom, not on different floors, but upon the same floor, upon the same writing desk, one upon one side and the other the other, who did not know where each other lived; they knew what rent or board they paid to the cent, but *where* was altogether another matter. Their families were perfect strangers." Such profound dissociation seemed freakish and unnatural to the South

Carolinian. He was by no means comforted to realize that one could seclude himself "and have no more to do with the world than Peter the Hermit yet be in the very midst of a half million of people, and as quiet as if you were ten miles in the rear of the Basin Spring, in North Carolina" (144).

The only circumstance that Bobo believed might catch the notice of an otherwise indifferent New Yorker was the prospect of a neighbor's infringing on his material prosperity. The instant one treaded on the toes of a New Yorker's business, the writer mordantly observed, he rose "in his stirrups," and then commenced "a competition and strife known only to quack medicine venders; but all in a business way; nothing personal" (144). Even when engaged most passionately in their greedy squabbles, Bobo believed that the city's residents remained determined to retain their attitude of studied impersonality. Interestingly, within a year of the publication of the South Carolinian's ruminations, native New Yorker Herman Melville would treat this same subject of urban alienation in a devastating and profound short story set on Wall Street entitled "Bartleby the Scrivener." But Melville's masterful work would be absent the sectional paranoia and the reactionary political and social attitudes that so mar Bobo's analysis of Gotham.

Unlike southern writers such as William Alexander Caruthers, Edgar Allan Poe, and William Tappan Thompson—authors who sought to have their works published in the North—William Bobo seems to have been content to have his travel narrative published in his native state in the city of Charleston. Given its astringent tone the prospects of his manuscript's being accepted by one of Gotham's publishing houses would have been bleak. It is unlikely, however, that this proud and choleric southerner cared a fig what New York readers, New York publishers, or New York critics thought about his book. He had obviously written it for like-minded southern readers such as his friend James Henry Hammond, and he clearly assumed that his genteel white audience shared his own exalted assessment of the South's social, political, and economic structure and that they would share his own dim view of Gotham's obsession with mammon and its damnable hypocrisy concerning the vital issue of slavery. *Glimpses of New-York* marks an ominous turn in southern writing during the early 1850s toward a more provincial and defensive regionalism as well as toward a progressively more malevolent view of New York City.

A cascade of unsettling events would continually disturb the increasingly charged political atmosphere of the 1850s. The controversial passing of the Kansas-Nebraska Act of 1854, the barbaric caning of Senator Charles Sumner on the Senate floor in 1856, the divisive Dred Scott decision of 1857, and John Brown's shocking raid on Harper's Ferry in 1859 guaranteed that the issue of slavery would continue to inflame the nation's consciousness. Moreover, the seemingly intractable nature of this conflict guaranteed that the South's condemnation of what it considered Gotham's feeble and irresolute support of slavery would become more intense. By the end of the 1850s no support for slavery that New York City strove to offer the South seemed adequate to appease the fire-eaters who now were beginning to dominate southern opinion and were driving the region toward secession.

Gotham's failure to appease the growing number of southern secessionists was nowhere more in evidence than in the events following the trial, conviction, and speedy execution of John Brown on December 2, 1859. On December 19 several thousand New Yorkers gathered at the Academy of Music for an event that had been organized by Gotham's pro-southern mercantile elite for the purpose of condemning John Brown's October 16 raid on Harper's Ferry, supporting his speedy trial and his execution on December 2, and defending the institution of slavery that Brown's raid had sought to destroy. One might have expected southerners to be gratified by such a massive demonstration of support, but, writing more than two weeks after the rally, the Richmond *Examiner* found "little reason to rejoice at the evidences of popular sentiment and feeling recently given in the most conservative city of the North." True, the editorial observed, those in the South hoping to preserve the Union—the editorial describes them as "timid and credulous Union idolaters"—had been initially elated by the prospect that "the dormant but potent conservatism of the Empire State [had been] aroused." But the early euphoria of naïve southern Unionists had been dashed by the subsequent arrival from Europe of New York senator William Henry Seward, one of Brown's most stalwart defenders. The same city that had produced thousands of supporters for slavery at the Academy of Music convocation now turned out a much larger crowd of tens of thousands of Seward's "Black Republican cohorts." In prose dripping with bitter irony the editorial described "the thunders of a hundred cannon. . . . The vociferous greeting of an immense multitude welcomed [Seward] to the commercial emporium of the Union; the authorities of the city voted him its freedom."[2]

In contrasting these two events the *Examiner* argued that the prospect of New York's coming to its senses and manifesting a united and unalloyed proslave political platform was an illusion. The lesson that southerners had painfully learned from Seward's reception was simple and clear. "We trust that the people of the South will close their ears to the delusive promises of the merchant princes in Fifth Avenue and hearken to no more tattle about popular reactions." At long last it was time for those New Yorkers who claimed to be political allies of the southern states to man up. Slave owners should demand no less than that "every public man" in Gotham, "either in office or a candidate for one, should stand at once upon defined and common ground with the people of the South."[3] The tumultuous reception given Seward furnished clear evidence that prosouthern apologists in New York City could not possibly have generated such unanimous support, but this is precisely what southern hard-liners were now demanding of Gotham's political leadership.

By the fateful election year of 1860 southern opinion on the slavery issue was at a fever pitch, and secessionist sentiment was rapidly on the rise, especially in the states of the Deep South. Denunciations of the city's inconstancy grew more numerous and harsher. Two southern novels, both published in 1860, demonstrate how on the verge of the Civil War hostility to Gotham had thoroughly saturated antebellum southern fiction. One of these works, *The Black Gauntlet: A Tale of Plantation Life in South Carolina,* was written by Mary Howard Schoolcraft, a longtime resident of Washington who had been born into the slaveholding elite of the Palmetto State. In her novel's introduction Schoolcraft boasted that her ancestors had lived in South Carolina "from its earliest settlement."[4] The narrative that followed was a rambling and disjointed account of life on the Low Country plantation of the aristocratic Wyndham family that served as a spirited apologia for what Schoolcraft considered the humane, civilized, and paternalistic institution of slavery.

Schoolcraft's narrative exhibits much of the same defensiveness that her fellow South Carolinian William Bobo had displayed in his earlier New York guidebook. Amid her rambling plot, she pauses to wonder why northerners, unlike more rational and reasonable southerners, seem always willing to believe the worst about southerners. "We of the South," she writes, "when we read of all these lawless crimes in New York and Boston, believe sensibly that they certainly are . . . the *exceptions,* not the general practice, in society there." By contrast "civilized, educated,

Abolitionists" seem compelled "to believe the monstrosities fulminated by lying runaway negroes, against their masters." It apparently never occurred to Yankees that, "as long as negroes are *property,* no master, unless he was a lunatic, would ever hurt them. Shooting or beating a slave to death would ensure the perpetrator's being sent to the asylum for the insane" (83). As for slaves murdering their masters, luridly recounted in numerous abolitionist tracts, what beside the insidious treachery of outside Yankee agitators could explain the striking down of kind masters who had magnanimously provided their slaves with "everything necessary to life or godliness—who had protected them from every foe, even the foes of their own lazy and evil nature—who had watched over them in sickness, supported them in old age, and tried to educate them, through religion, for happiness beyond the tomb" (253).

The primary purpose of Schoolcraft's idealized plantation setting seems to have been to convince her readers of the essential benignity of the South's peculiar institution. For, as she asserts in her narrative, not even the most "treacherous, double-faced, savage abolitionist" could have visited "Mr. Wyndham's South Carolina plantation without being forced, *nolens volens,* to the conviction that slavery, in the mild, humanizing form in which it now exists in the South, is a paradise of civilization and Christianity, compared with the misery of the runaway and free negroes at the North, and the abject, white pauper population of the cities there" (253). Expatiating further on this subject, the narrator goes on to contend that living conditions for blacks and poor whites in Philadelphia are hideous and that "it is understood . . . that the destitution of the colored population of New York City is even more hopeless" (255).

Toward the end of her novel Schoolcraft departs from her meandering plot long enough to look with favor on a single New Yorker, Horatio Seymour, a prominent New York Democrat who had served as governor in 1853–54 and would hold that office again in 1863–64. The author's approval of Seymour would have come as no surprise to informed southern readers of *The Black Gauntlet,* for he was a prosouthern peace Democrat and an active supporter of the Crittenden Compromise. Proposed in December of 1860 as a way of forestalling southern secession following the election of Lincoln, the compromise would have recognized slavery in all territories lying south of latitude thirty-six degrees and thirty minutes, thus opening the Southwest to the expansion of slavery. Seymour was a vigorous apologist for the South's peculiar institution who would become one of Gotham's most prominent Copperheads during the Civil War, and

Schoolcraft quoted him directly in her novel while presenting her case
for the southern slaveholder. In the author's view this esteemed New
Yorker had raised "pertinent" questions for abolitionists. "How came
slavery into these United States? Who brought the negro from Africa?"
The answer to these questions went to the heart of northern hypocrisy
on this issue. In Schoolcraft's view Horatio Seymour had been coura-
geous enough to remind his fellow northerners that "the men of New
York, of Massachusetts, and the men of Rhode Island were those who
stole [Africans] from their homes and brought them over to the sham-
bles here" (395).

Despite her admiration for Manhattanites like Seymour, when
Schoolcraft elects to set aside polemics and return to her plot she deliberately chooses to pillory New York City and to characterize it as a
soul-destroying metropolis that is both highly seductive to and highly
destructive of the characters of eager and engaging young southern gentlemen who travel there. A product of this malign influence is Edward,
the "highly educated, gifted" heir to the Wyndham plantation who is
sent to Gotham to complete his higher education. The dangerously seductive city becomes a source of ruin for this once able and pious youth.
Edward's father reacts with increasing alarm as his son's letters from
the North containing "tidings" and intimations of looming disaster. And
he must agonize helplessly from a distance as his son quickly becomes
"one of the most reckless, dissipated young men in the whole college"
(246). In order to court the young ladies of Gotham—Schoolcraft terms
them "silly Venuses"—the planter's son branches out "into every species
of extravagance, in horses, sleighs, and carriages, to take them to all
places of amusement, theatres, operas, balls" (246). Doggedly pursuing
the expensive pleasures of the city, Edward squanders his father's money
and virtually abandons his studies.

Neither young Wyndham's abiding courtesy nor his carefully cultivated gentility can save him from ruin in New York City, for his sense of
noblesse oblige and his gallantry toward ladies appear grotesque in the
hard, mercenary, and ruthlessly pragmatic setting into which Schoolcraft places him. The narrator mordantly observes that Edward's "chivalry" toward the female sex "was so great, that when he first went to
New York, and saw a handsome white girl walking into the parlor with a
heavy armful of wood, or coal, to make up the fire, he would instinctively
rush to relieve her of the load, to the great amusement of the Northern
dandies" (246–47). In short, the chivalrous attitudes Edward brings to

Gotham have the metaphorical effect of turning him into an innocent lamb ready for slaughter. Responding with alacrity to Manhattan's varied material blandishments, the young aristocrat is quickly and "thoroughly dissipated, which in New York, or any large city, means, walking straight in the road to perdition" (247). Indeed, Schoolcraft makes clear that Wyndham would have been destroyed had not his loving father, having initially refused to rescue his son by paying off $5,000 dollars in debt, relented and paid his obligations in full, allowing him a chastened return to the friendly haven of his native South Carolina.

Edward escapes Gotham's clutches, but not before exacting a measure of revenge on the Manhattan tailor who had most persistently and obnoxiously insulted him for not discharging his debt. When the proud young gentleman offers to pay him in full, this "knight of the goose and shears, perfectly delighted at the prospect of recovering a debt he had regarded so hopeless," hurries to Wyndham's hotel room. There Edward pays the tailor in full, locks his door from the inside, and "drawing out his cowskin," inflicts "on the wondering tailor a chastisement that proved, no doubt, a life-long alterative to his bilious system" (260). Before locking his thoroughly whipped prisoner in his room and hurrying to the ship that will take him home, Edward dispenses a final admonishment to the uncivil Yankee tradesman who needs to be taught to respect his aristocratic betters. "Sir, remember never again to insult a gentleman's son, in a land of strangers, as you have done me; remember that *Southern* gentleman *honestly* pay their debts" (260–61).

Despite the obvious pleasure with which Schoolcraft writes this scene, she seems entirely blind to the less humorous ironies implicit in her high-minded young southern gentleman's furious physical chastisement of his victim. A more thoughtful reader, however, can easily detect them. For the truth is that without the generosity of a loving and wealthy father Edward would never have been able to repay the enormous debts he had carelessly accrued in New York. One might also wonder how such a foolish and immature young gentleman could imagine himself worthy of punishing the man to whom he is indebted, no matter how insolent and churlish the Manhattan tailor might have been. In crafting this scene, the author reveals herself to be as heedless and arrogant as the youthful aristocrat she has created. The beating that Edward administers to his Yankee creditor richly amuses her, and she clearly judges it to be thoroughly deserved. Indeed, she relishes her scene in much the same way as many southerners had relished a few years earlier the near-fatal beating of Massachusetts senator Charles Sumner on the Senate floor by South Carolina representative Preston Brooks, an incident that Schoolcraft surely had in mind when she penned this episode.

It is noteworthy that both the historical Preston Brooks and the fictional Edward Wyndham were Carolina gentlemen who rationalized the brutal physical beatings they administered to their Yankee adversaries as the only effective way that a well-bred southerner could honorably respond to malicious verbal attacks from a social inferior. Brooks viewed his caning of Sumner as a necessary response to the calumny directed against his kinsman, Senator Andrew P. Butler of South Carolina, in a fiery speech concerning "Bloody Kansas" that the Massachusetts Republican had delivered on the Senate floor.[5] Wyndham likewise believed that he could not honorably leave New York without punishing the slander that had been directed toward him by a Gotham shopkeeper. Neither Preston Brooks nor Edward Wyndham would have considered defending their honor by challenging their adversaries to a duel, for neither considered his adversary to be a gentleman who properly understood and respected the code duello. They believed both their victims—an abolitionist senator and a Manhattan tailor—to be dishonorable Yankee knaves, and each was as deserving as the other of being whipped like a low-born villain or an obstreperous slave.

Mrs. Schoolcraft's novel amply demonstrates that four years after the Sumner incident most white southerners had not substantially amended their bizarre and distinctly paranoid conviction that the brutal caning on the Senate floor had been an assertion of southern nobility of character in response to malign Yankee insults. They remained defensive and dismissive in the face of northern condemnations of their culture and of the slavery that provided the foundation upon which their society rested, and Schoolcraft's scene, which delightedly details the beating of a presumptuous New York tradesman, is an assertion of this same kind of sectional arrogance and defensiveness. Having chosen Philadelphia's J. P. Lippincott as her publisher, the author might have considered whether she wanted to risk offending the sensibilities of the northern readers, who would furnish at least a portion of her audience by including such a scene. But by 1860 she and southern writers like her had ceased to care about the sensibilities of their Yankee readers. Indeed, her use of setting indicates that she was equally contemptuous of the sentiments of readers who might hail from New York City, the South's erstwhile political ally. *The Black Gauntlet* offered abundant fictional evidence of growing sectional intransigence in the slave states, and it ominously fore-shadowed the violent national upheaval that was to come within a year of its publication.

———————

By the time *The Black Gauntlet* appeared, southern criticism of north-erners had become well-nigh frenetic in its vituperative intensity, and for most southerners there no longer seemed to be any meaningful distinc-tion to be drawn between their former New York City allies and the other inhabitants of the barbaric lands lying north of the Mason-Dixon. The *Charleston Mercury* wrathfully concluded that nearly all Yankees were bigots, zealots, and hypocrites like their Puritan Roundhead ancestors, bent not on freeing slaves but on having "Southern fields upon which to make their descent and to pillage, [that] they may keep their hands from each other's throats and pockets."[6] It was amid this fevered political at-mosphere that another novel by a southern woman writer was published in Mobile, a narrative written by Mrs. V. G. Cowdin entitled *Ellen; or, the Fanatic's Daughter.* Unlike *The Black Gauntlet,* which was situated largely on a South Carolina plantation, *Ellen* was set primarily in New York City. And while Schoolcraft had mounted an extended and spirited defense of slavery in her novel, Cowdin's novel expanded the fictional horizon of her southern apologia to consider, in addition to contented and well-treated slaves, the fiendishness of abolitionists seeking to destroy slavery by fair means or foul and the horrors of Gotham's wage slavery.

Ellen opens with the arrival of a young gentleman from the Empire State named Horace Layton at the bucolic Louisiana plantation of Major Wallace. Layton has come south to teach, and he is an educated and reasonably refined youth who responds positively to the gracious hospi-tality of his host. Unfortunately, he also harbors abolitionist sentiments that have been nurtured under the powerful but malign influence of his brother-in-law, Parson Blake. This minister embodies the scheming vi-ciousness and profound hypocrisy that Cowdin associates with northern abolitionists, for she is quick to inform her readers that Blake is a man who uses his religion as "a mere cloak beneath which . . . his vices [are] effectively hid." He is a rabid and incendiary foe of slavery who "in truth" cares "as little for the slave as the slaveholder." Abolition is not for him a noble calling; it is a "popular theme" among New Yorkers that he is entirely willing to embrace and exploit, a wave of opinion upon which he comfortably rides. His ultimate objective is not the freeing of black slaves but the destruction of the South. Destroy the region, he covetously prophesies, and its wealth "must be given into our possession."[7]

Concealing the abolitionist inclinations inculcated in him by his brother-in-law, Horace Layton easily insinuates himself into the life of the Wallace plantation, and he quickly woos and weds Mary Danville, Major Wallace's niece and ward. Living now with his new relatives, Layton is introduced to what the author considers the unvarnished reality of the plantation's indulgent slave regime. In consequence his antislave convictions appear for a time to waver. One of the most powerful arguments for slavery that he hears comes from the mouth of Uncle Peter, a venerable house servant who, on a trip to New York City with his indulgent owner years earlier, had been "induced by abolitionists to leave his old master." His subsequently traumatic experiences in Gotham confirm his opinion that "the North and purgatory amount to much the same thing" (17).

Enticed away from his affectionate and generous master, the absconding Peter is quickly abandoned by the fanatics who formerly expressed such concern for his welfare. Now he is forced to fend for himself in a ruthless and indifferent city where ironically the inhabitants most exploitive of him are the free blacks and where he must somehow survive on the abysmally low wages paid for his labor. "It tuk all my earnin's to pay de free n—— for my board. . . . I was hungry all de time and fell away to skin and bones. I had no good close to wear, for dem free n——s stole ebery one of my fine things, and kept me workin', workin' for dem all day long and half de night" (19). Peter finds it impossible to gain higher wages in the city, for, as he observes, "you never did see sich a sight of poor white folks and n——s, all lookin' after a job to keep dem from starvin.'" But of all the indignities Peter suffers the most crushing comes on Christmas day when he attempts to enter a church, not having heard "a word of preachin' since I left home." "Begone," whispers a sexton, "you disturb de congregation—dis is no place for you." The shamefaced Peter leaves the church thinking that he "might live to be a hundred years old in do good old South, and never see a poor n—— driv out of church" (21).

Uncle Peter ultimately is the beneficiary of a scrap of good luck. A kind southern boat captain who encounters him near the docks takes pity on him and offers him passage to New Orleans. And his equally kind master receives him home by coming out of the great house and graciously shaking his shamefaced slave's hand. Mr. Wallace ironically tells the errant Peter that he doesn't think his "visit to the North has improved your looks any." "No master," he contritely replies, "but I have bin punished mightily for my wrong doin', and I deserved it; but, de Lord willin', I will try to keep de straight road hereafter" (21). The "straight road" for him means staying well away from abolitionist scoundrels and maintaining utter and unquestioning loyalty to his kind master.

Confronted with Uncle Peter's testimony and with the "well clothed, cheerful, and healthy" (4) slaves that surround him, Horace Layton almost converts to the southern point of view of Major Wallace. But the letters he constantly receives from brother-in-law Parson Blake full of abolition fervor ultimately draw him back into the fanatic's clutches. And upon the sudden death of Wallace, he determines to take his loving wife back to New York. There, under the direct influence of Blake, Layton turns his young wife's small fortune over to the preacher and enlists loyally in his abolitionist schemes. Indeed, he makes several trips below the Mason-Dixon as a secret agent engaged in "liberating the groaning slaves" (60). Just before his untimely death Layton comes to realize how his sanctimonious brother-in-law has betrayed and impoverished him, but his demise leaves his wife and his beautiful daughter Ellen destitute and alone. Cut off from friends in the South and faced with the malice and indifference of their fair-weather northern friends, Mary and Ellen, like Uncle Peter, must somehow survive in what Cowdin describes as the pitilessness and indifference of New York's urban jungle.

Though Mary possess no skills, her daughter is an exquisite embroiderer, and Ellen finds work with a seemingly friendly and solicitous lace maker named Madame Frivoli. But soon after securing the job the young maiden discovers to her horror that the Madam's lace-making establishment is a front for her real business, the prostitution of her youthful seamstresses. Ellen is fortunate enough the escape her employer's clutches, but now she and her mother, who is in increasingly ill health, must struggle to live in a very expensive city on the only job the beautiful and refined Ellen can find. She is required to make twelve shirts a week for the pitiful wage of a single dollar. As she frequently does in her novel, Cowdin pauses in her action to address Gotham's citizens directly and condemn their callous hearts. "One dollar for a whole week's hard work! . . . Oh, you who cry out against suffering and oppression in other lands: who turn up your eyes in horror at the word *slavery;* go forth from your sumptuous dwellings and luxurious tables; throw aside for a while your costly, gaudy trappings, and traverse the crowded, impoverished alleys of your far-famed metropolis" (135).

The sole shelter Ellen and her mother can afford on dollar-a-week wages is a filthy slum apartment. Here they manage to rent from a free Negro named Hugh Jackson a single dingy and hot attic room. Cowdin uses Jackson and his family to underscore what she believes to be the shiftlessness of this class of free black men. While the father serves as a kind of concierge for the deplorably maintained house, his daughter begs for a living and his wife, a useless drunk, has no visible occupation. The narrator describes their filthy apartment with disdain and disgust: "Soiled wash-tubs, cooking utensils, in the same predicament; unmade beds . . . painless window-frames, stuffed with old clothes . . . a few articles of soiled, torn, finery, hanging around upon rusty nails." The descriptive passage concludes with the author's characteristically caustic editorial irony: "Such was the appearance . . . of the abode wherein Hugh Jackson and his family, native New York negroes, enjoyed the *blessed privileges of freedom*" (113).

As deplorable as the condition and character of Gotham's free black population may be, Cowdin none too subtly suggests that the quality and character of most of New York's prosperous white inhabitants is no better than that of the blacks they oppress and look down upon. The owner of the tenement managed so haphazardly by Hugh Jackson is Mr. Lance White, a respectable bourgeois "married man, a leading abolitionist, a member of good standing in the church." Yet this seemingly upright New Yorker—a man who specializes in making what the narrator describes as "*inflammatory speeches against the unrighteousness, tyranny, and immoralilty of the South*"—continually harasses the helpless widow and her beautiful daughter, threatening to raise their rent unless Ellen submits to his sexual advances (116).

White is but one of many revolting examples of what Cowdin considers to be New York's fake gentility. Authentic chivalry of character and a sense of noblesse oblige are nowhere to be found among the author's "Broadway exquisites" (112) who swagger about Manhattan's streets. Accidently bumping into one of these self-styled gentlemen Mary is denounced as a drunk, and the offended bully responds to the imagined incivility by attempting "to push her bonnet rudely from her face." As the impoverished but dignified lady looks "with indignation upon the disgraceful specimens of human nature" who have set upon her, one of them sneers to his companion, "I say . . . did you see that look of insulted dignity? By the powers she may be Cushman in disguise, or Siddons come to life." His references are to two prominent nineteenth century actresses, Pauline Cushman and the famous eighteenth-century English actress Sarah Siddons. These gentlemen may fancy themselves cultivated connoisseurs of theater, but to Cowdin they are foul "specimens of New York City '*bon ton*'" (112).

During their time in New York Mary and Ellen are condemned to see themselves descend into the misery of the "troops of dirty, half-starved looking children, and intoxicated men and women . . . huddled together, several families upon one floor" (110) whom they had gazed upon with horror and aversion when they had first taken up residence in the slums. And their miserable poverty is compounded by Mary's poor health. Increasingly enfeebled and unable to work, she wastes away in her foul garret room, forced to listen twice a week to the fulminations of a "regular meeting of a branch of the Abolition party . . . in the room beneath her apartment" (117). As she languishes for lack of "bare necessities" and thinks of "the well-fed, well-clothed, careless slaves" of her childhood Louisiana plantation, she must endure the inflamed rhetoric of fanatical preachers ranting "about the unrighteous, immoral Southerners." The damnable hypocrisy of these abolitionists is as obvious to her as it is to Cowdin. "Mary thought of the starving, degraded herds of her own race, living like soulless brutes, in every alley and by-way of the city; crowds of young girls, just budding into womanhood, roaming homeless through the streets, ignorant, desperate, hungry, and ragged. Many of them beautiful as the fairest conceptions of Raphael—driven into sin, cast forth to die" (117).

Mary's grotesque vision of beautiful, innocent, and "budding . . . womanhood" defiled by corruption and lured or "driven into sin" by New York's unbridled materialism is often evoked in this novel. It is supremely ironic that in these lurid scenes Cowdin almost certainly drew her inspiration from the writings of what Jennifer Greeson has described as the city's "anti-prostitution reform groups." These reformers sought to "combat ills" in the "burgeoning" metropolis by bringing Gotham's sordid realities to life for their fellow citizens. By the early 1830s New York's rapid industrialism had brought both nascent attempts at labor organizing and efforts by reform-minded New Yorkers to compose "urban texts." These publications would create a new "urban discourse" that would unveil the civic vices that unrestrained commercialism had brought to the city in its train, especially the vice of prostitution.[8]

The first and probably most influential of these "urban tests," *First Annual Report of the New-York Magdalen Society,* was published in 1831 by

Arthur Tappan, later to become one of Gotham's leading abolitionists. This document fully articulated the anxieties of the city's reform-minded elite concerning the effects of modernization and rapid industrialization on poor women, and it deplored the intrusion of capitalism into "the intimate parts of human life." As decorously as it could express it, *the First Annual Report* made clear that the commercial spirit now dominating civic life was compromising even the sexual relations between men and women, witness what it described as an explosion of prostitution in Gotham. Among other information, it "presented the hitherto unimaginable fact . . . that the number of [prostitutes] in this city is not less than TEN THOUSAND!"[9]

Greeson points out that, even though Magdalen Society reformers focused their attention on prostitution in New York City, abolitionists like William Lloyd Garrison almost immediately established the connection between this northern urban vice and the more hideous sexual violation of female slaves in the South. "Illicit intercourse," he charged in 1832, "is constantly taking place at the south, between slaveholders and their hapless victims, and a large proportion of the colored children born every year at the south have white fathers who use and sell them as they do their cattle." American could choose to abolish slavery or "let the tide of pollution continue to swell" and "let the female slaves have no protection for their virtue." Garrison's sexual attack on slavery, as Greeson notes, would define "much of abolitionist discourse for the next three decades."[10]

It did not take southern polemicists and writers of plantation romance like Cowdin long to devise a two-pronged strategy for defending the South from abolitionist attacks launched by Manhattan zealots such as Garrison. Indeed, we see both schemes skillfully employed in *Ellen*. The first tactic was to simply insist, as southerners like James Henry Hammond had done, that the plantation South represented an Edenic social system with no significant traces of white-on-black coercion and brutality. The second strategy was to turn the fictional focus entirely on New York City's social evils, using the statistics and the shocking details compiled by the city's own social reformers as proof of prostitution's ubiquity in and pollution of Gotham's culture. Cowdin establishes in her opening chapters the benign governance that holds sway over Major Wallace's bucolic Louisiana plantation and dramatizes through the house slave Peter's traumatic experiences in Gotham the easy yokes that loosely bind southern slaves and their contentment with and even gratitude for their enslavement to masters such as the major. Having established

the South's peerless social cohesion, the writer can proceed to a mi-
nutely detailed account of the near sacrifice of his heroine's sexual innocence at the altar of Gotham's highest divinity—the great god mammon.

As highly sensitive and responsive as Cowdin is to the plight of her
virginal heroine in the snake pit of a Manhattan slum, her novel is utterly blind to the brutal miscegenation that William Lloyd Garrison had
described as a fundamental characteristic of plantation culture. She has
no interest in critiquing the plantation. She only wants to idealize it,
celebrate it, and hold it in opposition to a New York City commercial culture that sexually brutalizes innocent and pure white women like Ellen.
Entirely absent from her novel is Walter Johnson's Cotton Kingdom,
where "rape was an endemic feature of slavery" and being enslaved "was
not only a condition characterized by vulnerability to sexual assault—it
was always already a condition of sexual violation." Major Wallace bears
no resemblance to those plantation masters and overseers who in their
correspondence casually used "breed" and "breeder" when they wrote
about their male and female slaves.[11]

Black women have no part in Cowden's sexual analysis. She is exclusively concerned with the purity of white womanhood, and she shares
with other southern apologists the conviction that one of the most
sublime aspects of an aristocratic and chivalric plantation culture is
its dedication to both the honor and the racial and sexual purity of its
white women. For defenders of the southern slavocracy such appreciation for the feminine graces is nearly impossible to duplicate above the
Mason-Dixon. For in a brutally competitive commercial society where
vast wealth is accumulated through wage slavery and where everything
is destined to be sold to the highest bidder, womanly honor and purity
are commonly sacrificed at mammon's altar, as Ellen's honor is nearly
lost in the infernal slums of New York City.

Cowdin fully embraced the attitudes of southern male apologists of
her day, like "A. Clarkson." Writing for *De Bow's Review* in the same year
in which *Ellen* was published, Clarkson contended that true nobility and
refinement of character was a rare quality in a laissez-faire northern culture in which there was "no chivalrous devotion to the weak and helpless
female, no generous and manly protection of her, but all . . . calculating,
cold, and heartless as the metal they worship." Indeed, the author also
faithfully echoed the common complaint of southern polemicists that
northerners had compounded their crimes against womanhood by "liberating" their own women, allowing them to eschew the traditional duties of

their sex and to enter the masculine world of political action and reform. As one writer for the *Southern Literary Messenger* put it, how could feminine innocence survive among a people who encouraged their women to abjure "the delicate offices of their sex" and to desert "their nurseries" so that they might "stroll over the country as politico-moral reformers, delivering lewd lectures upon the beauties of free-love and spiritualism"?[12]

The conventional contrast that southern apologists like Cowdin were drawing in their novels between the purity and refinement of southern ladies and the coarseness and lewdness of the North's grotesquely desexualized female reformers is sharply reflected in a highly melodramatic scene in which Ellen is compelled to appeal for food for her dying mother to "the society of Women's Aid" (145). The censorious head of this society demands from the young girl a "certificate" authenticating her mother's dire condition, for how, she callously asks the destitute girl, can one expect those in charge of women's aid to dispense food to any worthless, indolent female who shows up and claims need? With as much dignity and calm as she can muster Ellen tells her inquisitor that all she asks is that the society "furnish her [mother] with something nourishing and suited to her condition. She cannot partake of the plain, coarse food, such as we have" (148).

At this point the writer glaringly contrasts the purity and nobility of her title character with the holier-than-thou sanctimony and the disgusting prurience of her puritanical and hard-hearted Yankee interrogator. "You seem to think," this woman observes scathingly, "that *your* mother cannot exist on *plain, coarse* fare! Ah, girl, I read your history in your face, the moment you entered the room. Fallen! Fallen!" And how can this self-righteous moral arbiter intuit Ellen's fallen state? "I see, plainly" she observes, "that you have once been in good society; it is indicated by your correct language, and you are now reaping the *just reward* of your sinful course; go, *poor evil one*" (148)! In Cowdin's novel New York's female reformers are incapable of perceiving in Ellen a quality that any well-bred southerner would instantly recognize—a refinement of character that is the product of upbringing and that exists quite independently of the vagaries of material wealth and social status. To the natives of Manhattan impoverished women of good breeding must necessarily be sexually fallen creatures.

The sanctimoniousness and incivility of Ellen's inquisitor and of her minions are matched by their lascivious curiosity about the life they imagine her to have lived. Gathering around her "with the hope of hearing a recital of sin and depravity," they aver that they will help her only if she confesses her evil deeds. "Tell us how you have sinned, and we will lend you good books to read—religious tracts—that will prove your lost condition to you, and the means of rescue from Satan." It remains for the impoverished and powerless but inherently refined southern heroine to courageously deliver her judgment on the puritanical fanaticism of these Gotham harpies. "Do you think yourselves Christians? Then you are deceived. Go to the fountain of all light, for you now wander in utter darkness" (149).

Not long after Ellen's emotionally charged confrontation with these self-righteous and hard-hearted Yankee do-gooders her sainted mother dies. Bereft and totally alone, the poor girl finds herself in debt to Lance White for three months' rent, and the lascivious abolitionist slumlord seizes his opportunity and mounts a final siege on her virtue. But in the nick of time she is rescued, much like the slave Uncle Peter had been saved earlier in the novel, by the fortuitous intervention of a kindly southerner. He is a handsome and courtly intern serving at the medical institution to which Ellen's mother's body has been delivered named Malcom Sterling, and by the most fortuitous of circumstances he turns out to be related to Major Wallace's family. He immediately assumes the role of protector and contacts the Wallace family, who have been trying for years to locate Ellen's mother. Ellen eventually marries Malcom, escapes the ruinous clutches of New York City, and finds refuge and happiness in the Wallace plantation's warm embrace. White and black residents assemble joyfully to greet "Miss Mary's" daughter. "Old, snowy-headed Peter . . . all welcomed the wanderer back, and neighbors and friends vied with each other in bestowing courteous greetings upon one of their own land, who had found so many sorrows in an uncharitable clime" (186). Ellen may have been reared in New York; but with her inborn nobility of character and her graceful femininity the author makes it abundantly clear to her readers that her title character, a New Yorker by accident of birth, is at heart a thoroughly well-bred southern heroine.

Though *Ellen* was published in the same year as *The Black Gauntlet,* Cowdin chose a Mobile publisher for her novel, rather than angling for a northern publisher like Mrs. Schoolcraft's J. B. Lippincott. Given the unrelievedly hostile treatment of her New York setting, there is good reason to believe this publishing choice was deliberate. Her novel reflects faithfully the feverish hostility of many southerners toward the North, and especially toward New York City, in the months leading up

to and following the election of Abraham Lincoln, and she seems to have
directed her work exclusively toward readers who shared her vision of
a covetous, fanatical, and hypocritical Yankee race and who understood
like her that Gotham had come to represent the black heart of a rapacious capitalist Yankee culture. Though New York had for decades
served as a hinge of union, connecting South to North both commercially
and politically, *Ellen* furnishes clear evidence that, at least for the South,
this hinge was breaking.

By the time of Abraham Lincoln's election to the presidency southern
writers like Mrs. Schoolcraft fully shared the judgment of diehard secessionists that New York City was, in the words delivered by a fire breath-
ing editorialist of the *Charleston Courier,* an enormous hive of "treacherous cowardice and hypocrisy" dominated by barbaric "merchants and
Mammon-worshippers." But in their bitter denunciations of Gotham's
treachery, secessionists like the Charleston editor could share at least
one consoling thought. They were convinced that New York's tepid and
ineffective support for the South's peculiar institution would ultimately
result in the withdrawal of the slave states from the Union and the rapid
decline of the city's economic hegemony over the South. Indeed, southern independence would annihilate New York's pretensions to being a
world-class metropolis. Writing from New Orleans James Dunmore De
Bow pursued this thesis by posing a question: "What would New York be
without slavery?" He answered his query by assuring his readers that,
once the southern states seceded, it would assume responsibility for its
own economic affairs and direct its slave-produced cotton away from
Gotham. De Bow was confident that southern sovereignty would swiftly
lead to the collapse of the city's economy; and he grimly and gleefully
predicted that Manhattan's merchant ships would soon begin to "rot at
her docks; grass would grow in Wall Street and Broadway, and the glory
of New York, like that of Babylon and Rome, would be numbered with
the things of the past."[13]

The widely embraced conviction of southern fire-eaters that Gotham's dependence on southern cotton rendered the city economically
vulnerable to southern retaliation had not risen spontaneously out of the
rancorous political climate of the 1860 presidential election; in fact, it had
been steadily advanced among southern nationalists through the 1850s.

The periodic economic panics that had roiled New York's economic waters through the early decades of the nineteenth century and that had brought numerous bankruptcies and spikes in unemployment in their wakes had not gone unnoticed below the Mason-Dixon. Indeed, Gotham's most recent financial panic of 1857 had convinced Virginia agronomist and secessionist Edmund Ruffin that Manhattan's seemingly indestructible economic foundations were in fact unstable and highly vulnerable to sudden economic dislocations.

In his diary entry of November 9, 1857, Ruffin had been pleasurably excited by the news that the mail of the day had brought to his plantation "awful accounts of awful omen, in the city of New York. Thousands of destitute men, who are demanding work and bread, have assembled and marched in procession, threatening to take by force what they need for subsistence, if it is not accorded to them for their offered labor. . . . They are instigated and led by foreigners. This before winter begins. What will it reach to hereafter?" If half of those thousands marching for work and bread turned completely desperate, he went on to reflect, they could easily "sack and burn the city, and murder its best citizens." Ruffin congratulated himself for having already forecast just such a disastrous fate for Gotham once the "dissolution of the union" that he so fervently desired had severed the city from the beneficially "conservative influence of the south and of its institution of slavery." These news reports, he remarked with grim satisfaction, suggested that the fulfillment of his apocalyptic scenario seemed "impending, or openly threatened, sooner than I expected."[14]

Just over two years after Ruffin's excited diary entry, with the tumultuous discords of the 1860 presidential campaign looming, the profoundly conservative and highly influential southern polemicist decided to launch his singular foray into the realm of fiction. He resolved to write a novel entitled *Anticipations of the Future,* in which he could dramatize what he believed to be the ineluctable course of southern secession and fully elaborate his augury of New York's City's doom. In hyperbolic and lavish detail, Ruffin's narrative would chronicle the obliteration of a city that—though he had visited it only once as a young man of thirty-three years—he had come to believe represented the most repugnant characteristics of Yankee culture. He would expose the colossus on the Hudson as a soulless metropolis established upon a foundation of capitalist greed and avidity; and, like other southern fire-eaters, he would judge it worthy of being "blotted from the list of cities." The ferocity of his fictional judgment on Gotham ratifies Fred Hobson's assertion that in his temperament and in his absolute devotion to his region's slavocracy he served as the slaveocracy's answer to John Brown.[15]

Written during the spring of 1860, Ruffin's novelistic prophesy of Manhattan's doom was uniquely his own creation, but his vision of a nation descending into civil war had been anticipated in fiction one year earlier by John Beauchamp Jones's *Border War: A Tale of Disunion.* The Baltimore-born writer was a strong supporter of slavery who believed that southern grievances were the natural responses to the agitations of extreme abolitionists. Jones, however, was also a staunch Unionist. In his novel it is the northern states who act as aggressors and who attempt to secede by force of arms, and in his haphazardly constructed narrative, these traitorous northern forces are ultimately defeated by federal troops fighting with the support of southern militias. The Union is thus preserved along with the institution of slavery. Edmund Ruffin was, not surprisingly, drawn to Jones's book. In his diary entry of February 29, 1860, he announced that he had just finished reading *Border War,* which he described as a *"prospective* account of the supposed consequences of disunion."[16]

Ruffin was as dedicated a secessionist as Jones was a Unionist, so it is not surprising that he found its version of the coming civil war to be "very foolish." He also astutely judged its plot as having been "wretchedly carried out." But reading the book did give him the idea of writing a fictional work "on the same plan" as Jones's novel. Within a few days he began writing his own version of the coming civil war, and the writing went quickly. By the end of April Ruffin had finished his manuscript. The Charleston *Mercury* promptly accepted *Anticipations of the Future* for serial publication in May and June, and in September S. W. Randolph of Richmond published it as a novel, just in time to add a bit more drama to the concluding weeks of the fateful presidential election of 1860.[17] Ruffin's novel would choose to make many major and minor departures from Jones's plotting and chronology in his description of the civil war to come, but one of his most striking alterations would concern the effect of the conflict on New York City. As Jones had imagined it, combined southern and federal forces would march to the gates of New York City, and its sacking would be forestalled only by the city's expeditious paying of tribute. In Ruffin's fevered vision Gotham's fate would be nowhere near as kindly resolved.

———————

Anticipations of the Future is set four years into the future; and its title page describes the narrative as "extracts of letters from an English resident in the United States," written to the London *Times* between 1864 and 1870. This fictional journalist was obviously inspired by the career of William Howard Russell, celebrated to this day as one of the first and finest modern war correspondents. In the mid-1850s the Irish journalist had achieved widespread fame at the *Times* with his telegraph dispatches from the Crimean War. His galvanizing and immensely popular articles had brought that war in both its glory and its gory reality into the homes of hundreds of thousands of Englishmen. Russell would eventually arrive in the United States in the spring of 1861, just weeks before the beginning of hostilities between North and South. Much like Ruffin's fictional reporter, he would send his dispatches to London until returning to England in the spring of 1862.

The first letter from Ruffin's English reporter, dated November 11, 1864, describes the election to the presidency of New York senator William Seward by a popular margin even greater than that achieved by Abraham Lincoln in 1860. The presidential succession that the writer imagines here—from a Lincoln victory in 1860 to a Seward victory in 1864—offers interesting insights into Ruffin's thinking as he was writing his narrative during the spring and making final alterations in the summer of 1860. Though he had absolutely no faith in Lincoln's ultimate intentions regarding the abolition of slavery, he clearly understood that the prairie Republican's position on the issue was widely perceived to be more moderate and less extreme than that of the hard-shell New York abolitionist Seward. Indeed, it was Lincoln's apparent temperance that had contributed to his rather surprising victory over Seward at the Republican nominating convention in May. By the time Ruffin finished revising his book in August, he had concluded that Lincoln's outward show of moderation would gain him the presidency. He was also convinced, however, that this lamentable victory would only delay what he believed would be the inevitable exit of the slaveholding states from the Union. He would have been delighted at the time had he known that his novel's chronology had underestimated the strength of the South's secessionist fervor and that the civil war he so eagerly anticipated was only about half a year away.

In the novel's opening letter, the *Times* correspondent informs his readers that Lincoln's policy during his time in office had not been overtly hostile to southern interests. Unfortunately—or fortunately from Ruffin's perspective—the president's relative moderation had been denounced and ridiculed as timidity by the rabid abolitionists of his own party. By 1864 infuriated Black Republicans led by Seward had attained complete control of Lincoln's party. They repudiated their own president and denied him his nomination for a second term, chose Seward as their candidate, and swept him into office. Depredations against the South escalated swiftly under the new president. The Supreme Court, now packed with abolitionist justices, took the Dred Scott decision under review. Federal fortifications in the South were strengthened, and the Underground Railroad flourished with tacit support from Washington. Finally, in the winter of 1868 facing the almost certain reelection of Seward, the states of the Deep South began to secede from the Union.

With an eerie prescience that the writer demonstrates on several occasions in his novel, Ruffin situates the flashpoint of his fictional civil war precisely where the actual conflict would begin seven months after his work was published—at Fort Sumter, situated strategically at the mouth of Charleston harbor. But unlike the spectacular bombardment of the fort that was to occur on April 12, 1861, the fictional seizure of Sumter in December of 1868 by southern troops is bloodless. This action does, however, precipitate a full federal sea blockade. By the summer of 1869 outright hostilities begin in the interior South with the invasion of Kentucky by a ragtag federal force dominated by white abolitionist and Negro troops. In Ruffin's fictional version of the civil war the conflict is short, not protracted and bloody, and it plays out primarily through naval battles along the southern coast and with ground engagements along the Ohio and Mississippi Rivers. The federal government's failure to subdue Kentucky is rapidly followed by decisive southern ground victories in Mississippi. Union reverses in the Deep South hasten the breakaway of Virginia and other states of the Upper South and trigger the rapid increase in strength of southern military forces.

By September of 1869 the conflict described in Ruffin's *Anticipations* is effectively over. Seward has evacuated Washington and that city is now the seat of the new southern government. The president has been forced to conclude a truce. Though newly independent southerners are jubilant, most northerners are despondent, demoralized, and enraged at the extreme abolitionist Republicans led by Seward, whose aggressions against the South precipitated the conflict. Ruffin's reporter predicts the withdrawal from the Union of many midwestern states and ultimately even of the states of the Middle Atlantic. But the collapse of the federal army in September of 1869 is not only the result of southern military victories in Kentucky and Mississippi. It is also a reaction to calamitous events that have taken place in New York City in August that have completely traumatized the North and destroyed its morale and its willingness to fight. Edmund Ruffin now turns his attention and focus on the destruction of the duplicitous city that he and other southern nationalists believed had so long engorged itself on the South's slave-produced wealth. In another stroke of remarkable imaginative prescience, his novel zestfully describes massive riots that erupt out of the seething resentments of Gotham's suffering underclasses and that in their near-apocalyptic violence and destructiveness both anticipate and far exceed the actual draft riots that would ravage large sections of Manhattan for four days in July of 1863. In Ruffin's fascinating and sensational fictional account New York is transformed within one week into a ghost city, a bleak and nearly deserted landscape of smoking ruins littered with thousands of corpses.

Ruffin begins his account of the destruction of New York by delineating an economic collapse that for years he had predicted would befall the city as a direct result of the South's withdrawal from the Union. First, he details the loss of "forty millions of debt" to Gotham's merchants and banks repudiated by southerners upon secession, which brings "bankruptcy to hundreds" of Manhattan's wealthiest families and commercial establishments and "heavy losses to thousands" of other citizens. This economic disorder is exacerbated by the "cessation of the purchase of northern fabrics, and of the employment of northern vessels by the seceded states" and by a drastic reduction in the supply of southern cotton that almost immediately results in the closing of textile factories and the firing of half of the North's textile workers. More dependent on the cotton trade than other northern cities, New York now experiences a huge surge in unemployment, and it must contend with masses of destitute workers who, if not provided food, threaten to "take it by force." One notably impressive "hunger procession" sends 40,000 men marching "through the wealthier streets" of the metropolis, taking special care "to exhibit their strength in the Fifth Avenue of sumptuous palaces" of Manhattan's "merchant princes." These formerly self-intoxicated and complacent plutocrats suddenly sit with unease upon their mercantile thrones.[18]

Hunger processions quickly degenerate into "hunger mobs and riots." By August of 1869, only a few months into armed conflict, the severe economic dislocations brought about by secession and the disruption of the cotton trade produce a spontaneous uprising among the subsistence wage slaves of the Gotham's fetid urban slums that reaches its height of fury and violence in what Ruffin terms the "sack of New York" (285). For the English reporter describing the disaster it is a catastrophe akin to the Turkish destruction of Constantinople, only this time the unfortunate Byzantines are Wall Street magnates. Within hours of the first apparently spontaneous confrontations between rioters and the police the number of mutineers has increased "to thousands, who force their admission into every shop and mansion, and plunder at their discretion" (286). "Terror-stricken property owners" are helpless in the face of large gangs of "plunderers," and those few who do resist are "promptly stabbed, and their bleeding bodies thrown into the streets." The city's police force, even when augmented by the local militia, is utterly unequal to the task of containing the disorder that rapidly assumes the characteristics of a guerrilla war. Within a day of the initial clashes "more than 30,000 miscreants" roam Manhattan's streets, "engaged in sacking the houses and shops, not only of the rich, but of all whose movables [are] supposed to be worth being plundered" (287–88).

The destruction of New York by huge mobs of protesters is accomplished with breathtaking speed. Not even the arrival of 4,000 Federal troops can stem the devastation. Most of these soldiers have been hastily trained and are untested in battle, and many of them surrender to the mobs or join in the massive plundering. Opposition to the rioters effectively ceases. Now, Ruffin's reporter observes, "every man who had a wife or children, endeavored, if possible, to flee with his family from the scene of horror, leaving his house and other property at the mercy of the plunderers" (289). Within two days of the beginning of the riots the city has collapsed into total chaos, and in scenes that weirdly anticipate John Carpenter's 1981 apocalyptic Hollywood blockbuster, *Escape from New York,* Manhattan has been transformed into a water-bound asylum run by maniacs from the confines of which terrified New Yorkers seek to flee.

Ruffin's novel describes with relish scenes of gruesome inhumanity that ensue from this unruly exodus. One wealthy New Yorker pays $1,000 for a "furniture wagon" to "take his wife and children, and as much luggage as would complete a load" out of the city. But the driver and his assistant choose "to emulate the worst crimes of the other plunderers." They seize the plunder and murder the merchant, his wife, and his two oldest children. Two younger children, "too young to report the crimes," are left on the street, "to perish by other means." As day turns to night "many thousands, mostly feeble females and children, and, in numerous cases, members of the richest families, intermixed with the poor inhabitants, now nearly alike destitute, helpless and despairing" crowd together and struggle on foot to reach the relative safety of Manhattan's upper and more lightly developed suburbs (290).

By dawn of the fourth day of rioting mobs effectively hold Manhattan, and total anarchy rules. Churches are now despoiled, and Ruffin zestfully roasts Gotham's mammon worshippers in the hellish fires of underclass insurrection. All the city's banks as well as the United States subtreasury are seized and "robbed of every dollar" (291). Rather than satisfying the mob's lust for lucre, the booty only serves "to inflame the rioters with insane lust of gain, and of blood." Upon attaining their treasure, a temporarily victorious group of thieves is set upon by "the later comers" who are "more numerous and equally greedy." Soon the city is pocked with heaps "of the dead and dying bodies of . . . plunderers" (292). The most enterprising of those who wind up on top of the gory heap determine to protect their spoils by seizing every available ship of good size anchored in New York harbor and sailing away with their plunder. Having sent all the Union's warships to the South to man their naval blockade, Seward and his Republican minions watch helplessly as a substantial portion of the Union's wealth vanishes along with the piratical armada. Ruffin seems to especially relish details that highlight the ignominy of the "Black Republicans" of Seward's ilk whose fanatical abolitionism, he believed, had precipitated the civil war. For example, one of the ships most heavily loaded with loot is manned "entirely by a gang of negro sailors, who [embark] under a negro captain, and set sail for Hayti" (293–94).

Ruffin concludes his description of the sack of New York City with an appropriately horrid and—to his mind, no doubt—entirely fitting climax. Gotham's teeming and subjugated masses attain their ultimate revenge on the haughty Fifth-Avenue plutocrats who have oppressed and reduced them to lives of grinding privation. In a final demonstration of hatred and fury they resolve to burn the city to the ground. Although the narrator attributes part of this hideous spasm of destructiveness to drunken folly and mob madness, *Anticipations of the Future* also illustrates the fascinating intellectual course by which a rabid defender of an anachronistic rural slavocracy like Edmund Ruffin could assume an intellectual posture strikingly akin to that of a radical nineteenth-century Marxist when he critiqued the excesses of northern industrial capitalism.

Like other southern polemicists Edmund Ruffin considered the laissez-faire entrepreneurs of the North far more exploitive of their wage slaves than paternalistic southern planter aristocrats, men who, he argued, were infused with a sense of noblesse oblige and who as a rule presided over their chattel with fatherly firmness and care. Such paternal concern, he argued, was entirely absent in a northern labor system devoted solely to the accumulation of maximum profits. *Anticipations of the Future* is adamant in its insistence that the strongest motive of New York's rioters is the "malignant hatred" that these "sufferers from want and hunger" feel "for the rich, and even for all property-owners," whom they view as their oppressors. Tens of thousands of Gotham's downtrodden proletariat "armed and bearing torches" spread through Manhattan and across the East River to Brooklyn, lighting the most flammable buildings. Within two hours, aided by strong winds, the "great and rich city, containing . . . 1,200,000 inhabitants," is "so covered by flames, that no possible human means" can prevent "the full consummation of the calamity" (295).

In a spasm of animosity directed against their capitalist oppressors Ruffin's furious plebeians generate an enormous firestorm, a "raging sea of flame" that rises "in billows and breakers above the tops of the houses higher than ever sea was raised by the most violent hurricane." The deafening "roar of the conflagration" sounds like a "continued rolling thunder." Storms of flying embers consume not only buildings but ships lying "at and near wharves, and even . . . many lying separate in the river." By morning only Gotham's "remote and thinly-built suburbs" remain standing. Not one house "in the closely built portions of New York proper and Brooklyn" has escaped destruction (295). The author has now exacted his full measure of vengeance on the city of shoulder hitters, extortionists, and mammon worshippers that he had so completely despised.

After the sack of New York, the Union's war against the South is essentially over. Ruffin's English narrator notes that public opinion in the North has turned massively against the conflict. Disasters on southern battlefields and in Gotham's streets make it highly unlikely that more troops can be sent to subdue the South, even if Seward and his allies remain determined to "persist in carrying on a war of invasion on the southern confederacy" (298). New York's shocking destruction precipitates the complete collapse of northern morale, and within days of the disaster troops of the southern confederacy enter a hastily evacuated

Washington. The narrator reports with unconcealed satisfaction the immediate expulsion by southern forces of free Negroes from the former capital of the United States of America.

By the conclusion of his narrative Ruffin has abandoned all pretense of reportorial objectivity on the part of his English journalist. Author and narrator are essentially the same. And they share the conviction that the sack of Gotham highlights the failure of the intellectually bankrupt ideals of laissez-faire capitalism and progressive democratic idealism that Ruffin considered the driving forces of Yankee culture. The horrific and vividly detailed sacking of Gotham represents Ruffin's proof positive that these systems are not, as northerners had long boasted, stronger and superior to those of the South. To the contrary, the narrative exposes the structures underlying northern society as fundamentally fragile and profoundly unstable. And Ruffin is certain that the city will remain vulnerable to such disasters if the values it embraces produce a society characterized by "great wealth . . . with great inequality of condition of the people" on one hand and "great destitution of the lower classes" on the other. He also contends that the social instability that is the natural product of such a highly unequal distribution of individual wealth is bound to be greatly aggravated by extending the suffrage to a broad mass of its citizens, however "poor, ignorant and vicious" they may be, and by giving this ignorant and deprived underclass "political privileges and power equally with the most worthy and intelligent" (297). *Anticipations of the Future* argues that it is exactly this lethal combination of economic and political ideas that has led inexorably to the smoking ruins of Gotham.

From his position as the defender of a patriarchal plantation slave society Edmund Ruffin acutely discerned the potentially fatal flaws in a system resting on the principles of untrammeled laissez-faire capitalism. He was also sensibly cognizant of the threat posed to modern liberal democracies by the presence within them of large masses of ignorant and underprivileged voters. He believed that New York City epitomized these destructive social conditions, and in his polemical work he described what he thought might well be the fate of a cosmopolis that worshipped both unrestrained capitalist greed and shallow democratic idealism. But discerning as Ruffin was in some respects, he was severely limited as a social philosopher in other significant ways. Sharply attuned to the exploitive and nakedly materialistic nature of the pure capitalist model, when he turned to consider his own region he wrapped the South's brutal exploitation of the master-slave relationship in the folds of a racist paternalism, choosing to cast a blind eye on the obvious and ugly parallels between the northern industrial economy he excoriated and the southern plantation economy he self-righteously vindicated. Devoting himself to the defense of an anachronistic way of life, he refused to consider the possibility that the South of his imagining had no future and deserved to have none. The concept of a Union free of the incubus of slavery was inconceivable to Ruffin, and he was equally incapable of imagining an American democracy in which the callous excesses of an unrestrained market system might be constrained and tempered by a government democratically elected by universal suffrage.

Anticipations of the Future vividly illustrates how enflamed and hysterical the state of southern opinion toward Republican abolitionists had become near the end of the acrimonious presidential campaign of 1860. By the time they were preparing to go to the polls most southern voters had, like Ruffin, bound themselves resolutely to the mast of the sinking ship of slavery. Through its vengeful destruction of Gotham Ruffin's novel also inadvertently exposed how lamentably far the South's intellectual and political leadership had drifted away from the nation's founding principles—values that had been valiantly defended and brilliantly articulated by Ruffin's own Virginia forebears—Patrick Henry, George Washington, Thomas Jefferson, and James Madison.

Like Mrs. V. G. Cowdin's *Ellen, Anticipations of the Future* was the fictional product of a tumultuous election year designed to appeal to southern prejudices and directed toward southern readers. Despite the author's reservations concerning his narrative's literary merit, however, he remained sanguine in his hope that the book would gain substantial critical attention and attract a wide readership, at least in his native region. Southerners, he trusted, would embrace his work "as an argument and incentive to defense and resistance by the South," and his justification for "disunion [would] have [a] noted and good effect." Alas this hope would prove unfounded. The *Southern Literary Messenger* did briefly mention *Anticipations,* observing that it would "be productive of much good" to those who read it, but no other southern magazines reviewed it at length, and very few southern readers purchased it.[19] Ruffin seems not to have realized that by spurning New York printers and choosing to publish his book in the provincial city of Richmond he had guaranteed it a smaller audience, even within his native South.

Ironically the only other positive notice his novel garnered issued from the pen of the Richmond correspondent to James Gordon Bennett's

prosouthern *New York Herald,* published in the city that Ruffin's novel
had completely and vindictively destroyed. Ruffin was pleasantly surprised by the *Herald* endorsement and gratified as well that James De
Bow had finally "thought proper to quote a long passage" from his novel
in his *Revue.* At least, he grumbled, the notice from the New Orleans
editor was proof that his novel had not "fallen dead from the press." He
was, however, bitterly aware of the failure of the southern reading public
to applaud or even notice his book. "It is to me a mortifying truth," he
wrote in his diary, "that, instead of being thus welcomed my book has
been scarcely noticed, and its very existence seems to be ignored by
the public, even in the more southern states, where, if nowhere else, I
expected notice and approval."[20] Denizens of the Deep South would not
disappoint Ruffin a second time. Some six months later in Charleston
they would bestow upon him the honor of firing one of the first shots
against Fort Sumter.

In the fateful summer of 1863, when news reached Virginia of severe
disturbances sweeping through New York City, Edmund Ruffin must
have been elated by the prospect that the destruction he had predicted
three years earlier in *Anticipations of the Future* was now at hand. Violent
riots did buffet the city from July 13 to July 16 in response to the federal
government's imposition of a widely unpopular draft lottery. Disorder
did quickly reach disturbing heights on Monday and Tuesday, July 13
and 14, in Manhattan, where thousands of rioters roamed the streets in
gangs, hanging, drowning, and mutilating black men, looting, and burning black homes, and attacking "Republican mansions and Protestant
missions." Just as Ruffin had anticipated in his novel, New York's mayor
appealed to the secretary of war for federal troops on Tuesday, July 14.
Luckily for Gotham the Battle of Gettysburg had concluded on July 3,
and Washington was able to divert five battle-tested regiments to help
quell the riots. By Wednesday evening of July 15, federal troops were
arriving and promptly joining with police, militias, and volunteer com-
panies of employees organized by Manhattan's merchants and bankers
to fight the mobs.[21]

Street fighting in the city on Wednesday night and all day Thursday
was fierce. Troops attacked rebelling crowds with "howitzers loaded
with grapeshot," mowed down rioters in the streets, and fought the miscreants from building to building. Opposition was at first intense, but
police, militia, and federal troops fought with determination. Edwin Burrows and Mike Wallace vividly describe the combat that raged through

lower and mid-Manhattan. "Rioters defended their barricaded domains with mad desperation. Faced with tenement snipers and brick hurlers, soldiers broke down doors, bayoneted all who interfered, and drove occupants to the roofs, from which many jumped to certain death below." By Thursday evening an uneasy peace had descended over a city occupied by 6,000 troops of the United States Army. Soldiers camped in Gramercy Park and Stuyvesant Square. By Friday telegraph lines were being repaired and omnibuses and horse cars were beginning to run again. By Monday morning—exactly one week after the disturbances had begun—nearly all laborers had returned to work. The infamous draft riot of 1863 was over, and Gotham stood relatively undamaged. It had been the largest episode of civil disorder in the nation's history, but though many contemporaries imagined the loss of life to have been in the thousands, in the end authorities could confirm a body count of only 119.[22]

On Saturday, July 18, 1863, two days after the New York riots had ended, Edmund Ruffin eagerly and suspensefully awaited the latest news from Gotham. Earlier in the month he had been emotionally crushed by twin Confederate disasters—the fall of Vicksburg on July 4 and the withdrawal on the same day of Lee's invading Army of Northern Virginia from Gettysburg. Desperate for any kind of good news, he had seized avidly on the early reports of massive antidraft riots sweeping Manhattan on the previous Monday and Tuesday. He was hopeful that "a widespread and bloody" disturbance such as newspapers were describing might be "far more important than all military events, and more disastrous, and still more ominous of evil for the North than would be a signal defeat on a battlefield." With undisguised satisfaction he observed that he had "long ago predicted" just such a "systematic sack and conflagration" of Gotham.[23]

Ruffin grasped for any straw that would confirm the North's dire condition as a result of the violence in New York. He judged it enormously significant that in response to the riots Washington had agreed to suspend temporarily the hated draft in the city. He was convinced that such official pusillanimity would encourage similar resistance to conscription across the North, an opposition to which, he predicted, Washington would also yield. The "non-execution of the draft," he concluded, would be "general, if not universal; and the effect of the New York riots would be "to detract from the military and physical strength of Lincoln's government, and Yankeedom, more than would the destruction of an army of 100,000 men." Though the outcome of the riots was far from certain to the Virginian that Saturday, he entertained the hope that "the atrocity and rage of the mob [might] be so extended, and unrestrained, as [to] lay in ashes the whole of the great city of New York, with all its appendages and wealth, as just retribution for its share of the outrages perpetrated on the people of the South."[24] He did not know that on the very day he penned these vengeful hopes in his diary New Yorkers were sweeping up the debris of the previous week's unrest and preparing to resume business as usual on Monday.

Ruffin was no doubt chagrined by the ultimate failure of his dire prophesies, and he must have been further disappointed by the relative ease with which New York City rebounded from the riots. Social and political tensions indeed remained high in the city after the violence was suppressed, but they were substantially diluted and mitigated by a war boom. Fortunes piled up as stockbrokers participated in an orgy of profit taking. Only a few weeks after the riots the *Herald* boasted that money was "pouring into Wall Street from all parts of the country." Fueled by decisive military victories at Vicksburg and Gettysburg, this speculative boom was aided and abetted by Republicans in Washington. In a move designed to induce apoplexy among diehard secessionists like Ruffin, Congress legalized cotton trading with the hard-pressed, blockade-bound Confederacy, and impoverished and nearly destitute southerners had no recourse but to sell what cotton they could grow to Gotham. By the latter half of the Civil War cotton bales by the thousands purchased in the Confederacy for twelve to twenty cents a pound were being shipped to New York, where they fetched nearly two dollars a pound.[25]

Only one year after the draft riots Englishman George Borrett visited Gotham as part of his grand three-month tour of Canada and the United States. A fellow of King's College, Cambridge, the young gentleman moved easily in the refined social circles of London, and he was "a stalwart Englishman with most of the traditional British prejudices in regard to American customs" and culture. Yet when he reached New York City on the final leg of his tour, he was forced to admit "reluctantly, that Broadway [had] no equal." Standing "at the top of the two mile straight in which the street stretches down to the ocean," he saw no evidence of the damage that had been wrought by the draft riots of the previous summer. He admiringly walked down "the gay avenue of life and color," past "the bright-fronted hotels of massive white marble, past the colossal stores . . . past the noble houses of pale-brown freestone." Borrett concluded his paean to Broadway by urging his readers to visit the avenue, "jostle with the crowd upon the sidewalks . . . and then say if you know of any street in the world . . . where you can find so much magnificence."[26]

Far from the killing fields of Virginia and Georgia, New York City sparkled brightly for the English visitor in the late summer sun of 1864. Of course, he observed with frosty condescension, all that glittered was not pure gold. The "convulsion" of wealth caused by bloody civil war had "tossed to the surface" of society nouveau riche Americans such as "Mr. Shoddy" and "Mrs. Shoddy." In a description of Gotham's gaudy extravagance that would have made Edmund Ruffin's skin crawl, the English visitor observed that because of enormous war profiteering the "great" jewelry establishment of Louis Comfort Tiffany had "grown fat" on "the extravagancies of the Shoddy." But Tiffany, he continued, was "not the only one of the fatted calves." Nearby on the corner of Broadway and Prince Streets, he noted, was the grand emporium of Ball and Black, famous for its finely wrought and very expensive sterling silver and boasting the largest French plate glass windows in America. Inside, customers enjoyed ascending floors in a steam-driven elevator. Its imposing façade, "constructed wholly of . . . marble and iron" and graced with "magnificent pure Corinthian" columns, gazed defiantly across Broadway toward Tiffany's.[27]

Despite several remarkably acute predictions that Ruffin had made in *Anticipations of the Future,* by the end of the Civil War the author's biggest prophesy had proved to be horribly inaccurate from a southern point of view. Secession had not brought Gotham's destruction; indeed, war had made the cotton trade more profitable than ever and the city more powerful, wealthy, and materially extravagant than ever. Yankee cupidity and Yankee laissez-faire barbarism had triumphed. The city's continued rapid expansion, the marble emporiums of Tiffany and Ball and Black on Broadway, and the upward thrusting of a new and ever-changing skyline were the visible symbols of this victory.

It is hardly surprising that Edmund Ruffin refused in the end to submit to what he considered a brutal and vulgar Yankee yoke and that he chose not to witness the coming apotheosis of Wall Street in a reunified nation. On June 19, 1865, slightly more than two months after Lee's surrender at Appomattox Courthouse, he penned one final entry in his diary in which he declared his "unmitigated hatred to Yankee rule—to all political, social and business connection with Yankees, and to the perfidious, malignant, and vile Yankee race." He then seated himself squarely in his chair, put the barrel of a loaded rifle in his mouth, and with the aid of a forked hickory stick pulled the trigger. The percussion cap exploded but failed to fire the rifle. Ruffin quickly replaced the cap and again pulled the trigger. When his son rushed into the room seconds later, he found him dead, still sitting in his chair, with his journal open to his final entry damning the "vile Yankee race."[28]

On September 27, 1860, at about the same time Edmund Ruffin's *Anticipations of the Future* was beginning to appear in southern bookstores, an officer of the city of Charleston's "Vigilant Police" barged into the room of Mrs. Catherine Bottsford. She was a widow, born and bred in New York City, who had arrived in Charleston in December of 1859 to pursue her trade as a seamstress. Though she professed that during her nine-month sojourn in South Carolina she had engaged in no personal conversations with slaves and that she had never mentioned the subject of slavery unless directly asked about her views, she had made no secret of the fact that she was an abolitionist in her sympathies. The officer promptly arrested her "without warrant" and conducted her immediately to the city's "common jail," where she languished in what she described as a "dank and filthy cell . . . without food" for two days. She was eventually taken to meet Charleston's mayor. In this interrogation she denied "tampering with slaves" but admitted being a supporter of abolition and an admirer of John Brown. The mayor found her responses to his questions to be both provocative and disrespectful. He determined that, although there had been no complaints lodged against her character, she was nonetheless required either to "give bail" or go back to jail. She went back to jail.[29]

Two days after her interview with Charleston's mayor Catherine Bottsford was again hauled before a magistrate, who warned her that only her sex prevented her being taken to the nearest tree in the municipal park and hanged there. Such threats seem to have had little influence on the feisty New York seamstress. When the magistrate asked her if she read Horace Greeley's abolitionist *Tribune,* she saucily replied, "No because I can't get it here." It was back to jail for Mrs. Bottsford, where she would languish for the next two months and become the talk of the town. She was not entirely destitute of friends. One of them was Dr. Howe, minister of the St. Phillips Episcopal Church congregation that she attended. He too asked if she was an abolitionist, and hearing the unpleasant truth that she was, immediately muttered, "Oh, that's treason, that's sedition, most decidedly." Still, he interceded as best he could for this "spirited and self-possessed" Gothamite.[30]

By the end of November Charleston's civic leaders had concluded that, because she could not or would not post bail, Bottsford was becoming an ever greater nuisance to the city by remaining stubbornly in her cell. She was finally released and escorted under guard to the steamer *Columbia,* bound for New York City. Officials had grudgingly purchased a three-dollar ticket for her deck passage. What followed was a standoff. Catherine said yes to boarding the boat but no to traveling as a deck passenger, refusing to sit for the duration of the journey exposed to the cold and surrounded by "sixty Irishmen." And Charleston officials refused to coddle the unrepentant abolitionist by paying for a more expensive ticket. Eventually the ship's captain resolved the dispute by kindly offering her cabin accommodations.[31]

Bottsford was eager to tell her story when she arrived in New York City, and Horace Greeley's antislavery *Tribune* was equally eager to publicize it. The editorial introduction to her newspaper narrative exposed the dire and hostile state of relations between Gotham and its erstwhile southern allies during the months that preceded and followed Lincoln's election. In "The New Inquisition" the *Tribune* compared the treatment of its innocent New York City heroine at the hands of Charleston officials to the barbarism of the Spanish Inquisition. That original reign of terror instituted by "bigoted Spain," the paper observed, had "withered before the light of civilization." Now the "atrocity" had been revived in the slave states. True, the paper remarked with bitter irony, burnings of the accused had been reserved for black slaves; but milder forms of barbarity, such as illegal imprisonment and exile, had been reserved for brave and principled women like Catherine Bottsford. If Spain's inquisitors could return from the dead, the paper concluded, they would no doubt approve of the methods employed by Charleston's interrogators.[32]

Paul Starobin's vivid and arresting analysis of the fevered political climate of Charleston in the summer and fall of 1860 views Catherine Bottsford's plight as an inevitable manifestation of the "madness" that had come to "rule the hour" in that citadel of reactionary southern conservatism during the election year of 1860.[33] In such an atmosphere it became almost impossible for most southerners to distinguish between northerners who were essentially sympathetic to them and northerners who were not. And if southerners had at one time been disposed to tolerate New Yorkers as useful allies, Bottsford's travails suggest that by the fall of 1860 New York natives could no longer take such magnanimity for granted. Indeed, the appearance of *Anticipations of the Future* in the fall of 1860, taken together with the persecution of the plucky New York seamstress, suggest that conservative southerners were no longer interested in giving a pass to residents of a city that they now considered a half-hearted and useless ally.

In *Anticipations of the Future* Edmund Ruffin's judgment on New Yorkers was even more draconian than that administered by Charleston authorities on Caroline Bottsford. The fire-eating Virginian chose as the setting for his apocalyptic vengeance a northern metropolis that had forged closer economic and cultural ties with the plantation South than any other American city, whose commercial and political establishment had sought for decades to support and defend as best they could the region's peculiar institution. The writer's gratuitous fictional destruction of Gotham demonstrates that southern nationalists, in their fury over the prospect of a Black Republican political ascendency in Washington, had effectively ceased trying to distinguish between their northern friends and their northern enemies. For them it was ludicrous to hope that a metropolis inhabited by people like Catherine Bottsford would somehow intervene to save the South and prevent the destruction of its way of life. To the rapidly increasing legions of southern reactionaries led by men such as Edmund Ruffin, it was thus fitting that Gotham and all who lived there be "blotted from the list of cities."[34]

WILLIAM GILMORE SIMMS, WILLIAM CULLEN BRYANT, AND THE BREAKING OF THE HINGE OF UNION

ON APRIL 17, 1856, South Carolina novelist William Gilmore Simms wrote a letter to Mary Lawson, the daughter of his New York literary agent and business manager, James Lawson, telling her that he might possibly pay her and her family a visit later in the year and bring with him his daughter Augusta, a good friend of Mary's. He explained that he was seriously thinking "of trying a course of lectures at the North this coming winter." Two days later he wrote to another friend, Boston publisher James Thomas Fields, proposing "to gather up a few of my Lectures and undertake a rambling Lecturing campaign in the North this coming winter" and wondering if Fields might lend his support to the launching of such an undertaking. Simms's idea was to "design one or two Lectures touching the scenery, the society, habits manners, of the South, especially for your people to establish better relations between North and South respectively." In the following months he successfully pursued this project, securing November speaking dates in Buffalo, Rochester, and Syracuse. To crown this initial phase of a tour that he expected to continue into New England, he received on November 3, 1856, a formal invitation from the Young Men's Lecture Association in New York City to follow his Syracuse lectures with presentations in Manhattan.[1]

The letter inviting Simms to speak in Gotham was signed by some of the most well-known and venerable members of the city's literary and cultural establishment. Prominent among the signatories were the names of historian George Bancroft, publisher and biographer Evert Duyckinck, and poet, journalist, and long-time editor of the *New York Evening Post,* William Cullen Bryant. All three were friends of long standing. Indeed, the Charleston writer's November appearance would seem to have represented a most felicitous joining of speaker and audience. Simms's colorful and romantic novels of colonial and revolutionary South Carolina—works such as *The Yemassee* (1835) and *The Partisan* (1835)—had been printed by northern houses, and after 1840 his works had been published almost exclusively in New York City. Indeed, northern readers had responded to them as enthusiastically as his southern audience had. For almost twenty-five years, occasionally accompanied by his family, Simms had traveled North in summer or fall in pursuit of his literary career to consult with his agent Lawson, cultivate publishers, and maintain his friendships with Gotham's literati. In his analysis of Simms's political writings Jon Wakelyn has noted that from his first visit to the city in 1832 the young novelist had been "an instant success in New York literary circles. He spent at least three months out of each year there, visiting friends, attending the theater, correcting the proofs of his many hurriedly written manuscripts, and haunting Northern publishing houses." He had come to know Gotham quite well, and he counted among his closest companions his agent, James Lawson, the Knickerbocker writer, James Kirke Paulding, and William Cullen Bryant. Indeed, these highly valued friendships helped him to adapt so readily to a Manhattan lifestyle that members of the extended Simms family came to consider him almost "as much a New Yorker as he was a Charlestonian."[2]

These intimate personal and professional ties to New York City buttress John Hope Franklin's astute observation that "the most prolific and most successful writer of the antebellum South" also cultivated "the strongest ties to the North," especially to the metropolis on the Hudson that was by the 1840s becoming the center of the nation's publishing and finance. Franklin discerned that Simms, being both a widely popular novelist and the owner of a sizable Carolina plantation, distinctively combined the interests of a professional writer with those of a full-time planter and advocate for the economic and political concerns of his region's planter aristocrats. In short, he was "as much at home in the literary and publishing circles of New York as he was in the world of southern plantations and politics."[3]

Of Simms's numerous New York friendships, none was more stimulating or pleasurable to him and his family than his decades-long association with William Cullen Bryant. The two men had established a strong bond during the recently widowed young South Carolinian's first visit to Gotham in 1832. James Lawson had introduced them, and Simms had quickly received an invitation to Bryant's house across the Hudson River in Hoboken. The two men both enjoyed leisurely conversing and long walks, and they went on several hikes along the banks of the Hudson. On subsequent journeys north Simms had visited Bryant both in his New York residences and at his summer house in Great Barrington, Massachusetts. On a few occasions he had brought his second wife, Chevillette, and their children with him, and the friendship had expanded to include both families. He had even sent his eldest daughter Augusta to school at Great Barrington so that she might continue to develop her friendship with Bryant's daughter Fanny. The entente between the families had not been solely nourished by the Simms family's trips north. In response to Simms's invitation to bring his wife "and all her little ones," Bryant and his wife Frances had spent three weeks at the writer's Woodlands plantation in the spring of 1843, and Bryant himself had made a return visit to the Palmetto State in 1849 on his way to Cuba.[4] Indeed the New York writer left a charming and affectionate record of his South Carolina visits in his portrait of Simms published in *Homes of American Authors* (1853).

The strong and abiding bond between Bryant and Simms might well have seemed an unlikely one, considering that Simms was a resolute supporter of slavery and of the interests of southern planters, while Bryant had opposed the institution from his early years as a young Massachusetts lawyer. Indeed, after he moved to New York City in 1825 he remained a steadfast opponent of bondage throughout his long and distinguished career as a writer and as editor of one of Gotham's leading newspapers, the *Evening Post*. But though he maintained the antislavery attitudes of his New England upbringing, he abandoned his family's rural conservative federalism, becoming a member of his adopted city's dominant Democratic Party. In his powerfully written editorials, he expanded his idea of freedom, augmenting his opposition to slavery with his advocacy of free trade, free speech, and the rights of working men. Like many New Yorkers he disapproved of the South's peculiar institution, but, also like most of them, he was kindly disposed toward distinguished visiting southerners like Simms whom he came to know personally. He was interested in their culture and way of life and respected their opinions.

Under his editorial guidance the *Evening Post* welcomed letters to his newspaper "from all sections of the country," and it often "quoted at length from southern journals."[5] When Bryant and Simms first met in 1832 and in the years immediately thereafter, the controversy over slavery had not so firmly established itself in the forefront of the nation's consciousness as it would be twenty years later, and neither man seems to have considered regional differences to be a serious impediment to their newly established friendship.

As their relationship grew through the 1830s and 1840s, Bryant's editorial openness to southerners exhibited on the pages of the *Evening Post* was more personally reflected in his increasing admiration for the Simms family and in his desire to know more about the culture that had fashioned them. In the fall of 1840, he wrote a letter to Simms, thanking him for inviting his daughter Fanny "to pass the winter at [his] plantation." It was, he admiringly observed, an invitation "urged with all the warmth of hospitality peculiar to you people of the south." Indeed, the graciousness of the Simms family had induced in him a desire to see them in their plantation setting. Bryant confessed that he nourished "a strong curiosity to visit your part of the country—to see not so much the cities of the South as the country and the rural life of the South. It is I admit a disproportionate curiosity . . . but such is my natural inclination." Simms responded to Bryant's letter with one of his own, brimming with excitement and anticipation, in which he rejoiced "in the partial promise which you gave me that you will yourself come and see me in the spring." Indeed, he hoped that Bryant could be persuaded to bring his wife with him "and, if practicable, all your family." He conceded that his native state featured a flat and unspectacular landscape, but he promised that its semitropical and newly blossoming foliage with "delicate varieties of forest green, the richness of the woods, their deep and early bloom, and the fragrance with which they fill the atmosphere" would delight and renew them all.[6]

It would be three years before Bryant could finally find the time to indulge his pronounced interest in the plantation South by traveling with his wife to Simms's South Carolina country house, Woodlands, for a three-week stay. They left New York on February 26, 1843, traveling by rail through Philadelphia and Baltimore to Washington and thence through Richmond and on to Wilmington, North Carolina. Here they left the train and boarded a boat for Charleston. On March 3 they passed Fort Sumter and arrived in Charleston harbor. Simms had promised that Bryant would not be disappointed with South Carolina, and in his account of the trip, sent to the readers of the *Evening Post* and later published as "A Tour in the Old South," he pronounced himself "most agreeably" impressed with his first views of Charleston. Upon disembarking he experienced the adventurous traveler's intoxicating sense of the exotic, of being, for the first time since he had left New York, "in a different climate."[7] For the next three days he and his wife would tour the city, examining a compact urban landscape that reminded him as much of Europe as America.

By the end of his brief visit to Charleston Bryant was thoroughly charmed with the city, and he expatiated on its many attractive features.

> The spacious houses are surrounded with broad piazzas, often a piazza to each story, for the sake of shade and coolness, and each house generally stands by itself in a garden planted with trees and shrubs, many of which preserve their verdure through the winter. We saw early flowers already opening; the peach and plum-tree were in full bloom; and the wild orange, as they call the cherry-laurel, was just putting forth its blossoms. The buildings—some with stuccoed walls, some built of large dark-red bricks, and some of wood—are not kept fresh with paint like ours, but are allowed to become weather-stained by the climate, like those of the European towns. The streets are broad and quiet, unpaved in some parts, but in none, as with us, offensive both to sight and smell. The public buildings are numerous for the size of the city, and well-built in general, with sufficient space about them to give them a noble aspect, and all the advantage which they could derive from their architecture. The inhabitants, judging from what I have seen of them . . . do not appear undeserving of the character which has been given them—of possessing the most polished and agreeable manners of all Americans.[8]

As pleasant as Bryant found the city of Charleston, his interest had always inclined toward experiencing the rural life of the plantation South. On March 8 he proceeded to Simms's Woodlands Plantation in the interior of South Carolina, halfway between Charleston and Augusta, Georgia, in Bamberg County. As Simms wrote to James Lawson soon after Bryant's visit, he had hailed the great American poet's arrival "with feelings of singular satisfaction." But like many anxious hosts endeavoring to create a perfect atmosphere, he had been foiled by circumstance;

and the long-anticipated occasion had turned out to be "an unfair and unfortunate one." Despite all his exertions, the host's entertaining had been spoiled by "very wretched weather" that had started stormy and cold and remained miserable for the entire three weeks. In consequence, he bitterly complained, Bryant "had few opportunities of seeing either our people or our climate. The latter is a month behindhand and the former everywhere would have enjoyed to give him welcome."[9]

Simms's anguish over Bryant's visit seems to have been excessive and misplaced. If Bryant's published account of the visit is to be believed, he and his wife spent three thoroughly pleasant weeks at Woodlands, visiting the small capital city of Columbia, roaming extensively over the countryside around the Simms plantation, and enjoying "the hospitality of the planters—very agreeable and intelligent men." Far from being substantially hampered by bad weather, he claimed to have enjoyed a host of interesting activities. In compiling a list of rural Carolina pleasures, the New Yorker observed that he had "been out on a raccoon hunt; been present at a corn-shucking; listened to negro ballads, negro jokes, and the banjo; witnessed negro dances; seen two alligators at least and eaten bushels of hominy."[10]

Regardless of the wretched weather, Bryant's host clearly strove to entertain his northern visitors fully and pleasurably; and if his intention had been to favorably impress his northern friends with southern plantation culture, he seems to have succeeded admirably. Bryant found Woodlands to be a pleasant and inviting house, "a spacious country dwelling, without any pretentions to architectural elegance, comfortable for the climate." And he viewed the character of the master of the house with even more admiration. For Bryant, Simms fully embodied the best qualities of the gentlemanly planter. "His manners," Bryant observed, "are singularly frank and ingenuous, his temper generous and sincere, his domestic affections strong, his friendships faithful and lasting, and his life blameless. No man ever wore his character more in the general sight of man than he, or had ever less occasion to do otherwise." Indeed, the visit to Woodlands expanded Bryant's admiration for his friend's character to include the Carolina gentlemen who were his friends. Writing to Richard Henry Dana soon after his return to New York, he described his trip as an "extremely agreeable" one, and he averred that "the frank, courteous, hospitable manner of the Southerners made it pleasant." "Whatever may be the comparison in other respects," he admitted, "the South certainly has the advantage over us in point of manners."[11]

Howard Floan has noted that the polished manners of the South Carolina gentry "suited Bryant's taste." Indeed, the innate courtliness of the New England editor's own temperament made him something of a kindred spirit to southern gentlemen. Simms himself admiringly observed after Bryant's visit that his guest had "made many friends" on his trip to the Palmetto State. "The Gentlemanly quietness of his manner, his unobtrusiveness, please in the South. All who met him were pleased with him." Floan also goes on to observe more acerbically that the "genial hospitality which he received along the way must have tempered his critical acumen."[12] One might argue that Bryant's acuity was more suppressed than tempered. Despite his long-held and frequently articulated opposition to slavery, the influential Yankee editor and proto-transcendental poet completely eschewed criticism of the institution in the accounts of his visit, and he took obvious care not to write anything on the subject that might offend either his host or the genteel South Carolinians who had been so gracious to him.

Perhaps there was nothing at Woodlands that was reprehensible enough for Bryant to notice and criticize. Certainly, Simms had assiduously striven to create for his northern guests the most favorable possible impression of life on his plantation. The corn-shucking that Bryant described as one of his host's many entertainments was given, he observed with no apparent sense of irony, "on purpose that I might witness the humors of the Carolina negroes." And what a production it must have been. Slaves from neighboring plantations arrived to help with the shucking, "singing as they came." "The driver of the plantation, a colored man, brought out baskets of corn in the husk, and piled it in a heap; and the negroes began to strip the husks from the ears, singing with great glee as they worked, keeping time to the music, and now and then throwing in a joke and an extravagant burst of laughter." Such laughter and ease and contentment—is it any wonder that after his visit to Woodlands Bryant concluded that Simms's slaves were "indulgently treated" and led "an easy life."[13]

In the description of his visit to Woodlands there is only one point at which Simms's carefully crafted representations of plantation life impress on Bryant a sense of unease and darkness. During the otherwise raucous singing at the husking the slaves suddenly turn to a song that does not have what Bryant terms a "comic character" but is instead "a singularly wild and plaintive air."

Johnny come down de hollow. Oh hollow!
Johnny come down de hollow. Oh hollow!
De n——-trader got me. Oh hollow!
De speculator bought me. Oh hollow!
I'm sold for silver dollars. Oh hollow!
Boys, go catch de pony. Oh hollow!
Bring him round the corner. Oh hollow!
I'm goin' away to Georgia. Oh hollow!
Boys, good-by forever! Oh hollow![14]

Why did Bryant choose to include in his otherwise lighthearted account the full lyrics of this mournful song, an agonized chant that starkly presents the chattel slave as human commodity to be bought and sold by his master like a bale of cotton? Did he intend for the song to serve as an implied counter-commentary to his otherwise rose-colored description of raucous and happy corn shucking on the old plantation? If his inclusion betrays a spasm of New England–bred conscience, it is, alas, a transitory display. There are no further ruminations on the content of the song or on the human anguish it reveals. Indeed a few paragraphs later in his narrative Bryant rather matter-of-factly opines that "the blacks of this region are a cheerful, careless, dirty race, not hard-worked, and in many respects indulgently treated." Bryant's firsthand introduction to slavery apparently did nothing qualify his positive feelings about the plantation South. A year later he wrote to Simms that he remembered his visit "as one of the pleasantest periods of my life" that had "left with me a favorable impression" of South Carolina "and a most friendly recollection of its inhabitants."[15]

In deference to his southern friends Bryant chose to assess the region's peculiar institution in transactional rather than in moral or philosophical terms. After three weeks of observation, he concluded that slavery was a system in which "the master has power of punishment on his side; the slave, on his, an invincible indolence, and a thousand expedients learned by long practice. The result is a compromise, in which each party yields something, and a good-natured though imperfect and slovenly obedience on one side is purchased by good treatment on the other."[16] By the conclusion of his tour of "the Old South" Bryant seemed willing to grant southern slaves an agency nearly equal to that of their white masters, and he also was amenable to judging southern slavery as an essentially benign anachronism. In mid-1840s America his was a position that would have greatly antagonized neither his northern readers nor his southern friend and host.

The friendship between William Gilmore Simms and Willian Cullen Bryant that was firmly established during the South Carolinian's first visit to New York City in 1832 and flourished during the 1830s and 1840s was nourished by temperamental and intellectual compatibilities and by common cultural interests that easily transcended whatever differences existed between the two men on the issue of slavery. Simms was a lifelong and stalwart defender of the institution, while Bryant had been strongly opposed to human bondage as a young Massachusetts lawyer, and he remained throughout his long life an eloquent foe of slavery. But when he assumed his position as editor in chief of the *Evening Post* in 1829 his stance on the emancipation of slaves was decidedly more melioristic than it would become in later years. He viewed southern slavery as an evil but one that could be over time gradually ameliorated. He believed that the institution could be firmly but judiciously opposed without resort to politically destabilizing rancor and vilification. He certainly did not uniformly judge the southern owners of slaves to be evil men, and he interacted easily with southern gentlemen like Simms who shared his interests and inclinations. Indeed, Bryant's attitude toward slavery placed him well within the middle range of New York City opinion during the 1830s and 1840s. His were the broadly moderate views of most of Manhattan's commercial and literary elite, views that created no serious impediments to friendships with well-mannered southerners of distinction like Simms.

In his nineteenth-century biography of Bryant, son-in-law Parke Godwin deftly articulated both his own and his father-in-law's Panglossian attitude toward slavery's prospects, a way of thinking that was commonly articulated in New York's social and political circles during the era of Andrew Jackson and Martin Van Buren. Like "nearly all the people of the North and with many of those of the South," Godwin observed, both he and Bryant "cherished the delusion that slavery, though an unmitigated evil, was in the process of extinction. Human reason and the sense of justice, they thought, would gradually alleviate its abuses, while the rapid material advances of the nation, rendering it unprofitable as a mode of industry, and more and more feeble as a political and social force, would ultimately reduce it to nothingness, as in the Northern States."[17] Though Simms was certainly aware of his new friend's sanguine assessment of slavery's future course and though he undoubtedly received the idea of its eventual withering away in South Carolina with inner skepticism, he no doubt tolerated what he probably considered his friend's naivety in the name of their newly established comradeship.

William Gilmore Simms and William Cullen Bryant thus entertained divergent, though not deeply conflicting, understandings of slavery when they first met in New York City in 1832; but they also shared a common political party allegiance and a common concern about the rise of a militant form of abolitionism that had originated in New England by 1830 and was beginning to spread through the northern and midwestern states. Politically and socially the two men shared much in common when they first met. Bryant had abandoned his New England federalism and embraced the more progressive tenets of Gotham's dominant Democratic Party, and both young men were Democrats and loyal supporters of Andrew Jackson. In his 1832 *Charleston City Gazette* editorials Simms had supported the president and bravely opposed the nullification theory of fellow South Carolinian John C. Calhoun, and in the *Evening Post* Bryant had also condemned Calhoun's concept as an idea dangerous to national unity. He had further endorsed the Jackson's drive to defund the United States Bank, which he editorially castigated as "an utterly corrupt and profligate" institution. Most notably the fellow Democrats saw eye to eye on the danger to regional comity posed by the rising abolition movement. Simms heartily concurred with Bryant's condemnation of "the agitation in certain quarters of the northern press for emancipation of slaves," and the South Carolina novelist certainly agreed with the New York City editor that the crusade against slavery threatened the fragile union of a geographically widespread, demographically diverse fledgling democracy and served only to encourage "deep-rooted and invincible local jealousy" between North and South.[18]

Simms doubtlessly would have been heartened Bryant's assertion in an 1833 editorial that there was no widespread support in the North for abolition. In none of his editorials of the 1830s did Bryant ever attempt to qualify or repudiate his moral opposition to bondage, but he was equally clear during the early years of the abolition movement's organization that his resistance to slavery did not mean that he supported immediate emancipation. "That the existence of slavery in the Union is regretted by the great mass of the population of the non-slaveholding states, we believe to be true." But, he added, "that there is the slightest opposition to interfere in any improper and offensive manner, except among certain fanatical persons, and those few in number, we regard to be as well settled as any fact in relation to public opinion ever discussed in the public journals."[19] This was the type of editorial reassurance that for a time would mollify the anxieties of southern planters like Simms who looked to New York's commercial and political elite for support against what they considered a rising abolitionist menace.

Bryant's general condemnation of the budding abolitionist movement extended to its most influential leader, fellow Massachusetts native William Lloyd Garrison. On October 3, 1833, the controversial editor of the weekly *Liberator* attempted to introduce Boston's budding fervor for emancipation to Manhattan's opponents of slavery. Garrison hoped to convene a sizable group of supporters, but when he arrived at his Manhattan venue an audience of between twenty and thirty cowered inside the building while approximately 5,000 objectors angrily milled around outside. The following morning Bryant applauded the fact that there had been no bloodshed or injuries, but he had no good words for the man who, he believed, had rashly blundered into a near catastrophe. "Garrison," he wrote, "is a man who, whatever may be the state of his mind on other topics, is as mad as the winds on the slavery question. . . . As to the associates of Garrison in this city, some of them may be of good intentions, but they are men whose enthusiasm runs away with their judgment—and the remainder are persons who owe what notoriety they have to their love of meddling with agitation subjects. . . . They are regarded as advocating measures which, if carried out, would most assuredly deluge the country in blood, and the mere discussion of which has a tendency to embroil the south with the north, and to endanger those relations of good will which are so essential to the duration of the Union."[20]

No southern journalist could have better or more effectively articulated Bryant's indictment of abolitionist social agitation. Not surprisingly, this editorial was widely reprinted in southern newspapers in the weeks that followed its New York publication. Under his editorial management the *Evening Post* had established correspondents in both Washington and Charleston. Indeed, the newspaper ultimately delighted in describing its South Carolina reporter as "our fire-eating correspondent," and it also shared its content with other southern newspapers, most notably Robert Barnwell Rhett's fire-eating *Charleston Mercury*.[21] Excerpts from

Bryant's editorial soon reached Charleston. As a prominent local journalist Simms would have read these, and he no doubt approved of his
new friend's political acumen.

———————

During the early years of their friendship and well into the 1840s, when
Simms was making his annual summer and fall visits north to New York
City and Bryant was venturing south to visit Simms, it would be fair to
conclude that there was no deep or unbridgeable gulf between the two
men on the issue of slavery and abolition that would have threatened or
compromised their good feelings for each other. However, some of Bryant's firm and unchanging positions regarding the subject would over
time become more and more difficult for Simms to accept. The New York
editor's increasingly strenuous opposition to slavery would prove to be
more problematic and ultimately fatal to their friendship. The two men
would gradually move further and further apart, for example, in their responses to the increasingly potent abolition movement. As we have seen,
Bryant, much like Simms, initially considered Garrison and his followers
to be half-mad extremists who constituted a clear and present danger
to national unity. Nonetheless, from the inception of the controversy
over abolitionism he also boldly raised his editorial voice in support of
Garrison and his supporters' constitutional right to speak and agitate
against slavery, and he consistently condemned the mob violence in the
northern states that was the all-too-frequent response of many citizens
to abolitionist provocations.

Bryant's eloquent defense of freedom of expression for all varieties
of opinion was on impressive display in his editorial of August 8, 1836,
entitled "Abolition Riots." In Cincinnati, the editor drolly informed his
readers, "a meeting of the people" had "proclaimed the right of silencing
the expression of unpopular opinions by violence." Bryant promptly proceeded to anathematize the outraged antiabolitionist citizens of that city:
"If they cannot put down the abolitionist press by fair means, they will
do it by foul; if they cannot silence it by remonstrance, they will silence
it by violence; if they cannot persuade it to desist, they will stir up mobs
against it, inflame them to madness, and turn their brutal rage against
the dwellings, the property, the persons, the lives of the wretched abolitionists and their families." In the early stages of the slave controversy
the transplanted New Englander was fixing his progressive editorial flag

in New York City. He was asserting the necessity of free expression of opinion on the slave question, a position that he never qualified over the ensuing decades of controversy. "We are resolved that the subject of slavery shall be as it ever has been—as free a subject of discussion and argument and declamation as the difference between whiggism and democracy, or the difference between the Armenians and the Calvinists. If the press chooses to be silent on the subject, it shall be the silence of perfect free will, and not the silence of fear."[22]

In 1836 a southerner like Simms would have been decidedly less enthusiastic than his friend Bryant about the free speech rights of abolitionist agitators in Cincinnati. Indeed, as early as 1831, less than a year before he would initiate his friendship with the *Evening Post* editor, Simms had taken a position on this question that was almost diametrically opposed to that of Bryant. Southern journalists had alertly noted and regarded with alarm Garrison's *Liberator* columns, and they were enraged by the threat his opinions posed to their peculiar institution. In North Carolina, the courts had gone so far as to indict the abolitionist editor, in absentia, for inciting violence among the state's slaves. In the *Charleston City Gazette* of October 8, 1831, Simms found it necessary to weigh in on the controversy. He began his editorial in a moderate key, pointing out that there was no legal way for North Carolina to extradite Garrison. But then he proceeded to recommend a course of action that, if enacted, would have smothered the free speech rights of abolitionists almost as effectively as the threats of physical violence by anti-abolitionist mobs in Cincinnati that Bryant would roundly condemn five years later.

Simms believed along with the great majority of white South Carolinians that the maintenance of slavery was essential to preserving the foundations of his state's plantation culture and its political order. Therefore, he advocated a constitutional amendment that would correct what he termed the "deficiencies of the Constitution" that had made it possible for abolitionist fanatics to abuse their free speech rights. Simms in effect was advocating a severe constricting of the first amendment, and he called for a united front of southern states and swift passage of "laws" for the slave states' "common protection." He concluded his editorial with this dire warning: "So long as any fanatic may scatter his brands through our community, in defiance of the laws as well of the land . . . we shall have no security and sovereignty of any kind."[23]

In his 1831 editorial William Gilmore Simms was strategically placing himself in the vanguard of those southern leaders dedicated to defending slavery and the plantation system whose foundations it supported. As antislavery voices grew louder and more numerous in the northern states during the 1830s the South united quickly to suppress and stifle these views, with the state of South Carolina leading the way. Indeed, Simms's 1831 editorial proposing to severely constrict freedom of speech on the topic of slavery might well have struck Charleston readers, only a few years later, as excessively moderate in tone. By the mid-1830s South Carolinians with the temerity to oppose publicly the South's plantation system invited severe and almost unanimous censure and even physical violence against them and their families. Not even postal clerks were exempt from this climate of hysteria. In 1835 a mob protesting the mailing of abolitionist tracts into the state burned the Charleston post office.[24]

Far from denouncing such mob violence, the conflagration drew the approval of the city's newspapers as a justified response to seditious abolition provocation. The *Mercury* proposed a convention of slave states to plan a comprehensive defense of slavery. Even the more editorially moderate *Courier* asserted, much as Simms had four years earlier, that censorship of the mails and the press in both the North and the South was essential to the South's self-preservation. In such a charged atmosphere Thomas Grimke, son of the prominent Charleston Unionist Thomas Smith Grimke, found it necessary to announce that his deceased father had been a loyal South Carolinian and that he, unlike his sisters, was an active advocate of the South's peculiar institution. In the words of Jon Wakelyn, "The younger Grimke even changed his last name to Drayton in order to avoid the social onus placed on his family by citizens of Charleston."[25] In contrast to William Gilmore Simms's intrepid defense of Andrew Jackson in the nullification crisis of 1832, his increasingly belligerent attacks on northern abolitionists faithfully reflected the waxing truculence of public opinion in his native state on the issue of slavery.

Simms's more fervid embrace of slavery during the 1830s may well have been more than a simple reflection of the increasingly reactionary temper of his fellow South Carolinians. When he first met Bryant in New York City in 1832 he had been recently widowed. His first wife, Anna Giles, the daughter of a Charleston merchant, had died earlier in the year, leaving behind an infant daughter. Four years later at the age of thirty-six he had taken as his second wife eighteen-year-old Chevillette Eliza Roach, the only daughter of a wealthy planter named Nash Roach. Roach owned a Charleston town house and two plantations, each containing roughly 7,000 acres. "Woodlands" plantation, where his son-in-law delighted in entertaining friends like William Cullen Bryant, was the most valued of these properties.[26] With Simms's sudden ascension in 1836 into the exalted class of major planter and slave owner the South Carolina writer's dedication to the institution of slavery was no longer purely ideological and theoretical. It also became intensely practical and material.

A year after Simms's propitious second marriage he seized the opportunity of expanding his reputation beyond that of an author of southern historical romances by writing a review of English social observer Harriet Martineau's *Society in America*. The author's strong support of abolition in this work had shocked and offended many readers in the South, and Simms used his review in Richmond, Virginia's, regionally prestigious *Southern Literary Messenger* to mount his first full-throated defense of southern slavery. In penning his vindication, he demonstrated his willingness to channel the anger of southerners who viewed Miss Martineau as both an ignorant and intruding foreigner and a stereotypical female do-gooder and busybody. The personal attack came early when Simms spurned the author as "biased and bigoted . . . to the last degree" in her treatment of the South and dismissed her as a scribbling female propagandist who had refused to "believe the truth when it spoke in behalf of the slaveholders" or to "doubt the falsehood, however gross," when it "fell from the lips of the abolitionist."[27]

After personally denouncing the author, Simms utilized his review to extoll southern slavery as a positive good and benevolent institution, one that existed in harmony with the natural development of human races. The emancipation of slaves in the northern states, he argued, had abruptly and artificially lifted "the coarse and uneducated negro" to "a condition to which his intellect [did] not entitle him." As a result, the former slave had become a "presumptuous . . . and consequently offensive" freeman. Slavery, by contrast, had never encouraged or allowed such dangerous presumption; consequently, in the South the "negro" had not been "hated" but "regarded as filling his true place, and as occupying his just position." The great majority of slaves had accepted this lowly but natural position in the human order and had consequently been met with the "favor and indulgence" of their masters. Indeed, Simms opined, southerners could all agree that there were "few people so very happy, hearty and well satisfied with their condition as the southern negro."[28] Six years after penning this article Simms would demonstrate to his visiting friend the truth of this assertion in his artfully staged Woodlands coon hunt and plantation corn shucking.

Simms next turned his attention to Harriet Martineau's charge that slavery had blighted the region by inciting widespread sexual license between white masters and their female chattel. Circumventing the sensitive subject of the sexual links between plantation mansion and slave cabin, he acknowledged the general truth that prostitution existed in the South. But how, he indignantly asked, did the author have the nerve to criticize the South on this subject when in the city of New York, "not including blacks," there were "ten thousand professional prostitutes" roaming its streets? At least southern prostitutes were "usually slaves," not white women as in the North. In addition, he boasted, the fruit of the southern variety of this universal vice was a highly desirable human issue: "the production of a fine specimen of physical manhood, and of a better mental organization, in the mulatto." Future illicit couplings, he cheerfully concluded, would continue to wash each generation of half-cast offspring lighter until ultimately the white man's eye would "cease to be offended" with the byproduct.[29]

Somehow Simms convinced himself, along with other apologists such as his friends John C. Calhoun and James Henry Hammond that slavery offered the best course for the ultimate improvement of inferior races. Indeed, he regretted that Native Americans had been denied the benefits of southern slavery that generously had been extended to African slaves. "Far better had it been for our native North American savage," he mused, "could he have been reduced to servitude by labor ... moderately accommodated to his habits" and thus "preserved from that painful and eating decay, which has de[a]lt but a raw and naked skeleton of what was once a numerous and various people." Ultimately, he predicted, slavery would save blacks from the fate that had befallen Native Americans. The "negro slave of Carolina" would be "raised to a condition" that would "enable him to go forth out of bondage." That going forth into liberation, he hastened to assure his southern readers, was destined for a future "very far remote." By contrast, one did not have to look far to observe above the Potomac the baleful consequences of attempts to unduly hasten this gradual developmental process. The free blacks living in the northern states, he contended, had declined, rather than advanced in the scale of human dignity. Out of their freedom they had "created nothing." They remained "the boot cleaners and bottle-washers of the whites, in a state of degrading inferiority which they are too obtuse to feel." They had sunk into permanent servitude "in compliance with their natural dependence and unquestionable moral deficiencies."[30]

Simms concluded his apologia for slavery by asserting that the African had been culturally and mentally elevated by his bondage. Not only had he grown over time incontestably superior to his "cannibal" ancestors, but he was also more culturally advanced than his free northern cousins. "We challenge comparison" he loftily proclaimed, "between the negro slave of Charleston and the negro freeman in the streets of New York." Southern slaveowners had essentially performed a social service for humanity; they had "rescued" and elevated the African slave through an essentially benign system of bondage. Even more impressively, by bringing Africans to America to sow and harvest their tobacco and rice and cotton they had accomplished God's work. Simms was certain that overall, the southern planter had not betrayed this heavenly trust. "Providence," he explained, had placed the slaves "in our hands, for his good, and has paid us from his labor, for our guardianship." He wound up his polemical review in a final paroxysm of southern self-congratulation. "The slaveholders of the south, having the moral and animal guardianship of an ignorant and irresponsible people under his control, are the great moral conservators . . . of the entire world."[31]

John C. Calhoun must have been proud of Simms. His fellow planters were certainly impressed with his polemical manifesto. In his review of Martineau's book Simms had paid with obvious enthusiasm his handsome entry fee into the exclusive company of other large slaveholding planters. And he was also handsomely rewarded with praise by the editors and the political leaders of his home state. Indeed, "Miss Martineau on Slavery" was reprinted outside South Carolina in the South's leading newspapers, and it was widely and often quoted from by the region's defenders of slavery. In Charleston, the local *Courier* was delighted that a talented writer of southern historical romance novels was now beginning to rise to the defense of the southern way of life.[32] New York friends like William Cullen Bryant, however, could not have been pleased by the essay's vicious personal attack on Martineau or the strident and overblown tone of its vindication of slavery. For Bryant, as for many New Yorkers, slavery was an institution that might be tolerated in the short run as it ran its course toward an eventual withering away. But it was impossible for him to agree with Simms's insistence in his essay that bondage was a positive moral good.

If Simms and Bryant were fated never to agree on the morality of slavery, they would likewise find it impossible to reconcile their conflicting views regarding its right to enter the rapidly expanding nation's new territories. Concerning the status of slavery within the Union in the 1830s, Bryant assumed a position like that of most of Gotham's political leaders, both Democrat and Whig. He accepted that the institution had been sanctioned by the Constitution and that it was therefore legal within the original states that had embraced it. But he opposed its extension into the federal territories, and he vigorously supported the Wilmot Proviso of 1848, drafted to block the introduction of slavery into the vast southwestern lands won by the United States in the Mexican War (1846–48). The Proviso was passed by the House but rejected in the Senate by the unanimous opposition of the slave states.

Bryant's position on the Proviso placed him for the first time in his editorial career, along with many other New York City Democrats, deeply at odds with southern Democrats like Simms. But his stance was firm and compellingly argued in an 1848 *Evening Post* editorial. "A man who does not approve of slavery," he observed, "may tolerate it where it exists, from the want of constitutional authority to extinguish it, or from regard to the actual conditions of society, and the difficulties of change; but how can he justify himself in instituting it in new communities, unless he believes with Mr. Calhoun, that it is in itself a 'great good'"? Calhoun's proposition that slavery was a positive contribution to human development was practically identical to the argument for slavery Simms had advanced in his *Southern Literary Messenger* polemical response to *Slavery in America* eleven years earlier. Bryant remained adamantly opposed to the ideas of both South Carolinians. He believed that no resident of a free state could in conscience sanction slavery as a moral good. The union of free and slave states thus rested on an imperfect but necessary compromise. "The federal government represents the free as well as the slave states; and while it does not attempt to abolish slavery in the states where it exists, it must not authorize slavery where it does not exist. This is the only middle ground—the 'true basis of conciliation and adjustment.'"[33]

The trouble with Bryant's "middle ground" was that, while it represented a compromise from the point of view of a New York moderate, from the point of view of a Carolinian like Calhoun or Simms it amounted to a plan for the eventual destruction of the slave system. These planters understood that slavery could survive only if it could spread and flourish. They perceived quite correctly that excluding the South's peculiar institution from new federal territories would lead to its eventual extirpation. Ultimately there would be no middle ground to be found between northern moderates like William Cullen Bryant and southern defenders of slavery like John C. Calhoun and William Gilmore Simms, as the bitter political conflicts of the 1850s would prove. The years following the failure of the Wilmot Proviso would move Bryant toward a more resolute opposition to slavery, and it would put an increasing strain on his friendship with Simms.

The disposition of the massive territorial gains of the Mexican War was, after long and difficult negotiations, resolved by the Compromise of 1850, brokered by Senators Henry Clay of Kentucky and Frederick Douglas of Illinois. The agreement defused at least temporarily a disruptive confrontation between the northern and southern states over slavery and forestalled for a time southern talk of secession. California was admitted into the Union as a free state, thereby ending the electoral parity that had existed in the Senate between free and slave states since the nation's founding. But to compensate the South for this loss the New Mexico and Utah territories were free to decide on slavery for themselves. And the Fugitive Slave Act, incorporated into the compromise, sought to mollify southern planters by requiring that slaves be returned to their masters, even if they had escaped to the free states. It also held the federal government responsible for finding, returning, and trying escaped slaves.

Few people on either side of the sectional divide were satisfied with Clay and Douglas's hard-wrought compromise, and Bryant was no exception. He was particularly dismayed by the Fugitive Slave Act, which proved hugely unpopular in the North. The riots in communities large and small that were precipitated by attempts to enforce the law drew from the editor a nuanced and heartfelt response. Bryant had consistently stood against civil agitation and violence that weakened the social fabric of the Union. But how, he asked, were law-abiding citizens of the North supposed to respond to a law that violated their basic "moral instincts"? He earnestly observed that ordinary citizens felt it "to be an impeachment of their manhood to be asked to assist in manacling, for the purpose of reducing to slavery, one who has lived among them the life of an industrious and honest citizen; whom for years they have been accustomed to meet in their daily walks, and with whom, perhaps, they have broken bread." Ultimately the Fugitive Slave Act struck Bryant as an act of folly. "The impulse towards freedom is one which no legislature can extinguish or control, and in legislating about slaves, it would be as great a folly to attempt it as it would be to require by law that fruit should not decay after it was ripe."[34] In its eloquent, downright, and Thoreau-inflected rhetoric, Bryant's editorial indicates that on the slave question he had progressed well beyond the shallow and condescending observations of slave life on Simms's plantation written nine years earlier.

If Bryant was dismayed and angered by the compromise, William Gilmore Simms in Charleston expressed equal disgust with it and complete skepticism about its hoped-for effectiveness in preventing a national schism over slavery. Indeed, by 1850 he had abandoned the Jacksonian nationalism that had led him to argue against state nullification eighteen years earlier. The admission of California as a free state had confirmed his conviction that the South could only preserve its peculiar institution by leaving the Union. He was equally cynical about the future of the Fugitive Slave Act. As he wrote in November of 1850 to Virginian and fellow fire-eater Nathaniel Beverley Tucker, the law would "in all probability . . . be repealed" in the next session of Congress. "The abolition of slavery" would follow "soon or late in the District of Columbia and all places directly under the control of the Federal government." Secession of the southern states would inevitably follow, "five years at the utmost." For Simms, the withdrawal could not come too soon. "Were I to trust my feelings," he confided to Tucker, "I should say to South Carolina, secede at once."[35]

Simms was slightly off the mark in his prediction about when the South would secede. But he was right in his conviction that the Compromise of 1850 would not extinguish the dangerous fires of passion erupting over the issue of slavery. Those fires would be reignited four years later with the passage of the Kansas-Nebraska Act on May 30, 1854. Drafted by Illinois Democrat Stephen Douglas, this law allowed the territories of Kansas and Nebraska to decide the issue of slavery by popular sovereignty; and it was passed thanks to the unanimous support of southern Democrats and southern Whigs. The act was an effective invalidation of the Missouri Compromise of 1820 that had prohibited slavery in the unorganized territory lying west of Missouri and north of the Oklahoma territory. The opening of slavery into territories that for over three decades had been declared closed to the institution violated the deepest moral convictions of Bryant and many other hitherto moderate New York Democrats. As men who had "long been faithful to the democratic party," Bryant and those in his camp were completely "exasperated" by the unwillingness of most party members to condemn the Kansas-Nebraska

Act.[36] After the act's passage the influential and widely respected editor began what would be for him a reluctant and momentous journey out of the Democratic Party and into the newly formed and militantly antislave Republican Party. It was a movement that would create a yawning political chasm between him and his old South Carolina friend.

By August of 1854 Bryant had joined with a group of antislave Whigs and Democrats to organize a convention at Saratoga Springs, New York, that would solidify opposition to Senator Douglas's odious legislative achievement. "We believe," he wrote to potential attendees, "that you appreciate the grave occasion which the passage of the Nebraska Act presents for consultations . . . between those who, having long been, politically, opponents, are brought near together by the wanton outrage upon rights and principles which they cherish." As a delegate to the September Saratoga convention Bryant ultimately voted with the majority to punish the New York Democratic Party by endorsing the entire state ticket of Whigs running in the fall election of 1854. In October he explained his actions to his *Evening Post* readers. The Democratic party had badly "misjudged . . . the strength of the antislavery feeling in this state." In the heat of such emotion lifelong ties of individuals to the party had been incinerated "like tow before the touch of fire" and had fallen "in pieces." Bryant and other like-minded party regulars spurned their candidates and turned to the Whig ticket. Democrats of Bryant's persuasion might well have been uneasy about the Whig propensity for favoring plutocrats. But for the time being they were willing to "shut their eyes" to "points of differences" and support an organization that had possessed the good sense and moral balance to "censure . . . the Nebraska Act."[37]

Bryant's position on the expansion of slavery thus remained impressively consistent over these years of heightened political conflict. The words he employed to explain himself to his readers in October of 1854 might have been used verbatim in his editorial of 1848 on the Wilmot Proviso. "While we deprecate the existence of slavery anywhere," he wrote, "we have claimed no right to interfere with the state governments where it is established, and where the federal government has no constitutional power over it. But the admission of slavery into the territories belonging to the federal government, and over which that government has legislative jurisdiction, is a question on which every state of the Union is concerned."[38] The Union itself possessed the legislative power and the obligation to decree that there would be no slavery in Kansas, no slavery in Nebraska, and no slavery in any other future territory.

New York City's citizens may have been divided about the necessity and manner of abolishing slavery in the South, but Bryant's position against its further expansion into the territories certainly reflected the views of a broad and growing segment of the city's population.

Bryant's movement out of the Democratic Party was not fully accomplished until September of the following year when the New York State Republican Party held its first convention. Here the influential editor formally switched his party allegiance. His editorial of September 29, 1855, clearly shows that the decision was both a difficult and poignant one. He could not announce his choice, he admitted, "without emotion." Nor could he "look with indifference upon old personal and political friends, whose joys have been our joys—and whose sorrows have been our sorrows—men whose honor and patriotism are above suspicion." Nonetheless leaving the Democrats was a judgment demanded of any man who was committed to America's progressive mission. Bryant understood that it would be challenging to "form new, and to some extent, perhaps uncongenial associations" with his new Republican brethren. But the course taken by his "old friends" in the New York Democratic Party in their August 1855 convention had left him no recourse. Theirs was a direction that had "ceased to serve the cause of freedom and justice" and that had subverted the interests and sentiments of New York to the interests of the slaveholding South. In their gathering state Democrats had chosen "to take their law of action from Washington." Instead of choosing to let "New York be ruled by New Yorkers," they had "taken counsel from" and bowed to the wishes of proslavery publications like "the Washington *Union*" and "the Richmond *Enquirer.*" By contrast, the first New York Republican convention had affirmed one essential and foundational principle: "the nationality of freedom and the sectionality of slavery." When New York Whigs adjourned their own meeting and marched en masse to join the Republicans at their convention hall, Bryant marched with them.[39]

Is there any way of knowing how the tumultuous political events that increasingly polarized the nation between 1848 and 1855 affected the personal relationship between William Cullen Bryant and William Gilmore Simms? There are few surviving letters between the two men during this period to give us clues. We know that they were on very close and congenial terms during and after Bryant's three-week sojourn at Woodlands Plantation in 1844. We know that Simms continued his annual summer and fall visits to New York City through the 1840s and that Bryant briefly visited Simms in 1849 on a tour he made with his wife to coastal Georgia and St. Augustine, Florida. We know that between 1844 and 1854 the two men found themselves increasingly at odds in their published writings over both the morality of slavery and its right to expand within the Union. And we also know that Bryant remained dedicated to the preservation of that Union, while by the 1850s Simms had determined, at least privately, that if the South were to preserve slavery, secession would be the region's only recourse.

Despite his increasingly militant stance as a defender of southern regional values, Simms's professional career as a writer remained tightly linked to New York City well into the 1850s. In 1852 he wrote to his old friend Bryant asking for a favor. As part of its upcoming book on *Homes of American Authors* (1853), G. P. Putnam's had decided to include a short description of Simms's Woodlands Plantation. Would Bryant agree to write this brief biographical sketch? "In providing him with a few paragraphs on these topics," Simms wrote, "you will equally oblige him and myself. You know what sort of book he is preparing; you know Woodlands; and you have known me, now for fully twenty years, since the week I first made the acquaintance of New York, Hoboken, and yourself together. Our intercourse has been too frank and unreserved during all this time, to leave you at a loss to report me pretty much as I am."[40]

There is nothing in this fondly couched request to suggest that the friendship between the two men had been significantly strained by the polarizing political debates of the day. Bryant responded with a generosity equal to the graciousness of Simms's request, praising his South Carolina friend in his contribution to Putnam's book for his "frank and ingenuous" manners and his "generous and sincere" temper. Yet Simms's letter, in its evoking of the writer's initial 1832 visit to New York and to Bryant's Hoboken residence, conveys the sense of both a life-defining introduction to a beloved place and a valued friend and a faintly elegiac apprehension of a golden moment gone. This sensation of loss is even more apparent a few lines later when Simms observes, not churlishly but rather sadly: "I never hear from you, and only occasionally of you."[41] Without freighting a letter with more significance than it can bear, this missive does suggest a friendship rendered less robust by advancing years and, perhaps, increasing political tensions.

Two years later in 1854 Simms would make his penultimate visit to Gotham, arriving on August 1 and departing in early October. But on this visit the author would depart significantly from his usual routine. For the first time in twenty-two years, he would leave the city without having contacted or seen William Cullen Bryant. Bryant might not have known of Simms's plan to visit Gotham, but with his trip to New York lasting over two months it seems highly unlikely that he remained unaware of his old friend's being there. Regardless of when he learned of the visit, Simms's failure to contact him did hurt Bryant's feelings. Indeed, the sense of injury seems to have been both lasting and mutually shared.

Fifteen months after his sojourn in New York Simms wrote a letter to Bryant informing him that a mutual friend who had recently visited Gotham had also met with Bryant and his family. This friend had reported that during this visit he learned that "there had been an expression in your family of surprise, amounting almost to displeasure, that, in my last visit to New York, I had not paid you a visit. I was at once glad and sorry to hear this. Glad, as it seemed to assure me of the continued regards of those whom I had ever honored; sorry, as it seemed that I had unfortunately given pain or offense." Simms's letter continued with an apology, but it was far from an unalloyed one. He explained that during his 1854 visit he had seen Bryant's son-in-law, Parke Godwin, and had "specially begged him to communicate my arrival, and my regards to you, and to beg that you would come and see *me*. I told him where I was staying, and that I was *alone*." Simms went on to observe in an almost complaining tone that he had "daily looked to see, or at least hear from you, but in vain. I was closely harnessed to the press while in N. Y., working almost incessantly . . . but had you called, sent or written, I would have made an effort to accomplish [a] visit, though I should have had to carry my work . . . with me."[42]

Simms describes himself as being very busy during his weeks in Manhattan, but another observation in this letter clearly indicates that his staying away from Bryant was more than simply a matter of being too occupied with business. "At the time I was in New York," he writes, "there were some things in the Post that decided me against calling at the *office*. But I did not ascribe these things to you."[43] Although the "things" Simms alludes to are not described, they almost certainly pertain to the ferment that was roiling through the city's political circles in August and September of 1854 while Simms was visiting. These were the days when Bryant was helping to organize the Saratoga Convention to oppose the Kansas-Nebraska Act and when he was joining with rebellious Democrats to support the antislave Whig ticket. It was also a period during which he was writing some of his most eloquent editorials in opposition to the expansion of slavery into federal territories. Bryant's political movement out of the Democratic Party was already under way, and his decision to spurn his party's electoral ticket in favor of the antislavery Whigs must have struck Simms with absolute dismay. To have met Bryant amid this ferment would have been difficult. To have entered the offices of a newspaper that had become one of the city's most fervent opponents of the South's peculiar institution was simply impossible for him. Fifteen months later he was careful to attribute the "things" in the *Post* that had obviously upset him to other journalists, not to Bryant. But the tone of his explanation is suffused with a tension inseparable from the political tensions of the time.

Simms's letter reminds us that, despite his open and frank temperament and the gracious and genteel manners that his friend Bryant so admired, he was also intensely partisan when it came to defending his region and his native state, and he had a temper. His early biographer, William Peterfield Trent, noted that "his Northern friends were a little afraid of Simms's vehement way of expressing opinions" and that his friendship with Bryant was cemented to some degree by the New Yorker's ability to hold to his "own opinions" without directly attacking or deprecating those of Simms. But in the increasingly combustible political climate of the 1850s accommodations between old friends on the question of slavery were becoming more difficult. And Simms was known for flying off the handle and offending northerners. New York editor and writer James Grant Wilson once heard him in company make this declaration, with a dramatic physical gesture suited to his words: "If it comes to blows between the North and the South, we will crush you as I would crush an egg."[44] Considering Simms's disposition, it was probably better that he did not meet his old friend in New York during the tempestuous fall of 1854.

Despite the political controversies that were beginning to strain Simms's relationship with William Cullen Bryant, the South Carolina novelist's letter of January 1, 1856, clearly shows that he continued to value the bond between them. He concluded his missive in an affectionate tone with news of his family and with the "hope, my dear Bryant, that the world is dealing gently with you, and that Time wears a mild and genial aspect." He was clearly unwilling to abandon either his friendship or the exciting city that he had enjoyed visiting for almost twenty-five years. The idea of a speaking tour to the North that came to him three months later in April of 1856 was doubtlessly generated to a significant extent by a desire to mend his bridges to Gotham and to Manhattan friends like Bryant by presenting through his lectures to a northern audience a view of southern culture that would foster what he described to Mary Lawson as "better relations between North and South respectively."[45]

By the time plans for his lecture tour achieved more definite form in May, the prospect of gaining substantial compensation for his lectures was also beginning to loom large in his consideration. As he explained to *Southern Literary Messenger* editor John Reuben Thompson, in the face of increasing "cares and children" he found it necessary to "earn $3000 per ann. apart from the plantation, to live decently in broadcloth." From both a personal and pecuniary perspective, therefore, Simms was certainly aware that in writing his lectures his wisest course lay in giving a rendering of southern culture and history that was as sympathetic as possible without grating the sensitivities of his northern audiences. As he put it to Thompson, the trick was to determine "what subjects would be most likely to please the Northern ear, from Southern lips."[46] Simms's articulation of his judicious approach to tackling a northern audience was penned in a letter written on May 20. Two days later in Washington, however, the Senate floor was stained with blood by the aggression of a South Carolina congressman against a Yankee abolitionist, an action that would enrage the great majority of northerners and substantially complicate the southern writer's planned ambassadorial lecture tour to New York.

On the afternoon of May 22, 1856, Representative Preston Brooks of South Carolina strode down the aisle of the United States Senate, carrying a walking stick, and stood at the desk of Senator Charles Sumner of Massachusetts. The Senate's morning session had adjourned a short time before, and Sumner, virtually alone in the chamber, was busily examining papers. For a moment he was unaware of Brook's presence. But when he did look up, the South Carolinian addressed him clearly and forcefully: "Mr. Sumner, I have read your speech. You have libeled my state, and slandered my relation, who is aged and absent, and I feel it to be my duty to punish you for it." Before the surprised Sumner could respond, he began hitting him with the walking stick, the blows becoming progressively harder and more savage. As Brooks later matter-of-factly recalled the astonishing scene, "I . . . gave him about thirty first rate stripes. . . . Every lick went where I intended."[47]

Tall and solidly built, Sumner found himself trapped within the confines of his writing desk, which was bolted to the floor. For several seconds, he was unable to rise and ward off the blows raining down on him. Finally, through a desperate exertion of strength, he succeeded in wrenching his desk out of its bolts. He staggered up the aisle of the Senate with Brooks continuing to beat him with the now-bloody stump of the snapped walking stick. At last Sumner collapsed unconscious on the floor. "Towards the last," Brooks later observed with undisguised contempt for his victim, "he bellowed like a calf. I wore my cane out completely but saved the Head which is gold."[48]

A few minutes after the attack, Brooks was calmly walking away from the capitol down Pennsylvania Avenue while a semiconscious Sumner lay on a couch in the Senate anteroom having his wounds attended to by a hastily summoned physician. Afterward he was taken by carriage to his Washington lodgings, his clothes soaked with blood. Before losing consciousness again he remarked, "I could not believe that a thing like this was possible."[49] It would be more than three years before Sumner would reassume his seat on the Senate floor.

What was the speech that Preston Brooks mentioned in his challenge to Senator Sumner, and how had it libeled Brooks's kinsman and his native state? The speech was "The Crime against Kansas," delivered in the Senate over two days from May 19 to 20. Its subject was the territorial conflict precipitated by the Kansas-Nebraska Act of 1854 that northerners like William Cullen Bryant had so deplored. By 1856 the Kansas territory had become a lawless battleground pitting proslavery settlers committed to extending the domain of the South's peculiar institution against antislavery settlers equally determined to stop slavery's spread into federal territories. These antagonists had already turned this frontier region into what became popularly known as "Bloody Kansas." Indeed, two days after Brooks's vicious caning of Senator Sumner an abolitionist named John Brown would retaliate against southern depredations in the territory by instigating the "Pottawatomie massacre" of four proslavery Kansas farmers.

Harvard-educated Charles Sumner, a leader of abolitionist forces in the Senate, viewed the strife in Kansas as an unambiguous battle between the forces of good and evil. He believed that the nation had reached a profound juncture, that Kansas must be the place where the growing cancer of slavery was contained. In his powerful "Crime against Kansas" speech he condemned the Kansas-Nebraska Act as "the rape of a virgin territory, compelling it to the hateful embrace of Slavery," and he called for Americans to "vindicate Right against Wrong" and to "redeem the Republic from the thralldom of that Oligarchy" that would enslave Kansas.[50]

Even today, one who reads Sumner's speech can understand why it outraged the southerners who were sitting in the Senate chamber in 1856. The same sense of righteous indignation that infused its antislavery substance also imparted a contemptuous and even cruel tone to its description of slavery's supporters. It was bad enough for southern listeners to hear Sumner identify their region with the antidemocratic and anti-American forces of oligarchy. But when Sumner proceeded to denounce a specific adversary, Preston Brooks's cousin, the venerable Senator Andrew P. Butler of South Carolina, his rhetoric became personally abusive. Worst of all, in attacking Butler he held up to ridicule the southern code of white chivalry, the foundation of the South's exalted view of itself as an enlightened, cultivated, and aristocratic slave society.

Sumner ridiculed Butler by metaphorically linking him to Spain's mad knight-errant Don Quixote. Like the deluded protagonist of the Cervantes novel, he observed, Butler had "read many books of chivalry, and believes himself a chivalrous knight, with sentiments of honor and courage." However, Butler had chosen an even more morally revolting mistress than Don Quixote: "The harlot Slavery is his 'wench Dulcinea.'" And if Butler could not keep his harlot, Sumner observed with acid irony, "then sir, the chivalric senator will conduct the State of South Carolina out of the Union! Heroic knight! Exalted Senator! A second Moses for a second exodus!"[51]

It was fortunate that the elderly and frail Butler was not present on the Senate floor, because Sumner concluded his long speech with an even more personal verbal attack. In the words of Sumner's biographer David Donald, "Uncharitably referring to the effects of the slight labial paralysis from which the elderly . . . senator suffered," Sumner scornfully described the way Butler had opposed the admission of Kansas as a free state in an address filled with what the speaker cruelly termed "incoherent phrases" in which Butler had "discharged the loose expectorations of his speech, now upon her representatives, and then upon her people."[52]

Having disposed of Brook's elderly kinsman, Sumner went on to vilify his native state and its "shameful assumptions for slavery." "Were the whole history of South Carolina blotted out of existence," he thundered, "from its very beginning down to the day of the last election of the Senator to his present seat on this floor, civilization might lose—I do not say how little; but surely less than it has already gained by the example of Kansas, in its valiant struggle against oppression." Kansas, he predicted, would one day enter the Union as a free state and would be "a 'ministering angel' to the Republic, when South Carolina, in the cloak of darkness which she hugs, 'lies howling.'"[53]

The reaction of southerners to Sumner's speech was an immediate and radiant hatred against Sumner and the abolitionism he represented that remained white-hot in the South in the months that followed the caning. It was epitomized by the speech of Senator James Mason, who stood before the Senate shortly after Sumner had finished his address. The Virginian repudiated the Massachusetts abolitionist and his brand of Yankee fanaticism as low, vile, and evil, an assessment with which his southern colleagues in the Senate chamber no doubt heartily agreed. In a voice trembling with rage he expressed his disgust: "I am constrained to hear here depravity, vice in its most odious form uncoiled in this presence, exhibiting its loathsome deformities in accusation and vilification against the quarter of the country from which I come . . . because it is a necessity of my position, under a common Government, to recognize as an equal, politically, one whom to see elsewhere is to shun and despise."[54] In anathematizing Sumner, Mason delivered upon him the worst judgment a southerner could make of an adversary: Sumner was no gentleman. He was a rabid abolitionist barbarian, a man without honor. Not surprisingly, southern venom was nowhere more concentrated than in the breasts of South Carolinians. One gentleman of the Palmetto State observed that immediately after the speech he "could not go into a parlor, or drawing room, or to a dinner party, where he did not find an implied reproach that there was an unmanly submission to an insult to his state and his countrymen."[55] It was just this "unmanly submission" that Preston Brooks determined to correct when he stood above Sumner on the Senate floor two days after the speech.

In contrast to this universal southern outrage, the initial northern response to Sumner's speech was decidedly mixed. Many northern senators felt that the rhetoric on display in "The Crime against Kansas" had been both intemperate and offensive. Massachusetts statesman Edward

Everett probably expressed the feelings of most politically moderate northerners when he observed that, though he generally approved of Sumner's position on Kansas, he had never heard a speech so offensive in tone "from a man of character of any party." Immediate editorial response in the North was also mixed. Many newspapers were troubled by the speech's harsh personal attacks. Others, including Republican Horace Greeley's *New York Daily Tribune* praised Sumner's effort as "one of the most searching and fearless exposures yet made of the Giant Crime which, in its legitimate consequence, has filled Kansas with violence and threatens now to deluge her plains with blood." Significantly William Cullen Bryant's *Evening Post* also approved of the speech's "inspiring eloquence and lofty moral tone" and celebrated it as "a triumphant senatorial achievement."[56]

Whatever ambivalence northerners initially felt about the intemperance of Sumner's speech completely vanished after Preston Brooks's savage attack on the Senate floor. The assault galvanized Americans living north of the Mason-Dixon. Democrats, Whigs, and Republicans united to condemn it as the cowardly attack of an uncivilized southern ruffian on an unprepared and unarmed northern adversary. The newly formed Republican Party was especially energized by the incident. It gave them "the perfectly matched themes of 'Bleeding Kansas" and 'Bleeding Sumner,'" which they would effectively employ in the elections of 1856 to increase their strength in Congress. More moderate northerners were also appalled. They might have disapproved of the tone of Sumner's speech, but they abhorred Brooks's violent response to it. Whig Congressman Robert Winthrop expressed this consternation most tellingly: "How could any high-minded and honorable man, as Mr. Brooks is represented to be in Carolina, have taken such a mode and place of redress and have proceeded to such extreme violence!"[57]

During the summer months that followed Preston Brooks's attack, feelings in both North and South remained high. North of the Potomac letters of support for the slowly recuperating Sumner poured in and lifted his spirits. Henry Wadsworth Longfellow did his best to console his friend. "I have no words to write you about this savage atrocity," he lamented. If Yankees judged the attack to be a manifestation of southern savagery, they apotheosized Sumner as a martyr to southern barbarism. The rapturous words of one admirer echoed the feelings of thousands: "You are glorious now. The crown of martyrdom is *yours*. . . . 'Every noble crown is, ever has been, a crown of thorns' and *you* have been found

meet to wear the one the Savior wore—oh thank God and murmur not."
Northerners expressed their outrage at the attack not just in editorials
and personal letters but in numerous formal resolutions. One of these,
signed by New Englanders Josiah Quincy, Henry Wadsworth Longfellow,
Richard Henry Dana, and Edward Everett, included pledges of money to
support the Senator's convalescence and praised his "dauntless courage
in the defense of freedom on the floor of Congress."[58]

New York City—with its extensive business ties to the South and its
strong political support for the region's slave-owning planters—might
have been expected to express less enthusiastic backing for Charles
Sumner. But as Philip Foner has tellingly observed, the Preston Brooks
caning marked the first major political rupture between Gotham's commercial elite and the cotton-producing southern planters with whom for
over three decades Manhattan's traders had so profitably engaged. Within
days of the incident the city's merchants organized a huge protest meeting
at which numerous speakers condemned both Brooks's barbaric assault
and the South's shocking and unseemly support of the caning. Samuel B.
Ruggles presciently warned the South that its overweening aggression
in defense of slavery would force northern conservatives into political
alliance with northern racial radicals to meet southern "force with force."
And he further advised the South "before they go further into this business to look into their arithmetic. There are more free white men within
one mile of this platform than in the whole State of South Carolina."[59]

The sea change that the Brooks caning precipitated in the attitudes
of many of Manhattan's social elite toward southerners can best be
measured in the diary entries of George Templeton Strong, prominent
Columbia-educated lawyer, founding member of the Union League Club,
and vestryman of Wall Street's Trinity Episcopal Church. Like most well-
bred New Yorkers, Strong was immediately shocked that a supposedly
civilized southern gentleman would approach his victim "unawares,"
stun him "with a cudgel," and continue to beat him until the cudgel broke
into splinters. Yet even more shocking to him was the fact that "Southern
editors and Congressmen" had praised "the 'chivalry,' 'gallantry,' and
manliness of the act." A day later he continued in his diary to take the
measure of the South's pretentions to gentility. Among most New Yorkers, he observed, a "notion" had "got footing" that southern gentlemen
represented "a high-bred chivalric aristocracy" regulated, not by the
values of Gotham's "money-making democracy" but by chivalric "codes
of honor." The caning of Charles Sumner, Strong concluded, had led him

to the opposite conclusion. Southerners were in fact "a race of lazy, ignorant, coarse, sensual, swaggering, sordid, beggarly barbarians, bullying
white men and breeding little n——s for sale."[60]

Antislavery New Yorkers were as delighted as they were amazed by
the turning sentiment of the city against both Preston Brooks and the
South. Horace Greeley's *Tribune* figuratively pinched itself in wonder
as it detailed the condemnations of the Slave Power coming from merchants who had hitherto been "conservative and cotton loving to the last
degree." And William Cullen Bryant's *Post* proclaimed that the city was
"awake at last."[61] As editor of one of New York's most influential newspapers Bryant was a leader in the defense of Sumner and the denunciation
of the southern barbarity that had almost killed him. His was a public
posture of which William Gilmore Simms could not have been unaware,
and it no doubt pained him, as had Bryant's migration the preceding year
into the Republican Party.

The day after the caning Bryant's brilliant editorial entitled "The
Outrage on Mr. Sumner" appeared in the *Post*. Here Bryant mounted an
eloquent indictment of Brooks's savage assault. He began by immediately
dismissing the notion that the beating had been a justifiable response to
Sumner's "wholesale denunciation" of Senator Butler. "No possible inde-
corum of language on the part of Mr. Sumner," he judged, "could excuse,
much less justify an attack like this." If Brooks believed that his kinsman
had been unfairly castigated, "the denunciation should have been repelled
and personalities rebuked by some of the fluent speakers of the powerful
majority to which Mr. Butler belongs, and the matter should have ended
there." Instead, Brooks had mounted a "sudden attack made with deadly
weapons upon an unarmed man . . . where he could not expect it or
have been prepared for it." Such conduct, Bryant argued, was not the
behavior of a gentleman. It was rather the "act of men who must be pol-
troons as well as ruffians. It was as indecent, also, as it was cowardly."[62]

In his editorial Bryant was dexterously turning the tables on southerners who had long argued that the South's plantation culture and the
institution of slavery which sustained it had combined to produce an
aristocracy distinguished by its high social cultivation and its refined
manners. These southern gentlemen had commonly looked down on
unrefined, bad-mannered, and money-grubbing Yankees. Bryant's public editorial, like George Templeton Strong's private diary ruminations,
ripped away this southern veil of politesse and revealed the honor-
obsessed Preston Brooks to be a bully and a ruffian. And it raised this

question: Were northern men of conscience to be brutally treated the same way as self-styled southern aristocrats had seen fit to treat their chattel slaves?

> Has it come to this that we must speak with bated breath in the presence of our Southern masters; that even their follies are too sacred a subject for ridicule; that we must not deny the consistency of their principles or the accuracy of their statements? If we venture to laugh at them or question their logic, or dispute their facts, are we to be chastised as they chastise their slaves? Are we too, slaves, slaves for life, a target for their brutal blows when we do not comport ourselves to please them? If this be so, it is time that the people of the free States knew it and prepared themselves to acquiesce in their fate. They have labored under the delusion hitherto that they were their own masters.[63]

Reading this editorial one is struck by the remarkably progressive evolution of Bryant's conscience on the slave question during the twelve years since he had visited Simms at Woodlands Plantation. In 1844 he had been ostensibly delighted by coon hunts and corn shucking. He had been amenable to viewing his friend's slaves as "indulgently treated" servants who led easy lives, and he had been inclined to admire the South Carolina gentry as men of refinement, social poise, and well-tuned manners, rather superior to his more brusque New York and New England peers. Indeed, he had commended his courtly host as a man who effortlessly embodied all these estimable southern traits. The Preston Brooks caning of Charles Sumner exposed to Bryant, as it had to George Templeton Strong, the darker, brutal, barbaric underside of southern culture, a reality that he had earlier been unable or unwilling to acknowledge.

As a popular writer and molder of southern opinion, Simms was intensely aware of the furious reaction of the northern press to what it considered a vicious attack on an unsuspecting victim who had possessed the integrity and the temerity to denounce southern slavery. And he could not have ignored the leading role that his friend Bryant was assuming in repudiating not only Preston Brooks but also the loathsome slave culture that he believed Brooks represented. However, through most of the summer Simms seems not to have allowed these attacks on his native region to throw a cloud over his coming fall lecture tour. On June 27 he wrote a letter to his friend, New York historian John Lossing, asking for advice in choosing his subjects. The eight presentations he was at that time considering included talks on poetry, on the "Moral Character of Hamlet," and on the "Choice of a Profession." Were these, he wondered, subjects "likely to prove of interest to the Northern audience"? He assured Lossing that he placed great value on his knowledge of the "usual appetites" of the New York audience that he was intent on pleasing.[64]

Even in August, after the July attempt to expel Preston Brooks from the House of Representatives had failed and thus further inflamed northern opinion, Simms seems to have remained sanguine about prospects for his literary expedition to New York. On August 23 he wrote to his New York agent that his "engagements . . . at the North this Winter" promised "to be very numerous" and that he was "now beginning to plan and prepare my Lectures." One week later he informed South Carolina politician James Orr that he was "immensely busied at this moment, preparing for a course of Lectures at the North, whither I have been summoned by a flood of invitations; and where . . . I am in hopes to earn a much-needed amount of money."[65]

Beneath Simms's sanguine assessments of prospects for his northern lecture tour, however, there lay a hard stratum of resentment. He was piqued at what he considered the self-righteousness of Yankee condemnations of Preston Brooks, and at the same time he was irritated with prominent South Carolinians who seemed to expect him to use his planned speaking tour to defiantly carry the southern flag into potentially hostile northern lecture halls. In his September 7 letter to political leader James Henry Hammond, Simms complained that he had been "flooded" with appeals to answer "the attacks of the Northern Press on South Carolina." Even Andrew Pickens Butler, the Palmetto State senator who had been the primary object of Charles Sumner's vilification, had pleaded with him as a "Historian" to defend his state's honor. It was Butler's "blunderings," Simms grumbled, that had "provoked" Sumner's hideous Kansas speech. This superannuated member of the state's political establishment had "fed all his life at the treasury bowls," while also contriving to keep journalistic outsiders like Simms "without feed at all." Now, he acidly observed, the senator who had been elected "for this very sort of warfare" was appealing to a lowly writer whom he had formerly ignored "to do [his] business" for him.[66]

Whatever hope Simms had for appeasing northern audiences in the wake of the Sumner caning, nothing transpiring in the halls of Congress during the tempestuous summer of 1856 altered by one iota his hard-shell secessionist sentiments. He may have been sincere to a degree in professing to Mary Lawson a few months earlier that the aim of his tour was to promote "better relations between North and South." But this affirmation in no way qualified his conviction that the preservation of slavery demanded that North and South go their separate ways, the sooner the better. His fire-eater convictions were on clear display in the letter he wrote to up-and-coming South Carolina politician J. L. Orr on August 30, 1856, in which he had also expressed enthusiasm for his soon-to-be launched goodwill odyssey to the North. In this missive Simms urged Orr "to calculate the value, at once to yourself and the South, of the Democratic Party."[67]

Though Simms had been for years a Democrat, he had ultimately concluded that the party was too weak and divided to serve the crucial interests of the South. Indeed, he was certain that all "existing organizations," Democrat as well as Whig, would soon "perish under the strife of sections." The inevitability of secession, Simms believed, made it crucial for his young friend Orr to "seize upon the proper moment, to show to your people that you are not simply a *national man,* which is the charge most frequently brought against you." He went on to urge him to explain himself to his constituents as a Democrat "only as that Party is able to promote the interests and safety of the South." If Orr were careful to associate himself exclusively with "the *extreme* Southern wing" of the Democratic Party, it would be easy for him to advance his political career in the future "under the new banner" of a prosperous and powerful southern nation.[68]

These three surviving letters—to James Lawson on August 23, to J. L. Orr on August 30, and to James Hammond on September 7—together suggest a weirdly schizophrenic split both in Simms's attitudes toward his upcoming lecture tour and in his understanding of the tour's purpose. Such warring mental postures would ultimately propel the celebrated South Carolina novelist and polemicist toward a disastrous reception in New York and deep personal humiliation. In his August 23 letter to his New York agent Simms had been excited about his numerous engagements and keen to begin preparing his lectures. His August 30 letter to J. L. Orr also brimmed with enthusiasm about the "flood" of invitations he had received and the prospect of handsome speaker's fees. Yet in this same letter Simms found himself counseling Orr to prepare for the inevitability of southern secession and the dissolving of the Union. Did he not recognize that his enthusiastic endorsement of secession conflicted with the idea of sectional harmony that he had months earlier proclaimed to Mary Lawson as the primary purpose and rationale of his fall lectures? Likewise, in his letter to James Hammond of September 7 Simms had complained about the responsibility thrust upon him by fellow South Carolinians to employ his lectures in vindication of his native state. But in a nation enflamed by the brutal attack on Charles Sumner, how could a committed secessionist and a writer dedicated to defending his homeland from scurrilous northern attacks be expected to find the words that, uttered from his "southern lips," would "please the Northern ear" of his audience?

The simple answer is that Simms miserably failed to proffer the appealing subjects and the conciliatory words that would have prompted New Yorkers who had read his historical novels with pleasure to applaud his 1856 lectures. During the weeks of September and October prior to his departure for Manhattan, as he plunged into composing his material, he decided to embrace the mission of using his presentations to defend his native state's beleaguered reputation. It was a duty that his letter of early September to James Hammond suggests he was initially reluctant to assume. But once he decided to accept the task, he pursued it with stubborn and dogged determination. John Guilds in his biography of Simms has sharply noted that during the weeks before he set out for New York "the writer's outlook changed from one of kindly benevolence intent upon instructing with charm to one of righteous indignation set upon redeeming the honor of South Carolina. . . . He changed, in short, from peaceful missionary representing only himself, to belligerent aggressor charged with righting a wrong done to his state and his people."[69]

Simms's transformation from southern cultural cicerone to zealous defender of southern sectional honor was ominously foreshadowed in the letter of acceptance he sent on November 3 to George Bancroft, William Cullen Bryant, and other distinguished members of the committee that had invited him to speak in New York City following his appearances in Buffalo, Rochester, and Syracuse. While professing himself honored by the invitation, he also made clear that he was eager to speak of his "native region." Gone were subjects like "The Moral Character of Hamlet" and "Choice of a Profession" that he had been considering earlier in the summer. They had been scratched and replaced by historical topics directly related to his state, such as "South Carolina in the Revolution" and "Marion, the Carolina Partisan." Simms was very clear in his explanation to the committee of the rationale for these changes in subject. His aim was to challenge his audience, "to disabuse the public of the North of many mistaken impressions which do us wrong."[70] Charles Sumner's speech, in which he had mocked South Carolina's contribution to the founding of the nation and contemptuously dismissed the state as destined to lie "howling" in its "cloak of darkness," had clearly burned itself into the South Carolinian's mind and had helped lead him to a drastic change in the focus of his lecture tour. The goal of enhancing sectional understanding and comity had been supplanted by a new intention, to engage New York audiences by directly pointing out to them their own "mistaken impressions" of the South that had wronged and damaged both his region and his state. Simms set forth from Charleston harbor bound for New York City on October 25, 1856. The central question about his dubious literary venture is how he could ever have imagined that a defiant apologia for South Carolina—the state that still proudly continued to claim Preston Brooks and his blood-stained, shattered walking stick—would be either favorably or neutrally received by northern audiences.

By October 28th William Gilmore Simms had arrived in New York City. About ten days later he set out by rail for his first speaking engagement in Buffalo, and he lectured there on the evening of November 11th. He had decided to begin his series with a presentation entitled "South Carolina in the Revolution." His choice of topic was for several reasons an entirely predictable one. Simms had cultivated a life-long interest in the American Revolution and had featured the period in eight historical war novels set in the Carolina Low Country, including one of his most popular works entitled *The Partisan* (1835). Like most South Carolinians he was extremely proud of his state's contribution to the war for independence, and he was especially offended by New Englanders who trumpeted their own region's participation in the conflict and discounted that of the southern colonies. Indeed, Massachusetts congressman Lorenzo Sabine's *The American Loyalists* (1847) had focused on South Carolina as a hotbed of Tory sentiment and lionized by contrast the patriotic Yankees who, Sabine argued, had assumed a primary role in leading the new nation to victory. Simms had been so agitated by this book that he had felt compelled to answer it in a long essay written for the conservative and staunchly pro-slave *Southern Quarterly Review* (1848).[71] It was this article with its chauvinistic and combative tone that Simms unwisely chose to draw extensively upon when he crafted his opening lecture to the Buffalo audience.

If Simms's purpose had been to ingratiate himself with northerners, one can only wonder why he thought that he could win them over by opening his lecture, not with a polite demurral of Lorenzo Sabine's Yankee-centric Revolutionary War thesis, but with a direct and vigorous personal attack on Senator Charles Sumner. Everyone in the audience would have been keenly aware that Sumner remained absent from his Senate seat, slowly recuperating from the grievous wounds inflicted upon him by a Palmetto State congressman. Yet this was precisely the approach Simms chose to adopt with his Buffalo audience. He began by declaring that it was imperative for him to respond to those living above the Mason-Dixon who, he believed, had libeled his South Carolina "ancestors" by accusing them of being "false to their duties and their country . . . traitors in the cabinet and cowards in the field!" And what specific northern villain had made such scurrilous claims? None other than "a senator in the Senate House" who, but a few months prior, had "poured forth with a malignant satisfaction" a "gratuitously wanton" assault on South Carolina "in sight and hearing of the assembled states." Simms proclaimed that it was his duty to "reject such calumny." Could it be, he mused, that the state that the "infamous 'senator'" had so gleefully excoriated was the same state that had contributed to the Revolution "Marion and Sumter, and Moultrie and Pickens—the very greatest among the revolutionary partisans?" And were these heroes "mere simulacra"? Were "Gadsden and Rutledge, Laurens and the Pinckneys" mere "common men"?[72]

After this opening verbal fusillade Simms launched into a detailed defense of the Palmetto State's contributions to the Revolution drawn from his original essay of 1848. But he had almost certainly lost the sympathy of a good portion of his audience. And any rapport with his listeners that remained was probably extinguished by his self-righteous and aggressive concluding remarks. He closed condescendingly with the observation that intelligent northerners—those who read "History, as they should, with no malignant determination to rake up the evil and suppress the good; to expose the base and deny the noble"—would be bound to concede "that the exertions of South Carolina were unexampled . . . and

that she was one of the most self-sacrificing of the whole Confederacy."
Simms did not implore his audience to extend sympathy to his native
state. He demanded "justice for my Mother Country. She has been more
faithful to you—more submissive—than she ever was to Britain; more
true to your cause than she has ever been to her own!" And what if New
Yorkers, having collectively beheld South Carolina's submissiveness in
the brutal Sumner caning on the Senate floor, refused to proffer the
respect and "justice" Carolina expected from them? Simms made very
clear to the assembled citizens of Buffalo the high price they would pay
for this treachery. His state would not be an "easy victim." "With her
lithe and sinewy limbs and muscles," he proclaimed, she would "twine
herself around the giant caryatides which sustain the anchor of the great
Confederacy, and falling like the strong man of Israel," would "bring
down with her, in a common ruin, the vast and wondrous fabric, which
her own prowess has so much helped to raise."[73] South Carolina, if forced
to preserve its way of life, would reduce to rubble the grand design of the
Union that Simms believed his state had done so much to create.

The morning after his Buffalo presentation Simms pinned a letter to
his New York literary agent, James Lawson, in which he expressed general satisfaction with his lecture and little apprehension of how its strident tone might have offended his patrons. Though he had arrived tired
from his journey from New York City with a sore throat and hoarse voice,
he had been received by a "very large audience" of "more than 1200
people" that, he thought, had "seemed pleased" with his presentation.
"The applause," he informed his agent, "was frequent, though I learn
that some of the Yankees took offence at a showing of the history which
they had never seen in Yankee books."[74] Simms had probably "learned"
of the far-from-unanimous approbation of his lecture from perusing the
reviews it received in the city newspapers the very morning he wrote
his letter to Lawson.

Critical response in Buffalo to "South Carolina in the Revolution"
ranged from lukewarm and qualified to devastatingly hostile. The *Daily
Courier* judged the historical portion of the address to be "interesting
and instructive." But it lamented the opening and concluding sections,
which had contained "severe animadversions on a portion of the North.
However merited his censure, it was hardly well timed before an audience assembled to listen to a literary lecture." The *Buffalo Commercial
Advertiser* likewise faulted the speaker's tendentiousness. Though South
Carolina's contributions to the Revolutionary struggle were obviously

a theme "dear to the lecturer, . . . It was unnecessary and in more than doubtful teste to build up its fame on a deprecation of the equally earnest and self-sacrificing struggle of the North. As a consequence, the audience was coldly polite."[75] The frosty and restrained response of the Buffalo listeners described by the *Commercial Advertiser* stands in marked contrast to Simms's own rose-colored memory of their "frequent" applause.

Other Buffalo newspapers were far less charitable to Simms. The *Evening Post* described his lecture as "an ill-digested, bitter and to at least nine-tenths of the audience, offensive defense of South Carolina politicians of the [Preston] Brooks school." The most annihilating critique of the presentation appeared in the *Morning Express* two days later. "Mr. Simms was invited by a Library Association," it tartly noted, "to address them as a literary man, the only one of note in the South. It was supposed that he would choose a subject proper for the occasion. With an impudence unsurpassed, he comes into our midst and makes an harangue abusive of a Northern State and running over with fulsome and false praise of the least deserving State of the Union. Certainly he was listened to quietly, because if Mr. Simms is no gentleman, the audience was too good-natured and civil to notice it, and they seemed to be rather amused than otherwise at his discourse."[76] For a South Carolina planter who considered himself a model of gentility, the judgement of this Yankee critic that he was "no gentleman" must have been as infuriating as it was humiliating.

Simms, who never missed a review of his work, would have read these Buffalo notices. At this point he might have considered dusting off or revisiting one of his earlier and less agitating inspirations, like analyzing the "The Moral Character of Hamlet." But he did not. He blundered on to Rochester's Corinthian Hall, where he delivered the same talk that his Buffalo critics had panned. This time his audience had been warned of what was to come for them. On November 13, the morning before Simms was to give his evening lecture, the *Rochester Democrat and Chronicle* informed its readers that the Buffalo newspapers had been "pretty unanimous in condemnation of a portion of Mr. Simms's lecture. . . . It is represented to have been interspersed with very much that was in bad taste, and positively insulting to a northern audience. Nevertheless, Mr. S. was courteously treated, as we hope he will be here."[77]

The best that could be said for Simms's Rochester appearance is that it provoked no outright riot. The day after the lecture the *Democrat and Chronicle* featured a scathing review entitled "Quattlebum in

Rochester—A Politico-Historico-Literary Lecture, of the Caudle Kind."
Though Simms may not have recognized the humorous implications of
this headline, local readers would have caught the reference to New York
satirist Philip Paxton's recently published *The Wonderful Adventures of
Captain Priest* (1855), which featured among its many characters a pomp-
ous southern braggart named General Quattlebum.

> Heaven protect us. Heaven defend us,
> War declaring, here they come,
> Breathing vengeance 'gainst the Union,
> Pillow and great Quattlebum.[78]

This Rochester review would prove to be both the most caustic and the
most personal of all the newspaper attacks on the South Carolina writer.

The reviewer's detailed description of Simms linked his physical characteristics closely to those negative characteristics of the planter class
that he was assumed to represent. "The author of *Yemassee* is a stout,
florid man, six feet, with coarse, wiry, gray hair, dressed like a planter,
with a loud, imperious, crackling voice, and manners suited to an overseer of a plantation, where slaves have to be daily cursed and flogged."
The reviewer went on to describe Simms striding onto the stage, "tread-
ing the boards as if conscious that he came from a region superior to
this, where greasy 'mechanics' and men and women who do their own
work and own no menials are not permitted to mingle with slaveholders and gentiles." The *ad hominin* attack continued as it described the
speaker's defiant and defensive attitude toward his audience. "On being
introduced he laid aside his notes for a moment while he attended to
what the Buffalo press had said of his lecture there. As he lived, he had
not intended to say a word that was insulting to Northern people; he had
alluded only to the past, and not mingled at all in questions of the present
day. If any were offended, it must be because *the truth* offends. His speech
was brief, his language plain, and his manner what we understand by the
term 'snappish.'"[79]

The *Rochester Democrat and Chronicle* concluded that the disagree-
ableness and insolence of the speaker had been horribly complemented
by the triviality of his lecture's content. He judged that "as a literary production" it was "destitute of merit" and that it reflected "no credit upon
the writer of a series of passable novels." As a lecture it was simply an
"imposition. . . . [T]he audience appeared indisposed to take offense at it

but were rather inclined to laugh at the absurd heat of the peppery fire-eater, who so valiantly and hotly assails a windmill of his own creation." The Rochester reviewer had obviously read with care Charles Sumner's Kansas speech of May 20, 1856. In that now-famous oration Sumner had mocked South Carolina Senator Andrew Butler as an enfeebled and ludicrous Don Quixote. Now a literary Carolinian was being ridiculed as a tilter against more self-created windmills. To nail down his analogy the reviewer raised this bitter question: "We should like to know how much [Simms] contributed to the Brooks' testimonial?" This "testimonial" referred to the infamous sliver goblet, possibly crafted by a Manhattan silversmith, that had been presented to Brooks and inscribed as follows: "From friends and neighbors and admirers of Hon. Preston S. Brooks, this testimonial is presented as full endorsement of his gallant conduct on May 22nd 1856."[80]

On November 15 Simms returned to New York City, three days before his scheduled appearance in Manhattan. There is no record of his having met his old friend, William Cullen Bryant, in this interval and no record of his thoughts about the disastrous visits to Buffalo and Rochester. Shortly after his return to South Carolina, however, he did convey to James Hammond his justification for his initial presentations. He was satisfied, he wrote, that he had "preserved" his "self-respect and the honour of our section. They saw no faltering in me." Unlike his letter to Lawson written in Buffalo, there was no further mention of audience applause, though he did seem to retain some degree of pride in the large numbers who had attended in both cities. He also continued to believe that he had given the Yankees exactly what they needed to hear. "I spoke to crowded houses at Rochester and Buffalo, more than 1200 people in each, and they howled under the arguments which they could not answer."[81]

It is possible Simms believed that he would receive a kinder reception in the city that he had loved and often visited for many years. Manhattan had been good to him, and it was a place where he could claim many friends and a degree of influence. In any event he had crossed a Rubicon, and he had no intention of altering or amending his lecture for a Manhattan audience. And though he no doubt harbored some anxiety about his reception in New York City, he probably could not have imagined the extent of the rejection and the degree of humiliation that he was soon to experience there.

On the evening of November 18 Simms gave his final reading of "South Carolina in the Revolution" at the Church of the Divine Unity on Broadway. In a December letter to John Henry Hammond, he estimated his audience at around 150, far below the thousand-plus numbers that had attended his Buffalo and Rochester presentations. One reason for the sparse turnout, he complained to Hammond, was that the event had been "badly advertised." But he also seems to have recognized the more likely source of this public relations disaster: that New Yorkers had been adversely influenced by news of "the furious demonstrations of the Buffalo press" against his lecture.[82]

The reviews of his Manhattan presentation that appeared the following morning in city newspapers were about as dismal as those he had received in Buffalo and Rochester. Assessments in the *Times* and the *New York Herald* were at best lukewarm. James Gordon Bennett's *Herald* had been from its inception in 1835 the city's most powerful and influential journalistic supporter of slavery. It might have been expected to respond sympathetically to the South Carolina fire-eater; and its reaction to the lecture, while not unreservedly enthusiastic, was one of restrained approval. It found the speaker's manner both "bold" and "rather prepossessing," and it observed that Simms had delivered his lecture "with great fluency" and that he had been "listened to with marked attention."[83] This wan critical endorsement, however, was far outweighed by the devastating critique that appeared on the same morning in Horace Greeley's powerful antislavery *New York Tribune*.

The *Tribune* review clearly demonstrated just how deeply many New Yorkers had been and continued to be outraged by Preston Brooks's caning of Charles Sumner. It also highlighted the disastrous miscalculation Simms had made when he had chosen to attack Charles Sumner at the beginning of a lecture designed to extoll the heroic contributions of South Carolina's Revolutionary heroes. The reviewer for the *Tribune* began by expressing feigned sympathy for Simms. "While Bully Brooks is feasted and loaded with presents and caresses on the strength of [his] single gutta-percha exploit," he snidely observed, "Mr. Simms, after spending a laborious life in efforts to write South Carolina into notice and admiration, is turned over, in his declining age, to the cold charity and empty seats of Northern lecture rooms." As for the body of Simms's presentation, the writer modestly offered "a few critical observations." First, he suggested, "considering he was addressing a Northern audience, it was not only a great lack of good taste, but a great lack of ordinary rhetorical prudence to commence his discourse by a pointed attack upon Senator Charles Sumner as a wicked and malicious maligner. Such an attack sounds too much like a covert apology for the brutality of Bully Brooks." The reviewer went on to express the hope that Simms would allow him to make one more suggestion: "That while seeking to extol and exalt the Revolutionary glories of South Carolina, it would be but policy to keep her doings of today as much as possible out of sight, both as suggesting disagreeable comparisons, and even tending to painful doubts whether such braggadocio and cowardly sons could, after all, have had such heroic fathers." The *Tribune* review concluded by questioning the discernment and propriety of a presumably well-mannered southern lecturer who to all appearances had relished in "denouncing all who have declined, or who may decline, to come up to Mr. Simms's estimate of South Carolina Revolutionary glory, as asses or reptiles."[84]

There were two open days between Simms's November 18 presentation and the second scheduled lecture on November 21, and William Cullen Bryant stepped forth and utilized his position as editor of the *Evening Post* to render what aid he could to his old friend's floundering speaking tour. On November 19, the *Post* had published a brief, but moderately positive assessment of the program. And on the day of the second scheduled program Bryant himself penned a supportive editorial that was probably written with the *Tribune*'s scathingly personal review in mind. He began by noting with disapproval "several instances of lack of courtesy in our contemporaries in their remarks upon Mr. W. Gilmore Simms, of South Carolina, in connection with a lecture recently delivered in Buffalo and in this city." Those attacking the speaker had made an unfortunate mistake, he believed, by conjoining a distinguished southern writer with "vulgar political agitators" of the Preston Brooks school. Far from being a demagogue, Bryant asserted that "since the death of [James Fenimore] Cooper" Simms had been, "in the range and extent of his works," the nation's "greatest novelist." The lecture topic that the distinguished novelist had chosen was one on which he was "thoroughly well prepared." Surely, the editor observed, "northern ears" were "not so delicate as to take offence at an occasional outbreak of local and very natural feeling in an exceedingly elaborate, painstaking, and . . . judicious performance." Bryant concluded with an undisguised plea to his readers to acknowledge and respect his friend's "literary labors of twenty years, no less than his generous personal qualities," which were deserving of "courtesy and respect. We trust, therefore, that in his next public appearance before us he will be honored by an audience worthy the occasion and the honorable feeling of the North."[85]

Bryant's heartfelt editorial tribute to Simms fell on deaf ears. On the evening of November 21, the South Carolinian was "honored" at the Church of the Divine Unity with practically no audience at all. Unfortunately for Simms, the *New York Herald*—which had printed a mildly positive review of Simms's first lecture but also seems to have cannily anticipated more controversy to come—sent another reporter to cover his second appearance. James Gordon Bennett's support for slavery was exceeded only by his newspaper's cultivation of the salacious and the sensational, and the events of that chilly November evening were perfect grist for its scandal mill. The *Herald's* amusing and satirical account of Simms's aborted second lecture was full of details that turned the speaker, consumed by his grand project of defending South Carolina's Revolutionary history, into a complete laughingstock.

After three stubborn and unsuccessful attempts to rhetorically batter northern audiences into a recognition of his native state's glorious and unappreciated contributions to the creation of the Union, Simms had finally accepted the necessity of changing his subject for his second program. According to the *Herald* account of November 22, the speaker had announced his intention of delivering an address that skirted the tendentious and political, entitled "The Appalachians: A Southern Idyll, Descriptive of Southern Life, Manners, and Scenery." This change was not widely publicized; and, in any event, it was made too late. The *Herald's* account made plain the full extent of Simms's humiliation.

> Five minutes before eight o'clock, the time appointed for the lecture, there was an audience of three persons present. The church was well lighted and warmed, but none of the committee having appeared, the sexton only admitted the people to the vestibule of the church. At eight o'clock, there was an audience of six persons, not including the reporters. From eight to eight and a half a few others dropped in, making an audience, all counted, of thirteen gentleman and four ladies. The lecturer still not appearing, the gas was turned off, the doors locked, and the assembly adjourned *sine die,* looking at their tickets.[86]

As Simms explained in his letter to Hammond, he was not present for his second lecture because he had been effectively disinvited from delivering it. The morning after his opening address members of the invitation committee had visited him and informed him that, because of his "allusion to Sumner" and to certain other "passages" of his "discourse," they could not only "not sell tickets," they could not "give them away." The predominant feeling among New York's citizens seemed to be this: "Damn S. C. and all that belongs to her—we want to hear no *blowing* about S. Car." He was forced to accept the fact that "the rancorous feeling in the city" was so strong that audiences were "willing to listen to nothing from the South." Simms may have appeared impetuous, obstinate, and condescending to his northern audiences, but he took seriously what he considered to be the obligations a southern gentleman. He promptly released the committee from a contract "in which they were to suffer loss" and canceled all his other scheduled appearances. By refunding his fees he lost approximately $2,300—worth about $70,000 today.[87]

The time Simms spent in New York City between the debacle of his second lecture and his departure for Charleston on December 1 must have ranked among the most miserable periods of his life. Days after the November 21 fiasco the press continued to hound him, led by the scandal-mongering *Herald*. On November 24, the newspaper printed another mocking commentary on the lectures. It averred that the speaker had been motivated by two purposes—"to bolster up the much-injured chivalry of South Carolina, and to palliate some of their recent exploits." This "Quixotical undertaking" had initially attracted the "curiosity" of "about one hundred persons," who had exhibited "but little sympathy" for the speaker's views. "The second lecture," the writer witheringly observed, "was not delivered, for the simple reason that only thirteen persons could be mustered to listen to it." In the end, the *Herald* concluded, New Yorkers had responded to Simms's provocations much more civilly than southerners would have done in the same situation. "How different would be the conduct of a South Carolina audience if any one were to go down there and lecture upon the intellectual preeminence of Massachusetts and the wrongs of Charles Sumner!" Horace Greeley's *Tribune* contributed its own postmortem, and, like the *Herald,* it focused on what it considered to be the speaker's gratuitous attack on Charles Sumner. It remined readers that it was "Bully Brooks" who on the Senate floor had responded to Sumner's condemnation of slavery by launching a "ferocious attack . . . well worthy of a cowardly South Carolina Tory . . . to which Mr. Simms also saw fit to allude in the beginning of his lecture, in terms reproachful to Mr. Sumner, and we must be allowed to say, very little creditable either to the head, the heart, or the taste of Simms."[88]

Since Simms spent the better part of the month of November in New York City, it is hard to imagine that he did not see William Cullen Bryant during that time. However, there is no record or evidence of their having met. Though Bryant was a member of the invitation committee, we cannot even be sure that he attended Simms's opening lecture. The *New York Tribune*'s account of the event mentioned George Bancroft and Richard Hildreth among the notables in the audience, but Bryant's name was conspicuously absent from that list.[89] Simms almost certainly read his friend's supportive editorial in the Nov. 21 issue of the *Evening Post,* and he might have been heartened by his old friend's vindication of his character and reputation. But though he was quick to quote the most scabrous and hurtful lines from the *Herald* and the *Tribune* reviews in letters to his South Carolina friends, he never quoted from or mentioned Bryant's defense of him. During the four years that followed Simms's humiliation, years that would lead ultimately to the bombardment of Fort Sumter and the secession of South Carolina he so ardently anticipated, there would be no more visits to New York and no more letters between the two old friends.

Even before Simms stepped off the boat from New York in early December, news of his disastrous reception in the city had reached his native state. In a letter of November 27 James Hammond informed him that he had read the account of his second lecture in the *New York Herald* just before dinner guests had arrived and had been so distressed by its contents that he had scarcely been able to entertain his company. "As I see it," Hammond continued, "you have gone North at a somewhat critical time for *you* and martyred yourself for So Ca who will not even buy your books and for Brooks whose course could at best be only *excused* and who in his supreme vanity will think your sacrifice only a slight oblation. What Demon possessed you, mon ami, to do this?"[90] Simms's reply to Hammond's letter made clear that he was in no mood to admit any major errors in judgment on his part regarding his suspended lecture tour.

Looking back on the fiasco, Simms insisted to his friend that "there was nothing in my lecture which should have given offense" to his northern audiences. Indeed, he asserted, he had simply presented them with "the true history of S. C." He had included "no allusion to Brooks, directly or indirectly," and he had attacked Senator Sumner quite properly "as the wanton assailant of S.C." By the time he ventured North he had made the decision—one that he had clearly communicated to the invitation committee—to use his lectures to "correct the vulgar mistakes or misrepresentations" of his native state's history. But his Yankee audiences had perversely refused to submit themselves to his correction. Such was the "rancorous temper of Black republicanism," so completely did "New England rule N. Y.," and so "malignantly" had New Yorkers come to regard South Carolina, that they had collectively closed their ears to the truth. Simms admitted that in confronting his northern audiences his "own blood" had been "in a ferment." But that was as far as he would go toward acknowledging his own remarkably tone-deaf approach to his New York audiences. In hindsight he would make only one admission: "If, at the outset, I had dreamed that I should have been denounced because of my local subjects, I would have taken others; but the step once taken, it was a matter of pride and honor, that I should insist upon these or none."[91] Ultimately Simms's sole consolation seems to have been that he had valiantly attempted to defend the honor of South Carolina before hostile and bigoted listeners and that throughout the disaster he had maintained his own sense of honor as a southern gentleman.

Simms's sense of humiliation at the hands of New Yorkers and of the city's press was enhanced by what he considered the lack of sympathy of his fellow South Carolinians. He complained to James Hammond that he should have been "too long accustomed to toils and sacrifice" for the Palmetto State "to feel her injustice now." But his sense of betrayal was nonetheless keenly felt. "My losses are all pecuniary," he acerbically reflected; but his fellow Carolinians would "never make them up to me." Nor would they "probably" ever "acknowledge [his] performances" on their behalf. Some days later, writing to James Hammond's brother, Marcus Claudius, he continued trying to retrieve a few shreds of his personal honor while also bitterly dwelling on the inconstancy of his native state. He assured Hammond that "private letters and assurances" from "the gentry and men of letters" of New York City had made plain their sense of "mortification" regarding his reception in Gotham. "The Georgia press" had warmly supported him, and even Missouri newspapers had sent him endorsements "using a language of sympathetic indignation." But he had "nowhere seen" such aid and comfort from South Carolina.[92]

At this point Simms might have chosen to withdraw from public activity while he licked his figurative wounds, but he was unwilling to relinquish his deep resentment of the indignities that had been visited upon him in Manhattan. And there was also the matter of the considerable sum of money he had forfeited by canceling his lecture tour. By January he had resolved to embark on a second tour in which he would detail the deep-seated northern animosity toward the South that he had encountered in New York and that had doomed his noble attempt to vindicate South Carolina's Revolutionary history. This new venture, however, would follow a very different itinerary and cultivate a very different audience. From early February to early March of 1857, he would deliver with considerable success a new lecture entitled "Antagonisms of the Social Moral. North and South," beginning his quickly organized lecture circuit in Washington and Baltimore and continuing to Norfolk, Petersburg, Richmond, Raleigh, and Greensboro.[93] He would now redeem himself and the South by damning the North and preaching to a sympathetic choir of southern or southern-oriented audiences.

Simms opened "Antagonisms of the Social Moral" by assuring his listeners that he had optimistically embarked upon his northern Odyssey convinced that Yankees were "surely not all hostile" and that most of them would "gladly listen to the truth" about the South. He believed that the "thousands of mistakes and misrepresentations" that had been spread by a small number of abolitionist newspapers and politicians had engendered an "ignorance" among northerners that he could correct through his lectures. Most of all, he asserted, he felt it necessary "that the North should be disabused of the nation that the South *is imbecile*— imbecile because of her slave institutions—imbecile in war—unproductive in letters—deficient in all the proper agencies of civilization,—and so, incapable of defense against assaults."[94]

Simms had assumed that it was possible to amend the ignorant misperceptions of his northern audience. But the people he encountered in the lecture halls of Buffalo and Rochester were decidedly inferior to the intellectual circles of Gotham with whom he had interacted most pleasurably for decades on his frequent trips North. The audiences of western New York State revealed themselves to be a "jealous, grasping, arrogant race" that had been corrupted by abolitionist dogmatism. They were people who had embraced an intolerant brand of political extremism that had been given most fulsome expression in Charles Sumner's "Crime against Kansas" speech. Yes, he freely admitted, he had attacked Sumner directly in his New York lectures. However, he asked his southern audiences, was the object of this verbal assault not "himself a wanton assailant. Did not his cold bloodied, venomous, deliberate assault upon our State, so entirely gratuitous, invite and justify retort?"[95]

After his Buffalo and Rochester appearances he had returned to New York City hopeful that it would afford him a more sympathetic and open-minded audience. Surely in Manhattan there would be "a sufficient body of high-minded people, solicitous of right and justice; calm and judicious; thoughtful and earnest" that would be less prone to the "fanaticism" of the more provincial cities of western New York State. He had been wrong in making such an optimistic assumption. The savage and bigoted reviews of his initial lectures had preceded him, and they had galvanized in the city a "vigorous, powerful, concentrated party" of detractors, "fanatical of mood, despotic of will." These abolitionist zealots had "cowed" more reasonable and open-minded New Yorkers from attending his programs, and they had intimidated the members of the invitation committee into demanding changes in his lecture that he could not have acceded to without compromising his purpose and his honor.[96]

New York City was a place that for many years had delighted Simms, stimulated his intellectual life, and nourished his literary career. It had been a source of many of his most valued friendships, including his long relationship with William Cullen Bryant and his family. For years it had served him practically as a home away from home. But, as his southern lecture tour made clear, the traumatic events of November had effectively severed that bond. Gotham had failed him, and in "Antagonisms of the Social Moral" he was willing to lump its citizens with all the other hostile fanatics he had endured on his ill-fated tour. From Buffalo to Manhattan, northern society had revealed itself to him as dominated by abolition-besotted fanatics, "warped and tortured . . . wild, disordered, anarchical, ready for chaos and disruption." Training his sight more specifically on Gotham, he observed that the extraordinary explosion of wealth that over the last thirty years had transformed the city into the newest of the world's great metropolises had also spawned a civic culture in which there was a complete "lack of veneration" for tradition and social order. Gotham had rapidly evolved into a crass urban society that refused "to recognize anything as sacred." Most of its inhabitants were consumed by a "morbid self-esteem" and lived "wholly for show and appearances."[97]

By the end of his calamitous New York speaking tour Simms had come to believe along with many other southern polemicists that the New England Puritanism that had spread to and now pervaded Gotham represented the quintessence of a religious fanaticism, which unopposed would destroy the Union. His scarring experience in Gotham had convinced him that the receptive and cosmopolitan city he had once loved, enjoyed, and found so appealing was now hopelessly enthralled to this fanatical spirit. He ended his southern lecture with denunciation and dire warning. Northerners were "the most intolerant people in the world and have been so from the days of Cotton Mather," and southerners could hope for no support or understanding from such people. Above the Mason-Dixon, he alerted his listeners, from newspapers and pulpits to living rooms and schoolrooms, "all classes" were now "united against" the southern states. With crude and stark metaphoric language that would have disturbed old New York friends like William Cullen Bryant, Simms ended his second lecture tour by reminding his audience that the North loved the South "as the tick, the cow;—as the leech the vein."[98] The sooner this northern tick was removed from the southern social body, the better.

One can usefully view the collapse of the Simms-Bryant friendship in allegorical terms. Their close personal relationship—cemented by mutual intellectual and cultural interests and carefully nurtured during the decades of the 1830s and 1840s—mirrored the strong economic, cultural, and political bonds forged during this same period by the burgeoning and mutually profitable cotton trade between New York City and the plantation South. Likewise, the gradually widening personal gulf between Simms and Bryant on the issue of slavery—a gulf that became a chasm after Simms's disastrous 1856 lecture tour—was a personal fracture that reflected the deep and growing divisions between southerners and more moderately inclined New Yorkers over slavery's place and its future within the Union, divisions that grew practically unbridgeable during the turbulent 1850s. The personal union between William Gilmore Simms and William Cullen Bryant would founder on the shoals of slavery in 1856, and four years later so would the political, commercial, and cultural entente between Gotham and the South.

SIX

EXECRABLE
NEW YORK

IN SEPTEMBER OF 1857 financial panic seized New York City as its overheated economy suddenly came crashing down. Though centered in Gotham, this was the first severe economic downturn to spread through all regions of the nation. Indeed, its adverse effects on the South gave impetus to southern nationalists, who for years had complained that southern economic well-being was too dependent upon that of New York. During the height of the crisis the *New Orleans Daily Crescent* had trained its editorial sights on the financial colossus on the Hudson. The paper had condemned it for its "rotten bankruptcies permeating and injuring almost every solvent community in the Union," and they had anathematized it as "the center of reckless speculation, unflinching fraud and downright robbery."[1]

Three years after the financial panic, on October 13, 1860, the *Crescent* again turned to New York City, but its editorial tone had changed drastically. Now, rather than launching a predictable southern attack on Gotham's corruption and perfidy, the newspaper chose to respectfully pose to the citizens of the Empire State an urgent question. "Will New York," it asked, "prove herself equal to the occasion? Will she now come forward, as the largest and most powerful State of the Union, and save us (and herself) from the consequences—social, political and commercial—of Lincoln's election? Will her chief city, built up to colossal proportions by the commerce of the whole Union, permit that Union to be endangered, if not destroyed, by the fanatical folly and madness of her own people? Are there not enough conservative men in the city and

State, if they will only postpone their petty disputes and combine in solid mass, to save the State from the grasp of that party whose triumph will still further embitter the South—already fearfully exasperated—against the continuance of our Federal Union?"[2]

The political party that the editor of the *Daily Crescent* could not bring himself to name directly was the new, antislavery Republican Party, rapidly ascending in membership and power in the northern states since its organization in Ripon, Wisconsin, in the spring of 1854. By 1860 it was more commonly and contemptuously referred to by many southerners as the "black Republican party." Indeed, University of Virginia law professor James Philemon Holcombe had published a pamphlet during the tense and bitter campaign of 1860 entitled "The Election of a Black Republican President: An Overt Act of Aggression," in which he claimed to have exposed the key assumption of the "Black Republican organization." The fanatics supporting this new party and the Lincoln candidacy, he asserted, were unanimous in their conviction that "between the free labor of the North, and the slave labor of the South an irrepressible conflict must take place until one gives way to the other."[3] Increasing numbers of southerners like Professor Holcombe believed that Black Republicans were intent on leading the nation to a violent racial Armageddon in which the South and its system of chattel slavery would be completely destroyed.

The *Daily Crescent*'s appeal to New Yorkers opposed to Lincoln's candidacy to "postpone their petty disputes and combine in a solid mass" was an acknowledgment that the burning issue of slavery had turned the presidential campaign into the most fragmented and chaotic electoral contest in the nation's history. The political controversy over slavery had created the new Republican Party and destroyed the old Whig Party, driving many New York Whigs and antislavery Democrats such as William Cullen Bryant into the Republican camp. The issue had also deeply divided the Democratic Party, with northern and southern Democrats nominating separate presidential candidates at separate conventions. In the fall of 1860 four candidates vied for the presidency—Abraham Lincoln, the Republican; Stephen Douglas, the northern Democrat; John Breckinridge, the southern Democrat; and John Bell, nominated by former Whigs and Know-Nothings. Politically astute southerners knew that winning New York State was the key to denying Lincoln the presidency and that victory depended on the three other candidates joining or fusing their votes against him. It was just such a fusion ticket that the *Crescent* was urging New Yorkers to cobble together.

Though the outcome of the fast-approaching election was uncertain, the *Crescent*'s editorial writer was convinced that New York was the South's "only hope of escape from . . . the evils that threaten us." The slave states now looked "to New York alone" for "effective resistance" to the Black Republican menace. "Upon the great Empire State," the editorial concluded, "the hopes of the South now rest." The *Daily Crescent* was not alone in bestowing such importance and investing such hope in the state's potential political efficacy. A few weeks earlier the Crescent City's *Daily Picayune* had also lauded it as "a mighty conservative power" and a linchpin of the Union. And it had offered a southern vision of the future in which New York would stand with the slave states in defense of a powerful and unified nation that recognized and sanctioned the continued existence of slavery. "If the South but shows its determination to stand by the Union," it concluded, "it may be believed New York will stand there too."[4]

The editors of the *New Orleans Crescent* and *Picayune* were not wildly off the mark in their estimation of what New York might do to save the South from Abraham Lincoln. Despite the rancorous criticisms and acidic tirades against Gotham emanating from the pens of southern fire-eaters such as Edmund Ruffin and William Gilmore Simms, New York City had generally maintained its reputation as an emerging commercial giant dependent to a significant degree on the cotton trade and correspondingly sympathetic to the interests of southern planters. In the presidential campaign of 1860 Republicans themselves had largely written off their prospects in Gotham. Indeed, they had capitalized on its overwhelmingly Democratic political orientation to appeal to upstate rural voters' distrust of the city's cosmopolitan and ethnically and racially diverse population. Horace Greeley's pro-Lincoln *Tribune,* for example, claimed that the wealthy merchant class of Manhattan hated Republicans because the "rich Jews and other money lenders" of Wall Street, like the "great dry goods and other commercial houses" lining Broadway, were beholden to and politically in league with the slaveholders of the South.[5]

Contrary to Greeley's editorial stance, affluent New Yorkers were by no means monolithic supporters of the South and the southern-oriented Democratic Party, and Republican voices condemning slavery were not so rare in the city as to be a source of shock or consternation to the financial district. Still a strong majority of the city's mercantile elite remained firmly opposed to Lincoln. It was indeed these merchants and bankers who successfully engineered and promoted the fusion ticket, as the *Daily Crescent* had urged them to do, to block Lincoln's victory in New York State. And although some of the city's largest newspapers—like the *Times,* Greeley's *Tribune,* and Bryant's *Post*—strongly attacked slavery and endorsed Lincoln, other major papers virulently opposed him and starkly appealed to the bigoted and racist inclinations of their readers. The *Daily News* predicted that if the Republicans prevailed, New Yorkers would find "negroes among us thicker than blackberries swarming everywhere." In a similar vein James Gordon Bennett's *Herald* cautioned the working men of the city that if Lincoln were elected "you will have to compete with the labor of four million emancipated negroes." Indeed, in his final election-eve appeal this reliably prosouthern editor reached a rhetorical crescendo of anti-Republicanism in which he implored the respectable wives of the city to persuade their husbands not to cast their votes for Lincoln. What, he asked these women, if the "energy and gayety" of Gotham "should be suddenly eclipsed by the triumph of the Black Republicans? What if the child is now born who will see the grass growing on Broadway? Think of these things, matrons and maidens of New York."[6]

Throughout the presidential campaign Gotham's business and political establishments continued to vigorously oppose Lincoln. "On election day," observe Edwin Burrows and Mike Wallace, "thousands of stores closed and hung out signs urging patrons to vote the Union (Democratic) ticket. Many businesses circularized their employees, saying that if Lincoln were elected 'the South will withdraw its custom from us and you will get little work and bad prices.'" The editors of the *New Orleans Daily Crescent* could have found little to complain about regarding the efforts of New York City's Democrats to thwart a Republican victory. And indeed, when the votes were counted 62 percent of New Yorkers had cast ballots for candidates other than Lincoln. But the 38 percent voting for him in the city combined with a huge Republican vote in the interior and western parts of the state to provide Lincoln with a comfortable electoral majority of 54 percent, awarding him all the Empire State's thirty-five electoral votes and assuring his election as president.[7]

The election results in New York State answered the anxious question that had been posed by the *New Orleans Crescent* one month earlier. As southerners would see it, neither the city nor the state of New York had proved equal to the momentous electoral moment of November 6, 1860. To have passed the *Crescent*'s test Gotham would have had to provide, not just a landslide of over 60 percent, but an annihilating landslide of anti-Lincoln votes that would have overwhelmed the upstate New York returns. But New York was not Charleston, New Orleans, or even Richmond, which cast 99 percent of its vote against Lincoln. New Yorkers, often hostile to what they considered extreme abolitionist sentiments and generally tolerant of southerners, were also uninclined to commit themselves to the long-term perpetuation of chattel slavery within the Union, much less its expansion into the western territories.

One of New York City's swing voters was George Templeton Strong, a Columbia-educated and socially prominent Wall Street lawyer. Strong approached the presidential election with no illusions about the dangers involved in electing Abraham Lincoln. In a remarkable diary entry written shortly before the vote he observed that Republicans were obstinately refusing "to believe secession possible (in which I think they are wrong), and maintain that were it accomplished, it would do us no lasting mischief. I am sure it would do fatal mischief to one section or another and great mischief to both." Yet even though he was no abolitionist and no Republican, he decided four days before the election to support a Republican ticket. If New Yorkers voted for the Democrat fusion ticket, he concluded, they would be choosing to "accede to Southern exactions, we must re-open the slave trade with all its horrors, establish a Slave Code for the territories, and acquiesce in a decision of the United States Supreme Court . . . that will entitle every Southerner to bring his slaves into New York and Massachusetts and keep them there. We must confess that our federal government exists chiefly for the sake of n——-owners. *I can't do that.*" With a real sense of trepidation Strong cast his ballot for Abraham Lincoln because, he wrote, he wanted "to be able to remember that I voted right at this [time of] great crisis."[8]

Some days after the fateful presidential election Strong returned to his diary, and in it he pondered how New Yorkers of conservative persuasion like himself had gradually become alienated from their southern friends. Until around 1850, he noted, the city had largely ignored the "vaporing" of Manhattan's "abolition handful." "Our feeling . . . till that time was not hostility to slavery, but indifference to it, and reluctance to discuss it. It was a disagreeable subject with which we had nothing to do." But ten years before, the "clamor of the South about the admission of California" into the Union as a free state had served to place slavery squarely before the North's conscience. Strong believed that this controversy and the Compromise of 1850 that came out of it had begun to teach New Yorkers "that the two systems could not co-exist in the same territory. It opened our eyes to the fact that if we allowed slaves to enter any territorial acquisition, our own free labor must be excluded from it." The nastiness of the political brawling of 1850 might have been forgotten "had not [Stephen] Douglas undertaken to get Southern votes by repealing the Missouri Compromise. . . . Then came the atrocious effort to force slavery on Kansas by fraud and violence [and] the brutal beating of the eloquent and erudite Sumner with the cordial approbation and applause of the South."[9] This concatenation of proslave outrages had by 1860 depleted the good will that moderately conservative Manhattanites like the diary writer had habitually extended to southerners. Their consciences would no longer allow them to consent to what they considered the outrageous demands of the slavocracy. From a southern point of view the trouble with New York City in 1860 was that there were too many men of conscience like George Templeton Strong living there.

The entry of New York State into the Republican electoral column no doubt compounded the South's sense of betrayal at the hands of their half-hearted political and economic ally, and it seemed to confirm the malignant judgements of Gotham by hard-shell secessionists like William Gilmore Simms and Edmund Ruffin. But would it also confirm the prophesies of these fire-eaters concerning New York's fate in a dismembered Union? Only two months earlier Edmund Ruffin had published a novel in which he had gleefully predicted the collapse of the city's economy following the secession of the southern states and zestfully detailed the ensuing riots of the desperately impoverished working class and the catastrophic incineration of Manhattan. Nearer to home conservative New Yorkers themselves had raised the specter of grass growing between the cobbles of an abandoned Broadway. Would New York's dependence on the lucrative cotton trade and its failure to appease the South and forestall secession prove its undoing?

Burrows and Wallace astutely observe that Edmund Ruffin's "first predicted catastrophe arrived as if on cue. Triggered by the interruption of southern commerce, [an economic] panic struck New York City in 1861 that in some respects was more severe than that of 1857." Southern planters renounced their debts to northern creditors, and merchandise destined south of the Mason-Dixon began piling up in New York shops, as did business bankruptcies. Unemployment rose precipitously, and

Ruffin's fictional scenes of bread riots and violent social disorder seemed a more and more concrete possibility to more and more New Yorkers. Merchants and bankers moved quickly to mollify their southern creditors as best they could. In mid-December more than 2,000 gathered to affirm their solidarity with the southern states. The declaration of one of the attendees expressed the prevailing racist sentiment of the crowd. "If ever a conflict arises between races," he proclaimed, "the people of the city of New York will stand by their brethren, the white race." In January of 1861 the New York City Chamber of Commerce, claiming to represent the "voice of the commercial emporium," compiled and sent to Washington a petition with 38,000 signatures calling for "mutual concessions" from North and South that would allow the nation's trade to "assume its accustomed channels."[10]

The trouble with petitions such as that of the Chamber of Commerce was that a month after election day the United States no longer resembled a bona fide Union. Secession sentiment was boiling over in the Deep South, and South Carolina was already on its way out. The response of concerned New Yorkers to the Palmetto State crisis was a foreshadowing of the futility that would greet the efforts of the city's conservative establishment to hold the nation together in the months to come. Richard Lathers, a South Carolina native who had amassed his fortune in Manhattan and had been long a resident of the city, penned a letter in early December to leading Charleston merchants expressing his concern about the possibility of his native state's secession and the fear among prominent New Yorkers that "the usual influence of conservative men, like yourselves, has not been exercised to check undue excitement." Might Charlestonians, Lathers inquired, receive a delegation of Gotham's "leading men," who he assured them were all sympathetic to the South. Charleston's reply came quickly. The city, like the state, was completely fixed on leaving the Union. The visit of a New York delegation, no matter how sympathetic to the South, would prove "unprofitable and unpleasant."[11]

From December through the following March bipartisan groups of wealthy New Yorkers and groups of equally wealthy Manhattan Republicans would journey to Washington to discuss with the outgoing Democratic administration and the incoming Republican administration possibilities of compromise with the South and urging further concessions to save the Union. But incoming Republicans were repelled by southern arrogance and intransigence and were tired of trying to placate the

South. The exhortations of financial titans as powerful and as influential as Peter Cooper and William B. Astor were to no avail. Sven Beckert has perceptively observed that the failure of "New York's bourgeois Republicans . . . to persuade Lincoln to appease the South [stands] as powerful testimony to the limited influence they enjoyed in a party dominated by farmers in general and westerners in particular."[12]

New York City's strenuous efforts to pacify the slave states were scorned by southerners even more completely than they had been by newly ascendant Washington Republicans. By the beginning of 1861 the South seemed to be finished with Gotham. An editorial appearing in the *Richmond Examiner* on January 6, 1861, made this dismissive attitude toward the city abundantly plain and no doubt warmed the hearts of secessionists like Ruffin and Simms. According to this editorial the ruling ambition of the "buying, manufacturing, trading, speculating populous" northern states was to obtain by popular majority rule "uncontrolled power over the producing and sparsely populated southern section of the Confederacy." As the epicenter of this ravening capitalism, New York City would always champion northern domination of the Union. Thus, for its own survival it was incumbent for the southerners to close their ears "to the delusive promises of merchant princes in Fifth Avenue," plutocrats who prattled on about their conservative principles and counseled compromise on the slavery question. The South could no longer afford to foolishly look to Manhattan's merchants "for comfort or succor."[13] There was no real help to be found in Gotham and there never had been.

Lincoln's electoral victory in the Empire State gave fuel to the fire of anti–New York southern polemicists. The *Vicksburg Daily Whig* called for both the secession of Mississippi and an end to the South's spineless acquiescence to New York's commercial dominance. "By mere supineness," it complained, "the people of the South have permitted the Yankees to monopolize the carrying trade, with its immense profits. We have yielded to them the manufacturing business . . . without an effort . . . to become manufacturers ourselves." The editorial went on to observe bitterly that Mississippians should not be surprised that Gotham's "merchant princes" lived in "gorgeous palaces" and reveled in "luxuries transcending the luxurious appliances of the East." The southern states needed to acknowledge that they now lay supine at the feet of one city: "New York City, like a queen of commerce, sits proudly upon her island throne, sparkling in jewels and waving an undisputed commercial scepter over the South. By means of her railways and navigable streams, she sends out her *long arms* to the extreme South; and with an avidity rarely equaled, grasps our gains and transfers them to herself—taxing us at every step—and depleting us as extensively as possible without actually destroying us."[14] A new Confederacy of southern states would bring an end to Gotham's rapacious economic imperialism.

Swept by a surge of anti-Lincoln hysteria, the South moved inexorably toward secession, and fire-eaters of the Edmund Ruffin school relished the prospect of New York City's receiving at last its justly deserved economic comeuppance. *De Bow's Review* in its December 1860 issue confidently predicted that secession would bring several small southern cities into active competition with Gotham. There was no reason, it argued, why in a new confederacy "Charleston, New Orleans, Mobile, Savannah, and Augusta should not become points of distribution, and be relied on entirely for supplies. Charleston can become so without waiting to establish lines of steamers to Europe. If she can obtain her fair portion of the jobbing and distributing trade, she will soon number 200,000 in population, and the lines of steamers will follow, and so will the ability to build railroad outlets." A newly independent South, *De Bow's* assured its readers, would redirect trade from New York to southern cities, where it "rightfully" belonged. New York City would "immediately retrograde in population," it rather maliciously predicted, and would "settle down to be the Liverpool of the United States, instead of the 'London of America.'"[15]

New York was aware of these southern pronouncements of its coming economic ruination, and the city's petitions and multiple delegations to Washington during the winter months preceding Lincoln's March inauguration clearly show that it had a substantial degree of respect for such predictions. However, at least a portion of the city's public opinion remained reasonably sanguine about Gotham's future. They believed that conservative New Yorkers had become enthralled by southern polemicists and that they were too willing to ratify these voices of doom. Some of the most eloquent expressions of the city's optimistic spirit could be found in the *New York Times*. In its edition of December 7, 1860, it published a substantial article arguing that the notion that a Lincoln victory and southern secession would bring ruin to New York was a threat "greatly exaggerated" by conservatives wishing to appease the slave states.[16]

If the South were to successfully end its trade with Gotham, the *Times* observed, a state like South Carolina would have to refuse absolutely to buy from or sell to the city. But could South Carolina persist in such a scheme if doing so was "a violation of her own interest"? Where would it find a better market for its cotton, and where would it find an emporium offering cheaper prices for manufactured goods? No such place existed. Self-interest thus dictated that "South Carolina can no more stay away from us than matter can refuse to obey the laws of gravity." Indeed, for South Carolinians to gain full economic independence they would need to "construct" their own "commercial system." They would have to send their cotton to Europe, "bring back the proceeds in their own bottoms," and create a "great depot of commerce rivaling New York."[17]

Could South Carolina or any southern state create such a rival metropolis? "For some fifteen weary years," the *Times* sarcastically observed, "great Commercial Conventions [have] been held at various points in the Southern States, where annually it has been resolved that the South *ought* to become a great manufacturing and commercial people." But what had been the effect of these high-flown resolutions composed by "the foremost minds of the South"? Had they inspired "a love of industry . . . or of maritime adventure in the soul of a single *Southron?*" For the *Times* the notion that a culture established on chattel slavery could successfully rival the commercial efforts of a city like New York was risible. The article concluded rather magisterially with this prediction: "We shall . . . continue to carry cotton, except in case of war, precisely as we have done, and so long as we can underbid competitors to the extent of a cent a bale. After the gusts of passion have subsided, this cent will always place us on as good terms with our Southern brethren as have ever existed between us."[18]

Despite the bravado of the early-December *New York Times* feature, the city's pro-Union rallies, petitions, and delegations to Washington indicate that most New Yorkers remained highly nervous about the deleterious effects of the fracturing of the Union on Gotham's economic fortunes. An alert reader might well have noted, for example, that the *Times* had guaranteed the confident predictions of its conclusion "except in case of war," and by New Year's Day of 1861, as a worsening commercial panic swept the city, war itself seemed a more-and-more distinct possibility. During the two months preceding Lincoln's March inauguration Gotham's mood grew progressively darker and more anxious. Indeed, the Manhattan's economic disarray and its fractured sense of confidence were avidly seized upon and embellished in reports telegraphed by correspondents to the South's prosecessionist newspapers. Dispatch after dispatch gave weight to the catastrophic prophesies that had been delivered just a few months earlier by Edmund Ruffin in his *Anticipations of the Future*. They also seemed to confirm the southern fire-eater's conviction that New York's day of reckoning was at hand.

Less than three weeks after Lincoln's election, the New York correspondent for the *Charleston Courier* was regaling his readers with details of the city's rapidly metastasizing economic distress. Two manufacturers of felt hats, facing a collapse in orders, would "leave for the South, scouting new locations" for their company. And "their first look," the reporter assured his readers, would be "on South Carolina." These businessmen were wise to be planning an exit from a city on the verge of collapse. "The opinion here among cautious, conservative men," the dispatch concluded, "is that the Banks cannot stand out longer than twenty days." A few days later the *Charleston Mercury* proclaimed that the loss of southern trade and the repudiation of southern debt portended a bleak winter for Gotham. "People not accustomed to be frightened think that they hear the rumble of a financial and social earthquake compared with which [the financial panic of 1857] was a mere bagatelle."[19]

Southern reporters also readily played on the notion that New Yorkers would never fight to keep the South in the Union. On December 3 the *Mercury* excitedly reported that Representative C. C. Vallandighham of Ohio had declared before a Manhattan audience that he would never "vote one dollar of money whereby one drop of American blood should be shed in a civil war." In the reporter's words, "the merchants and solid men of the free and patriotic City of New York" attending the meeting greeted Vallandighham's vow with "vehement and long-continued applause . . . rising and cheering as one." Three days later the *Norfolk Day Book* reported that an "intelligent gentleman residing in New York" and passing through Virginia had asserted that support for the Republican Party had collapsed and that if the presidential election were being held in December "Lincoln would be defeated in New York State by at least [a] 100,000 majority." This dramatic turnabout in voter sentiment could be largely attributed to "the refusal of the South to send their cotton."[20]

A dispatch to the *Mercury* of December 11 nicely encapsulated the two primary thrusts of southern journalistic propaganda—that New York was petrified by the fear of economic collapse and that it would never fight to prevent the South's leaving the Union. Probing the "true sentiment of New York" concerning secession, the reporter claimed to have heard many expressions of sympathy for the South. He was convinced that any attempt to coerce the slave states would elicit "much material aid" from the city, especially from the Irish, "who hate the n—— as they do the devil," and would "fight to sustain our [southern] rights" along with many other like-minded New Yorkers. Rather than risking violent conflict with its prosouthern citizenry, he predicted that the city would countenance the slave states' going "quietly out of the Union." Such a course would be led by Manhattan's merchants and traders, who "believe that if the South is allowed to take its own course" southerners "will return to them to purchase our goods and sell our cotton."[21]

Throughout the winter southern correspondents in New York City, especially the reporter for the *Charleston Courier,* continued to cultivate the idea that Gotham was on the verge of economic disintegration. In December he had focused avidly on details of the escalating business panic, observing that businessmen were overwhelmingly talking "in the gloomiest manner" and that men in the clothing trade were "all being swept along remorselessly with the tide into the devouring maelstrom of ruin." Devoid of their southern clientele, Manhattan's hotels were also doing "a wretched business. . . . at the St. Nicholas the dinner tables show about one third of the usual number of guests." Months later the *Courier* continued to harp on the dire economic condition of the city. "The papers of this city," it noted, "are constantly denying in the most flippant manner that there is more than the usual distress here this winter. The facts tell a different story." The dispatch reported that aid societies had been overwhelmed by rising numbers of unemployed and that business "failures continue to be the order of the day. A number of very large houses went under on Saturday." The prevailing hard times were reflected in rates for rental properties. Rents had "considerably decreased in certain portions of the city," especially for properties below 14th Street. "Private residences, which last year let for $1500, are now obtained at $1200."[22] Given the tone of these dispatches from Gotham, southern readers would have been justified in believing that New York was too enfeebled by business depression and too vulnerable to southern economic retaliation to stand as a bulwark against the dissolution of the Union.

———————

On January 6, 1861—with South Carolina out of the Union and the states of the Deep South poised to follow its example—Mayor Fernando Wood rose to address the New York City Council. The "dissolution of the Federal Union," he declared, was "inevitable"; and it could not "be preserved by coercion or held together by force." As mayor he believed it was requisite that the city recognize and adjust to these new realities. Manhattan had traditionally cultivated "friendly relations" and a "common sympathy" with the slave states, though the same claim could not be made by the state of New York. Interior and western areas, he opined, had unfortunately been infected with the "fanatical" abolitionist spirit of the New England Puritans. Luckily Gotham had largely rejected such provincial zealotry. Instead, it had expanded its cultural and economic horizons and extended itself commercially into every section of the Union, thereby assuring its mercantile dominance and its prosperity. But if the city was to sustain such economic preeminence, it was incumbent that it strive to assure an "uninterrupted intercourse" with all regions of the nation, South as well as West.[23]

Mayor Wood continued his address by reminding council members that business relations with the southern states had always been mutually beneficial. Indeed, in recent years New Yorkers had come to realize that they had more to fear from the "usurpations" of Albany than from the demands of fealty coming from the South. The state of New York, he contended, had robbed Gotham of municipal rights that had been guaranteed by the British Crown. Dominated by abolitionist Republicans, Albany had become in effect a "foreign power," and as a result, the city's "burdens" had been "increased, our substance eaten out and our municipal liberties destroyed." In response to these depredations, he offered, "Why should not New York City, instead of supporting by her contributions in revenue two-thirds of the expenses of the United States, become . . . independent" of both the nation and the state? Such an independent city-state, he argued, would bring prodigious benefits. "As a free city, with but a nominal duty on imports, her local government could be supported without taxation upon her people. Thus, we could live free from taxes, and have cheap goods nearly duty free. In this she would have the whole and united support of the Southern States as well as of all other States to whose interests and rights under the Constitution she has always been true."[24]

Fernando Wood's proposal for the creation of an independent city-state was not dismissed as a bizarre idea by those conservative New Yorkers who strongly supported the South. Indeed, the plan was approved by most of the city council, and the idea that Gotham might declare its independence had been circulating in Manhattan for several weeks. The prosouthern *New York Daily News,* boasting one of the largest

circulations in town, had floated the idea to its readers two weeks before Mayor Wood's presentation. The editorial had contended that in
the event of southern secession the independence of New York would be
"an object exceedingly desirable, not only to the interests of its citizens,
but also to those of the State and the whole of the North." A free city
would cement "a bond of peace and continued commercial relations between the two separated Confederacies." Burrows and Wallace note that
Wood's scheme was discussed widely among the city's business elite. Not
surprisingly, southerners were also eager to give the plan credence. John
Forsythe, Confederate commissioner to the national government, wrote
to Confederate president Jefferson Davis that influential and powerful
New Yorkers not only supported an independent city but also, in the
event of succession, planned to seize control of the Brooklyn Navy Yard.[25]

Despite the approbation of many of the city's stoutly prosouthern
Democrats, within a few days of the publication of Wood's speech it
became apparent that most conservative New Yorkers were markedly
skeptical of his project. A torrent of editorial ridicule predictably issued
from the pens of Gotham's antislavery newspapers. Horace Greeley's
Tribune, for example, labeled the mayor a "traitor" to his country. But
it was telling that even John Gordon Bennett's anti-Republican *Herald*
refused to endorse the idea, and the most calmly considered critique of
Wood's proposal appeared in the January 8 issue of the *New York Journal
of Commerce,* the orthodox journalistic organ of Wall Street. This editorial agreed with Mayor Wood that the policy of the Albany legislature
toward Gotham had been "infamous" and "subversive of the plainest
principles of local government," but it did not believe that the establishment of an independent city-state was a practical solution to the city's
dilemmas. New Yorkers, it concluded, had "a more important part to play
in the theater of events" than "to reduce [itself] to a 'free city' confined
to Manhattan Island." Above all, it cautioned, local politicians needed to
avoid imitating the "hasty actions of South Carolina."[26]

Through January and February of 1861, as southern states seceded
one after another and Lincoln's March 4 inauguration loomed ever
nearer, concern in Gotham over the survival of the Union grew ever
stronger. The mayor's city-state proposal remained before New Yorkers
as a possible option, though in the weeks that followed its introduction
it failed to gain popular traction. Events that swiftly followed Lincoln's
ascension, however, brought a precipitate end to what Wallace and Bur-
roughs have termed "Wood's fantasy" of independence for the city. Seven

days after the Lincoln inauguration, the provisional government of the Confederacy declared that as of April 1 customs duties on imports arriving through southern ports would be reduced to half the rate of those required by federal law and applying to New York City, and it expanded the access of European shipping to its harbors. At long last, the new Confederacy's economic vengeance on Gotham seemed to have been set in motion. The *Charleston Mercury* crowed that a new southern nation was now positioned to free itself from the "New York money changers" and "trade directly with our customers." And the *New York Times,* which a few months earlier had made light of the South's threats to devastate Gotham's economy, abruptly changed its tone. Employing metaphorical rhetoric akin to that of the prosouthern *Herald,* it warned its readers that if the recently established Confederacy successfully implemented its new tariff policies, "we shall not only cease to see marble palaces rising along Broadway but, reduced from a national to a merely financial metropolis, our shipping will rot at the wharves, and grass will grow in the streets."[27]

Conservative New Yorkers were convinced by the events of early March that to prevent the city's economic collapse southerners had to be persuaded not to leave the Union. Further compromises thus needed to be wrung from Lincoln and the Republicans. But how was Gotham to force such concessions? Some of Manhattan's financial titans sought to temper what they considered Lincoln's hardline policy toward the South by threatening not to buy the federal government's loans, but Republicans howled and defiantly vowed to bypass the city's financial institutions and sell bonds directly to the American people. And would New York City really use its financial clout in such an existential crisis to bring the national government to its knees? Michael Zakim has perceptively noted that in order to avert the financial mayhem Gotham's financiers so feared in the spring of 1861, it was essential for them to preserve both the financial integrity of the city's markets and banks and the fiscal stability of the federal government. One could not be saved without saving the other. There was no alternative course, and during the second half of March Manhattan's business establishments and its banks moved successfully to guarantee federal solvency. The crowning irony of these events, Zakim concludes, was that by unleashing its tremendous resources to stabilize the incoming Republican administration, Gotham's commercial magnates undermined their "own campaign for sectional compromise."[28]

Fernando Wood's proposal for an independent city of New York was probably the only initiative that, had it been implemented, might have restored Gotham to the good graces of most southerners. But both the mayor's scheme and the city's subsequent threat not to purchase federal bonds turned out to be political exercises in magical thinking. New York could not serve the interests of the slaveholding South over its own economic interests. The explosive issue of slavery had finally destroyed the golden age of cultural and economic comity that had linked the city to the plantation South from the 1820s into the 1850s. By 1860 Gotham remained substantially dependent on trade with the slave states, but thanks ironically to its cotton trade, it had also developed into the new nation's financial capital and its chief commercial emporium. It needed the South, but it needed the nation and the world even more. And it could not achieve its ambition of being a world-class city by accommodating itself either to the southern vision of the United States as a slave republic or to the region's design of establishing an independent slave Confederacy.

By the end of March many New Yorkers of all political persuasions had concluded that they could not preserve the Union by further compromises or concessions to the slave states. What's more, as Philip Foner has perceptively noted, the Confederacy's new tariff policies had also "cleared away the clouds of confusion" in their minds regarding the city's best response to southern secession. Until early March civic leaders like Fernando Wood had overwhelmingly supported the peaceful departure of the southern states. Now merchants and financial titans were coming to the realization that they could not "sit by idly and watch the South destroy a business system which had been built up over so many years." For August Belmont, longtime southern sympathizer and New York financier, the preservation of the Union was now paramount. The South must not be allowed to dismantle the United States. It was no longer a question of slavery, he believed; it was "now a question of national existence and commercial prosperity." Wealthy shipper and cotton merchant E. K. Alburtis expressed the emerging consensus of Gotham's merchant elite even more savagely. Alburtis avowed that he was no "philanthropic abolitionist" and that as a voter he had always positioned himself "upon the side of the South." But now, he declared, the time for compromise and accommodation was over. "The Slave Power ... has tried to snatch away our liberties; they have corrupted our people; they have proved themselves incapable of understanding or tolerating constitutional liberty; therefore, that power must be curtailed; yes broken, if not altogether annihilated."[29]

At 4:30 on the morning of Friday, April 12, 1861, shells from an arc of gun emplacements manned by over 500 Confederate troops began to descend on the eighty-man federal garrison at Fort Sumter, located at the mouth of Charleston harbor. For well over thirty hours more than 3,000 shells fired from forts and batteries around the city rained down upon the battered fortress. Early on the afternoon of Saturday, April 13, the fort's tattered American flag emblazoned with thirty-three stars was lowered, and a white flag was raised in its place. The following day Major Robert Anderson and his small contingent of federal troops were evacuated from the smoking ruins of the fort and held for the night in a Confederate naval vessel. On Monday, April 15, they were transferred to the USS *Baltic*. Carrying with them their tattered American flag, Anderson and his men began their four-day voyage to New York, arriving in the city harbor on Friday, April 19. The American Civil War had begun.

During his journey north Major Anderson must have wondered how the evacuation of Fort Sumter would be received in the North, and he doubtlessly speculated about what kind of reception he and his men would be given upon their arrival in New York City. He would not have been alone in his surmising. In the days after the fateful bombardment both northerners and southerners were attempting to gauge the temper of the nation's largest metropolis. Now that war had come, what course toward the conflict would Gotham's leaders and its general populace embrace? Considered for decades to be a nest of southern sympathizers, would New York City support the new president or actively spurn and thwart his efforts to preserve the Union by force of arms?

Southerners themselves were generally confident of the answer to these questions. They believed that as a result of its economic vulnerability and its political divisions the city would continue to encourage compromise, oppose hostilities, weaken the North's fighting spirit, and facilitate secession of the slave states from the Union. *London Times* correspondent William Russell was initially willing to give this prevailing southern assessment credence. He informed his readers in early April that "the South believed New York was with them" and that he was inclined to agree. Indeed, he had personally heard from several "Southerners in Washington, that it was very likely" that the capital city itself "would go out of the Union." The idea that Gotham was paralyzed by the prospect of economic disintegration and was thus unwilling to coerce the South into submitting to federal authority had been nourished by the southern press through the winter, and this journalistic scenario of collapse, civic division, and demoralization continued to be purveyed by southern newspapers right up to the bombardment of Sumter. In late March, for example, the *New York Tribune* presented its readers with what it obviously considered the fantastical reporting of the *Charleston Mercury* on conditions in Gotham. In this article the southern correspondent informed its readers that "the whole City of New York" was "on the verge of bankruptcy." Confederate tariff reductions would inevitably divert the bulk of Gotham's trade to southern ports. The "pauperism" arising from this disruption, he predicted, would become so pervasive that "risings and riots" would sweep the city. In fulfillment of Edmund Ruffin's apocalyptic fictional prophesy of the preceding fall, the unemployed and destitute, described by the reporter as "white slaves of commerce and capital," would rise en masse and violently administer to Fifth Avenue plutocrats "the poisoned chalice which they [had] prepared for the planters of the South." In the unlikely event that the South required troops to help defend itself, it need only go to New York City. "Thousands of native Democrats" living in Manhattan were aligned with the southern cause, and there was scarcely one "unemployed Irishman" who would not gladly enlist in the Confederate army if offered the chance.[30]

These exaggerated evaluations of Gotham's economic condition and its conflicted and divided state of mind were not without some basis. After Lincoln's inauguration New Yorkers like George Templeton Strong had been alarmed by and distressed with the climate of opinion in their city. In March of 1861 Strong declared that he would not fear the prospect of civil war "were we at the North only united, of one mind, loyal to the government." The problem, he complained, was that New York City was not united. Newspapers like William Gordon Bennett's *Herald* seemed to be actively supporting secession, and even some of Strong's own friends were engaging in "wild ultra-Southern talk." His old companion, Walter Cutting, had stood in the opera house lobby only the night before and declared that he was "ready to go in for a fight and to give up all he's worth in the world and his life, too, to exterminate these d——d Abolitionists." Rumor was sweeping through town that Lincoln was poised to evacuate Fort Sumter. Though the possibility of such a withdrawal was being "generally received with favor" in Gotham, Strong was downcast and demoralized by the prospect. Americans, he feared, were "a weak, divided, disgraced people, unable to maintain our national existence." If forced to travel abroad he would be ashamed to "show [his] nose in the meanest corner of Europe."[31]

During the hours that immediately followed news of the Friday morning bombardment of Fort Sumter, the South's confidently optimistic prognostications about Gotham's response to the attack seemed to have been confirmed. Even before the shelling had ceased on Saturday the prosouthern *Daily News* predicted that within a week the conflict would be over. The wealthy merchants of the city, it declared, would "not supply means to depreciate the rest of their property by prolonging this unnatural war." George Gordon Bennett's *Herald* joined the Copperhead chorus on Sunday by reporting that "the leading merchants, traders, and professional men of the City of New York" intended to hold "a preliminary meeting . . . preparatory to a grand mass meeting . . . to declare in favor of peace and against civil war and coercion."[32]

These early announcements of support for southern secession proved to be disastrously premature. The lowering of Sumter's tattered American flag and the surrender of Major Anderson's hugely outmanned troops on Saturday afternoon had produced an instantaneous and astonishing effect on New York's collective morale. James Gordon Bennett apparently could not detect this sudden seismic shift in opinion on Saturday evening when his newspaper was penning its call for a mass antiwar protest, but by Tuesday, April 16, he had heard the new voice of the city loud and clear. The *Herald* now chose to report approvingly on a different gathering. This one, "a meeting of prominent citizens," had been convened "to make arrangements for a grand mass meeting at an early day to strengthen the hands of the [Lincoln] administration in repressing the Southern revolution."[33] On the issue of southern secession Bennett's newspaper had, within a span of forty-eight hours, turned on a dime.

How had this almost unbelievable shift in New York public opinion happened? As with so many events taking place during this tumultuous period, George Templeton Strong's diary provides invaluable insights into the precipitate shift in the thinking of tens of thousands of New Yorkers who, like the diarist, found in the violent events at Fort Sumter a liberation from the uncertainty and confusion that had plagued them in the months after Lincoln's election. On April 13 with the fortress ablaze and under constant fire, Strong sat down and penned these words: "So Civil War is inaugurated at last. God defend the right." Gone was the despondency of his March entries. Though the battle in Charleston harbor had not yet concluded, his entry exhibited a new confidence. Only a day after news of the attack reached New York, he sensed that "the Northern backbone" had "much stiffened already. Many who stood up for 'southern rights' and complained of wrongs done the South now say that, since the South has fired the first gun, they are ready to go all lengths in supporting the government." Strong was prescient in his prediction that the *Herald* would be "upholding the Administration and denouncing the Democratic party within a week. It takes naturally to eating dirt and its own words." He concluded his entry with these stirring words: "Would I were in Sumter tonight, even with the chance of being forced to surrender (seventy men against seven thousand) and of being lynched thereafter by the Chivalry of Charleston. The seventy will be as memorable as the 'four hundred' of the Light Brigade at Balaklava, whatever be their fate."[34]

Strong's diary entries for the days immediately following the surrender of Fort Sumter concretely dramatize the immense tide of patriotism that spontaneously swept through what had previously been considered a city of Copperheads and trimmers. On April 16 the diarist celebrated the complete "conversion of the New York *Herald*" to supporting the war, a conversion that he had predicted three days earlier. James Gordon Bennett's "capitulation," he wrote, "is a set-off against the loss of Sumter. He's a discreditable ally for the North, but when you see a rat leaving the enemy's ship for your own, you overlook the offensiveness of the vermin for the sake of what its movement indicates." Bennett's journalistic white flag was quickly followed by those of New York's other prosouthern newspapers. On April 17 Strong personally witnessed a large crowd assembling before the offices of the conservative *Journal of Commerce*, which had advocated the South's peaceful secession. In response to this demonstration the "American flag was hung out from the window" of the newspaper office. The assembled citizens immediately "sent up a cheer" and then "moved promptly up Wall Street again, cheering lustily."[35]

Just days after the assault on Fort Sumter, Gotham's prosouthern Democrats were expressing dismay at the eruption of popular support in the city for the Union and for Lincoln's determination to preserve it by force of arms. In a letter of April 15 prominent Manhattan lawyer Sidney Webster uneasily admitted to a political ally that democrats would probably "lose some persons who will feel constrained now to follow Lincoln's lead." Republicans, he complained, seemed to be succeeding in putting "northern men who differ from the administration in an attitude of disloyalty" to the country. In this alarming atmosphere New York City suddenly appeared to have formed itself into "a unit in support of Lincoln and his policy." Two days later Webster's dismay had turned to despair. Democratic opposition to the president had collapsed, he lamented, and "despotism" in Manhattan was now "supreme." "Men who have houses of business," he observed, "do not dare to denounce the war or even to criticize the acts of Lincoln." In less than a week Democrats had found themselves "compelled to adjourn discussion of party issues and not dissent from the act of Mr. Lincoln."[36]

If some New Yorkers of Democratic persuasion were privately dismayed and shocked by Gotham's abrupt turn toward war fever, many others were as exhilarated by the city's sudden emotional unity as George Templeton Strong had been. Ezra White described this prevailing sentiment in an April 17 letter to a friend. "There is but one feeling here now. That the government must be sustained, and our glorious Republic preserved. . . . My feelings are intense as is almost our entire community." White's words echoed almost perfectly those of Nathaniel Niles, written two days earlier. "There is but one feeling here and that is to sustain our flag and the government at all hazards." Niles predicted that there would be "but one party of the North" and "no half measures" from the federal government. Preservation of "the Union, the country, and our honor" was now "the paramount obligation." "Southerners," he believed, had "brought this war upon us," and there was no alternative but to "reduce them and the whole country to a state of legal [peace] and submission to the laws."[37]

London Times correspondent William Howard Russell seems to have been as mystified as he was surprised by Gotham's sudden soaring of patriotic spirit. Being fond neither of the city nor of its inhabitants, he judged the volt-face to be as phony as it was "absurd." Why, he skeptically asked, had New Yorkers been suddenly enraged by the insult to the national flag at Sumter when in the previous weeks that same standard had been "torn down from the United States' arsenals and forts all over the South." Underneath this newly minted patriotism he smelled the distinct odor of rotten Yankee cupidity. When Manhattan's merchants, he concluded, "saw that the South was determined to quit the Union, they resolved to avert the permanent loss of the great profits derived from their connection with the South by some present sacrifices." These financial titans had promptly denounced their former southern allies and "rushed to the platforms—the battle-cry was sounded from almost every pulpit—flag raisings took place in every square."[38] For Russell New York avarice had been conveniently tricked out in patriotic rhetorical finery.

Russell was not alone in indicting Gotham's greed. The city's rapacity had long been the central theme of southern fire-eater attacks. And there is no question that economic interests had long dictated the course of New York's relations with the plantation South. But neither the English journalist nor the southern correspondents reporting from the city were willing to acknowledge the substantial degree of altruistic sentiment that New Yorkers felt for their nation and their Union at this perilous moment, a sentiment that could not be valued in dollars and cents. Eleven days after the bombardment George Templeton Strong surveyed the chaos and political tensions that had racked the city and the nation over the past six months. Ever the realist, he recognized that the United States was entering a "terrible, ruinous war" and facing an uncertain future. He also frankly acknowledged the fearful losses the crisis had inflicted on many men of fortune like himself. His assets had been "reduced fifty per cent, at least," and he could "clearly see" that the coming of war had been a "most severe personal calamity." Yet, he declared with complete sincerity, "I welcome it cordially, for it has shown that I belong to a community that is brave and generous, and that the City of New York is not sordid and selfish."[39]

This strain of national idealism was as widely imbedded in the characters of the city's prosouthern Democrats as it was in their Republican political foes. Charles and Maria Daly may be considered as typical representatives of Gotham's dominant Democratic Party. Charles was the son of Irish immigrants, but as Chief Justice of the Court of Common Pleas he had attained eminence within Manhattan's political, cultural, and social circles. His wife, Maria, was not descended from such humble immigrant origins, but she fully shared her husband's Democratic politics, his sympathy for southerners, and a common New York hostility toward New England Yankee abolitionists. In her fascinating and intelligently observed diary she candidly displayed the antiabolitionist spirit that frequently linked New Yorkers of different political persuasions, such as Mrs. Daly and George Templeton Strong. In one particularly revealing 1861 entry she described being in a social setting with members of "the *Tribune* circle—all rabid abolitionists," not an uncommon occurrence at Gotham social gatherings. Mrs. Daly was introduced to the wife of the New England poet John Henry Stoddard, with whom she engaged in a polite but brief debate on the slave question. She freely admitted to Mrs. Stoddard that she was "no friend to free blacks," and when her

interlocutor continued to assert the "moral principle" in her opposition
to the South's peculiar institution, Daly made this bold proposal: "Let
those who feel so concerned for the slaves at the South and who ask
such sacrifices from slave-owners each buy one and then liberate them
by degrees. Then I shall believe in the principle—the philanthropy which
actuates the abolitionists."[40]

Such an unapologetic defender of southern slaveholders might reasonably have been counted a loyal member of Manhattan's Copperhead
corps of secessionist enablers, Democratic leaders like Fernando Wood
who were urging the creation of an independent city-state. Yet in the
hours following the bombardment at Fort Sumter Maria Daly wrote
an entry in her diary brimming with patriotic spirit. Her words were
sharply reflective of those penned by other New Yorkers of various political persuasions. Gone was her contempt for the Republican president,
whom she had earlier in her diary referred to as "Uncle Ape" and "the
clod." Also vanished was her solicitude for the southern states. Without
a trace of the sympathy that she had expressed for southern slaveholders
a few months earlier, she wrote that "the attack . . . [had] united all the
North as one man against the South. Party is forgotten. All feel that our
very nationality is at stake, and to save the country from anarchy . . .
that every man must do his best to sustain the government, whoever or
whatever the President may be. It is a sublime spectacle."[41]

It was Gotham's spontaneous demonstration of patriotic unity following the reports from Fort Sumter that allowed George Templeton
Strong, after months of disillusionment, finally to feel proud of his native
city. And it was this same civic and political concord that struck died-
in-the-wool Democrat Maria Daly as a "sublime spectacle." Three days
after hostilities had begun the *New York Times* detected and celebrated
the irresistible current of patriotism that was now coursing through
the city. In an eloquent April 15 editorial, it exulted in Manhattan's near-
miraculous transformation. The "reverberations from Charleston harbor," it declared, had accomplished "what months of logic would have
been impotent to effect." At last, the North was "now a unit." No place
had proved the truth of this simple assertion more clearly, it proclaimed,
than the city of New York. Even in the metropolis "most tainted by the
Southern poison" nothing had been able to withstand this "electric fire"
of nationalism—neither the "thick insulation which the commercial spirit
puts between the conscience and duty" nor "the obliquity engendered by
long years of the most perverse political education." From abolitionist

Republicans to "life-long Democrats," and even to the "very roughs of the City"—all had been galvanized by the "fiery heat" of "one intense, inspiring sentiment of patriotism"[42]

During the four days Major Robert Anderson spent at sea onboard the USS *Baltic* he had no knowledge of the extraordinary transformation of New York's mood that the *Times* was celebrating. On the night of Thursday, April 18, as his boat dropped anchor outside the harbor for the night at Sandy Hook, he remained so battle-weary and depleted in energy that he could not write his obligatory report to the War Department. Still uncertain of how his conduct would be judged by his superiors in Washington, he dictated the following telegram instead: "Having defended Fort Sumter . . . until our quarters were entirely burned, the main gates destroyed by fire . . . four barrels and three cartridges of powder only being available," he had accepted Confederate General Beauregard's terms of evacuation and "marched out of the fort on Saturday afternoon . . . with colors flying and drums beating . . . and saluting my flag with fifty guns."[43]

On the morning of Friday, April 19 as the *Baltic* entered New York harbor Captain Abner Doubleday, second in command of Fort Sumter, was surprised when he saw that "all the passing steamers saluted us with their steam-whistles and bells." To the astonishment and delight of the troops assembled on deck "cheer after cheer went up from the ferry-boats and vessels in the harbor." The American flag that Major Anderson had carefully carried from the fort, now "almost in rags," billowed in the breeze behind the *Baltic*'s mainmast. The crowds assembled at lower Manhattan's Battery Park were so immense that the ship anchored offshore near Governor's Island. With masses onshore cheering heartily and city dignitaries crowding aboard his ship, Anderson was described by one sympathetic observer as being "too exhausted and too much overcome by his emotions to speak." He and his troops had not imagined being greeted as heroes, but by this mid-April morning New York had unanimously determined that a heroes' entrance was due these soldiers. There was no tickertape at that time and no canyon of skyscrapers yet towered over Wall Street. But even as early as 1861 Gotham was known for the scope and impressiveness of its civic receptions, and its celebration of the Fort Sumter veterans would not disappoint expectations. Anderson was "immediately carried off to dine," and his men became instant celebrities as well. Doubleday remembered that it was impossible for any of them "to venture into the main streets without being ridden on the shoulders of men and torn to pieces by hand-shaking."[44]

President Lincoln clearly understood that Robert Anderson had become a public relations bonanza for his administration. Physically weak and battle-weary though he may have been, after his luncheon he was hurried on to Broadway where, from the balcony of the Ball and Black Jewelry Company, he waved the tattered and now-precious American flag to a wildly cheering crowd and saluted the departure of the city's famed 7th Regiment to Washington to defend it from Confederate forces then massing both north and south of the capital. Strong's diary records that the "silk stocking regiment," composed of the husbands and sons of Gotham's finest families, marched "not as on festival days—not as on the reception of the Prince of Wales—but nobly and sternly, as men who were going to war. . . . [W]e saw women—we saw men shed tears as they passed." Oren Gross, watching the departing regiment with a friend, confessed that it was impossible for him to translate either the "excitement" or the emotion of the occasion. How could one, after all, adequately convey the intensity of feeling released along Broadway as fathers and mothers urged "their sons and friends to go and sustain the honor of the country."[45]

Though the departure of the 7th Regiment on Friday afternoon was deeply moving, Manhattan had saved its most impressive display of mass patriotism for Saturday, April 20. Shortly before the arrival of the *Baltic* Democrats and Republicans had come together at the Chamber of Commerce to organize an enormous gathering to honor the men whom they considered to be the heroes of Fort Sumter. Indeed, Maria Daly's diary makes clear that as far as most New Yorkers were concerned, Anderson and his men had left the destroyed fortress with their honor fully intact. Southerners, she bitterly observed, might be celebrating their "inglorious victory." But their "7000" well-armed men had prevailed over "160" inadequately supplied Union troops, "who, without provisions and with their magazines surrounded by their burning officers' quarters, were at last obliged to leave it." They had not surrendered the fort. They had "evacuated it . . . with the honors of war, saluting his flag—that flag which has never before been humbled since it first floated on the breeze!"[46]

The organizers of the Saturday mass event had cannily chosen as a venue the aptly named Union Square, then functioning as an imposing northern entrance to the heavily developed city proper lying south of 14th Street and distinguished by the equestrian statue of George Washington. On Friday the *Times* anticipated that the event would "doubtless be the largest public meeting ever held in this City, or indeed on this continent," and their prediction was correct. More than 100,000 New Yorkers flooded the square and the streets around it. In addition, the *Times* reported that "a surging mass of human beings" filled Broadway from Fourteenth Street all the way down to the Battery. George Templeton Strong observed that "the crowd, or some of them, and the ladies and gentlemen who occupied the windows and lined the housetops all round Union Square, sang 'The Star-Spangled Banner,' and the people generally hurrahed a voluntary [spontaneous cheer] after each verse." In his diary Oren Gross reported that "the war-beaten flag of Fort Sumter in its shattered flagstaff floated from the statue of Washington."[47] Not since Francis Scott Key had "The Stars and Stripes" been employed so effectively in the service of national unity.

The enormous event was capped by the appearance of Major Anderson. To some members of the press, he appeared "nervous and agitated." But he was "with the greatest difficulty" ushered by the police through the tightly packed but adoring crowd. Far beyond his expectations Anderson had been transformed into "the Hero of Fort Sumter," and, perhaps feeling overburdened by his new role, he modestly acknowledged the tumultuous applause of the masses with a simple wave. Within eight days of the attack on Fort Sumter New York City had achieved an astonishing unity of purpose. Oren Gross expressed the feeling of hundreds of thousands when he observed that at the Union Square rally "but one sentiment prevailed—that is the Union must and shall be preserved—death to the traitors was the war cry." Even Fernando Wood had surrendered to the prevailing zeitgeist. Strong reported with great delight that "the sagacious scoundrel" had stood before 100,000 New Yorkers and committed himself fully to the war by a plain, unadorned, "straightforward speech."[48]

The patriotic fervor of the city that was raised to the highest pitch by the Union Square rally did not rapidly diminish in the following days. One-week after the event Strong's diary described a city festooned with decorations and flags. "Here," he wrote, "the flag is on every public building, every store, every private house almost. . . . The supply of bunting has been far short of the demand, and the stars and stripes multiply slowly, but steadily." Even city churches had joined the display. "The steeple, tower, or pediment of every church building, almost, displays the national colors, and symbolizes the sympathy of the Church Catholic . . . with law and order and national life." Truman Smith, who had traveled from Washington into the city, reported on April 27 that the "state of feeling [was] much stronger in favor of asserting the authority of the government and putting down the rebellion than I had supposed it was or could be."[49]

———————

When *London Times* reporter William Russell arrived in Charleston, South Carolina, two days after the bombardment of Fort Sumter. he found the city in a jubilant mood. Charlestonians were celebrating the establishment of a new southern Confederacy and their deliverance from hated Black Republican rule. But their joyful temper was not unalloyed, he reported. It was also mixed with popular indignation "against the City of New York, on account of the way in which the news of the reduction of Fort Sumter has been received there. New England has acted just as was expected, but better things were anticipated on the part of the Empire city." Charleston and the South at large had expected that Gotham would receive the bombardment as proof of the inexorability of secession and that it would consequently support the peaceful exit of the southern states from the Union. Instead, days after the shelling ceased the *Courier* was describing to its readers a meeting of the New York Chamber of Commerce in which, rather than urging its members to oppose Lincoln's policy of coercion, the Chamber was exhorting fellow New Yorkers to "rally in support of a Constitution and Government the best in the world." The paper declared itself stunned and outraged by the unanimous approval of a resolution completely "devoted to an uncompromising support of Lincolnism and military despotism."[50]

The New York Chamber of Commerce's firmly Unionist response to the attack on Fort Sumter and the *Charleston Courier*'s outraged response to the Chamber's proclamation suggest that the Confederate aggression in Charleston harbor had been the product of miscalculations made by both northerners and southerners. As George Templeton Strong had presciently observed directly after the election of Abraham Lincoln, Republicans had badly misjudged the strength of secessionist sentiment in the South. Likewise, southern secessionists had badly underestimated the strength of Unionist sentiment in the North and especially in New York City. Leaders on both sides had exhibited a complacent attitude toward the possibility of a frightfully destructive civil war.

Careless thinking on the part of both regions would ultimately prove most destructive to the southern states. A January 1860 entry in Maria

Daly's diary illustrates just how just how completely southern political leaders misjudged New York City's response to the coming conflict. The Dalys had traveled to Washington as members of one of several delegations that Gotham had sent to forestall the fracturing of the Union. They had been present in the Senate gallery on January 26, when the announcement came that Louisiana had seceded. Afterward Judge Daly had encountered Louisiana Senator Judah Benjamin outside the capitol and walked with him up Pennsylvania Avenue. In their conversation Benjamin had assured the judge that southerners would be back in Washington "in two months, and you will join us. New York and several other states will come in. We don't care for most of the Eastern ones; they may stay out if they please; New York will certainly come." Daly strongly opposed such magical southern thinking. "It would be very unwise for you to act on any such supposition," he warned Senator Benjamin. "Believe me, you will be entirely mistaken. No Northern states will ever enter your confederacy if you take these forcible measures to separate yourselves, except upon the point of a bayonet. You will unite us as one man in defense of this government." The senator casually dismissed this warning. "Oh Judge, you are not a practical politician as we are. We know how people feel at the North." "I have lived all my life in New York," Daly replied firmly, "and was born there. I think I ought to know something about the people, and, depend upon it, you will find the result to be as I tell you."[51]

If southern politicians like Judah Benjamin were blind to the thinking of New Yorkers in the winter and spring of 1861, their wildly optimistic misapprehensions had been shaped to a substantial degree by the propagandistic dispatches from Gotham that were spewing from the pens of southern journalists—accounts that southerners were willing to swallow hook, line, and sinker. Even in the weeks after the commencement of hostilities these dispatches continued to promote the vision of Gotham as an anarchic city ruled by mobs of fanatical abolitionists. Reporting on "The War Feeling in New York," the *Charleston Courier* described hordes of disreputable troublemakers descending on prosouthern newspapers like the *Day-Book,* the *Express,* and the *Journal of Commerce,* and then attacking the New York Hotel, an establishment favored by southern travelers, forcing it to raise the American flag. The account was careful to note that these mobs contained "a goodly number of ragged juveniles and infirm topers," who cheered the orations of patriotic rabble-rousers "heroically with their Irish accent."[52] The Irish, heretofore praised as white supremacist proletarian allies of the South, were now being excoriated as abolitionist scum.

Southern postings from New York City through the month of April illustrate William Russell's observation that Gotham's sudden repudiation of secession "filled the South, first with astonishment, and then with something like fear, which was rapidly fanned into anger by the press and the politicians." A *Charleston Courier* article of April 24 illustrates this progression. Confounded by the city's massive upwelling of Unionist sentiment, the southern reporter attributed it to mob emotion, not to popular feeling. New York, the reporter asserted, was now "in the hands of an abolition mob, protected and urged on by a Black Republican police force." As a result of this Republican-inspired anarchy no man's property was "safe who happens to be born in the South. The reign of terrorism is inaugurated as effectually as Robespierre did in France." A city that before Fort Sumter had been praised as the South's ally had now transformed itself into one possessed by a "universal . . . feeling against the South" that contained "a most malignant and persistent element of hellish hatred."[53]

To the southern mind New York City's abrupt shift in sentiment against the South and its new determination to stand against secession and with President Lincoln were the crass betrayals of mammon-worshipping and opportunistic fair-weather friends. The reliably pro-southern *New York Herald*'s overnight conversion to "Lincolnism" was proof of this inconstancy and a particularly bitter pill for the South's political writers. In its April 25 edition the *Courier* reprinted George Gordon Bennett's newly minted militant attitude that "half a million men, put in motion by the North" would "prove the cheapest, shortest, and most effective argument for peace." But the bitter headline that the *Courier* used to introduce his editorial gave expression to the South's sense of being the victim of both Bennett's and Gotham's treachery: "The Renegade *Herald.*"[54]

On April 29, four days after its reporting on the *Herald*'s betrayal, the *Courier* published a letter reputedly sent to a Charlestonian from a friend living in New York City. The tone of this missive, however, starkly contrasted with the frenzied reports of lawless abolitionist mobs that the newspaper had been featuring for over two weeks. It now reported a "great change" in the mood of the city in the days immediately following the bombardment. "Before that," the writer observed, "I hardly thought it possible that an army could have been raised here to oppose the South." Remarkably, as soon as news reached Gotham that "the Federal Flag had fallen at Sumter . . . Republicans and Democrats [had] joined hands." Now the letter writer painted a picture of Manhattan much like that of

George Templeton Strong's diary. "I never saw so much enthusiasm displayed in my life as there had been of late." Cockades and bonnets of red, white, and blue were ubiquitous on city streets, and flags were "floating from stores and private dwellings, drums beating, soldiers marching."[55] At last, the *Courier* had decided to print a report that realistically reflected actual conditions in the city of New York. But dispatches like this came too late. Armies were already massing in both North and South, and less than a month after the publication of this letter Union forces would cross the Potomac from Washington into the recently seceded state of Virginia and occupy Arlington Heights, the home of Robert E. Lee.

———————

By May of 1861 the slaveholding southern states were marching to civil war. Southerners were convinced of the righteousness of their cause and sanguine about the prospects of victory and of an independent Confederacy. But as it had been with Charlestonians, their exuberant mood was not unalloyed. Amid their war euphoria, they continued to turn a gimlet eye on the city of New York, the erstwhile ally that had betrayed them. One of the most indignant and rhetorically charged editorial condemnations of Gotham was launched by the *Richmond Daily Dispatch* on April 24, 1861. Headlined "Execrable New York," the opinion began by asserting that "of all the execrable spots on the American continent, the city of New York bears off the palm. Sodom, to which, on account of its horrible profligacy of morals, it has often been likened, had in it at least one man who stood by his principles. . . . If New York has one, he has not the courage to let his voice be heard." Never, the writer declared, could one have believed that a city that had been "enriched by Southern trade, and had ever professed to be true to the Constitution and the South, would one day be converted into our bitterest enemy, panting for our blood." Men had been transformed into devils, all because "Fort Sumter, a fort in a Southern harbor, was deprived by Southern citizens, without spilling a drop of blood, of its power to assail and destroy an innocent and unoffending people."[56]

The hideous April transformation of New York might appear to be a "monstrous . . . miracle of Satan's own working." Yet, the editorial argued, it represented merely the "falling of the veil" of "Hypocrisy" that had heretofore hidden the city's true visage, "the face of the most intense Selfishness and Greed." Gotham had risen in both "wealth" and "vice" to become the "Babylon of the New World," and the river that had fed her "affluence, her pomp, her pride, and luxury" had flowed "from the South." It was the fear that this flow of southern trade would be cut off that had "crushed out" all "vestiges of gratitude, delicacy, and honor" and nerved Gotham to commit "any crime and outrage against God and man" that would enable her to "secure her hold of the section which has hitherto been the chief tributary to her trade and commerce." No published volume, the *Daily Dispatch* concluded, would be large enough to illustrate "the unparalleled perfidy and vileness of New York."[57]

Three days later the *Charleston Courier* joined the editorial chorus, condemning "the treacherous cowardice and hypocrisy of the Merchants and Mammon-worshippers of New York." The editorial culminated with this annihilating judgment: "The interests of Christianity, civilization, humanity, and intelligent self-government, require that New York, the metropolis of shoulder-hitters, prize-fighters, blackguards, and mercantile gamblers, should be blotted from the list of cities. . . . If Sodom and Gomorrah were rightfully destroyed New York . . . cannot stand." The malignant editorial judgments of the *Richmond Daily Dispatch* and the *Charleston Courier* were echoed by southerners throughout the South. Writing to his mother, Carolinian Milton Willis asserted that when the "American Gibbon" arrived to write "his history of the downfall of this republic," he hoped that the author would "be permitted to point his finger to the great city of New York in ruins, and say *Behold the effects of national ingratitude, and Yankee Fanaticism.*"[58]

One month earlier these late-April editorial fulminations against New York by some of the South's most influential newspapers would have struck terror into the hearts of the city's business and civic leaders and precipitated pleas for further concessions to the slave states. But Philip Foner has insightfully observed that now, for the first time in over thirty years, New Yorkers responded to these southern attacks without panic. The die had been cast. The city was now overwhelmingly unified in its opposition to the fracturing of the Union. Accepting the potentially dire economic consequences of the disruption of their southern trade, thousands of Manhattan's merchants signed a memorial pledging their "unfaltering support in a vigorous prosecution of the war, until every rebel has laid down his arms, and every state returned to its allegiance."[59]

As war irresistibly approached, Gotham's newspapers did not hesitate to report on the confident state of mind of southerners and on their widely expressed contempt for the North's fighting spirit. On May 13 the

Tribune quoted liberally from a letter sent by a young resident of New Orleans to a New York merchant. This Louisiana gentleman was convinced that "the Black Republicans" of the North would never fight and that Gotham would never fully support the war effort. How could northerners hope to prevail when, the southern correspondent claimed, "more than two-thirds" of New Yorkers remained "opposed to bloodshed, if not decidedly in favor of the South." He ended his letter by boldly predicting that Jefferson Davis, not Abraham Lincoln, would ultimately preside as President in Washington and that the New England states would be "sent to Canada probably." Rather than publishing this letter as a cause for concern, however, the *Tribune* headlined it as a "Southern Delusion" and dismissed it as a demonstration of "how wild [were] the ideas of even the most intelligent among the Southern people."[60] Just a few weeks earlier such southern arrogance and aggressiveness would have been a source of concern. Now it had become a source of dismissive condescension.

And what of the South's vow to bring Gotham to its economic knees? As hostilities began in the summer of 1861, visitors to New York such as Georges Fisch, pastor of the French Evangelical Church of Paris, could find little evidence of a disastrous economic implosion. "Although there was a stagnation of affairs," he observed, "the commercial movement was still immense. Liberality, instead of declining, seemed to be more and more stimulated. After having furnished the national loan, private individuals of New York subscribed nearly five millions sterling as voluntary donations in aid of public expenditures." Months after its reception for the defenders of Fort Sumter the "immense city of New York" remained, to Fisch's eyes, "dazzling in its *fete* dress. Every window had its one or more flags. . . . Omnibuses, and even the horses of the common carts, were decked out with flags." The economic reverses that had been unleashed by the South's economic blockade had not significantly weakened Gotham's resolve. Fisch saw ample evidence that "the most furious Democrats, and the most ultra-abolitionists . . . [had] rallied round Mr. Lincoln."[61]

The long-hoped-for commercial catastrophe that the South's fire-eaters had predicted for Gotham would never arrive. Though the abrupt loss of trade with southern planters seemed to portend dreadful economic ruin in the spring of 1861 and though thousands of the city's businesses suffered or went bankrupt through the first half of that year, by fall the business of war had combined with Gotham's entrepreneurial genius to resurrect and dramatically reorient its ailing economy. Thanks to poor European harvests in 1860 and 1861, the demand for midwestern wheat skyrocketed, and within the year wheat had replaced cotton as the city's principal export, exploding from nine to fifty-seven million bushels. With the federal blockade of the Mississippi closing the port of New Orleans, westerners swiftly shifted their shipments of wheat, corn, and lumber from north-south river routes to east-west rail and water links. With its excellent rail, canal, and Great Lakes links, New York City rapidly transitioned to accommodate the new flood of wheat from Illinois, lumber from Michigan, and oil from the newly discovered fields of northwestern Pennsylvania.[62]

The Civil War enormously boosted Gotham's industrial output. Shipbuilding was stoked by war contracts, and war orders quickly revived the city's languishing clothing trade. Ultimately the struggle to preserve the Union forged what Burrows and Wallace describe as "powerful new bonds" between New York's manufacturing and financial systems and the rest of the nation. By the end of the war the city was nowhere near as dependent on trade with the South as it had been at the beginning of the conflict. And its industrial output was "roughly equal to that of the entire Confederacy." Gotham would not become, as southerners had fondly anticipated, a fallen Babylon, and grass would not sprout between its abandoned cobbles. It would instead take its place as the newest of the modern world's great cities. Its stock exchange, now second in importance only to London, would occupy its impressive new Tuscan-palazzo quarters only a few months after the surrender of Robert E. Lee's Confederate army at Appomattox.[63]

The forty-year love-hate affair between the plantation South and New York City had finally dissolved in a flood of bitter southern tirades and mutual recriminations. The South self-righteously imagined itself the blameless victim of an unfaithful partner. In the end, even as it celebrated its independence from what it viewed as the yoke of Yankee tyranny, it was consumed by the desire to avenge itself on the one city that it had nourished economically and by which it had been ultimately betrayed. The vengeance it yearned for would never come. New York City, for its part, had at last thrown in the towel, exhausted with trying to appease the unappeasable South, deciding in the end that it could no longer bind itself to a region dedicated to the inhumane and anachronistic system of chattel slavery. Both partners had their freedom, but only one would prosper.

NOTES

ONE

THAT MOST SOUTHERN CONNECTED
OF NORTHERN CITIES

1. Ann Wagner, letter to Effingham Wagner, 13 May 1818, Cheves-Wagner Papers, Southern Historical Collection, University of North Carolina.

2. Ibid., 17 October 1818, 13 May 1818.

3. Philip S. Foner, *Business and Slavery: The New York Merchants and the Irrepressible Conflict* (Chapel Hill: UNC Press, 1941), 5.

4. David Quigley, "Southern Slavery in a Free City: Economy, Politics, and Culture," in *Slavery in New York*, ed. Ira Berlin and Leslie M. Harris (New York: New Press, 2005), 269, 271.

5. John Hope Franklin, *A Southern Odyssey: Travelers in the Antebellum North* (Baton Rouge: LSU Press, 1976), 90; Quigley, "Southern Slavery," 271; see also Gene Dattel, *Cotton and Race in the Making of America: The Human Costs of Economic Power* (Chicago: Ivan R. Dee, 2009), 86–87.

6. Sven Beckert, *Empire of Cotton: A Global History* (New York: Alfred A. Knopf, 2014), 217–18.

7. Ibid., 222–23.

8. Jill Le Pore, *New York Burning: Liberty, Slavery, and Conspiracy in Eighteenth-Century Manhattan* (New York: Alfred A. Knopf, 2005), 21, 20.

9. Leslie and Michelle Alexander, "Fear," in *The 1619 Project: A New Origin Story* (New York: One World, 2021), 103–4.

10. Leslie M. Harris, *In the Shadow of Slavery: African Americans in New York City, 1625–1863* (Chicago: U. of Chicago Press, 2003), 34, 39.

11. Le Pore, *New York Burning,* xii.

12. Nicole Hannah-Jones, "Origins," in *The 1619 Project: A New Origin Story* (New York: One World, 2021), xvii.

13. Franklin, *Southern Odyssey,* 91–92; Ira Berlin and Leslie M. Harris, "Uncovering, Discovering, and Recovering: Digging in New York's Slave Past Beyond the African Burial Ground," in *Slavery in New York,* 23.

14. Quigley, "Southern Slavery," 271; Eric Lampard, "The New York Metropolis in Transformation: History and Prospect," in *The Future of the Metropolis: Berlin, London, Paris, New York,* ed. John B. Goddard and Horst Matzerath (New York: Water de Gruyter, 1986), 40.

15. Quoted in Leslie M. Harris, *In the Shadow of Slavery: African Americans in New York City, 1628–1863* (Chicago: University of Chicago Press, 2003); Foner, *Business and Slavery,* 14.

16. Berlin and Harris, "Uncovering, Discovering, and Recovering," 4; "In Pursuit of Freedom," exhibition, Brooklyn Historical Society, 2014–18; Edwin G. Burrows and Mike Wallace, *Gotham: A History of New York City to 1898* (New York: Oxford, 1999), 348–49.

17. Patrick Rael, "The Long Death of Slavery," in *Slavery in New York*, 114, 132–33.

18. Jonathan Daniel Wells, *The Kidnapping Club: Wall Street, Slavery, and Resistance on the Eve of the Civil War* (New York: Basin Books, 2020), 8–9.

19. Ron Soodalter, "The Day New York Tried to Secede," Historynet.com.

20. Quigley, "Southern Slavery," 276–77.

21. Samuel J. May, *Some Recollections of the Anti-Slavery Conflict* (1869; rpr., New York: Arno, 1968), 127–28.

22. Davy Crockett, *An Account of Col. Crockett's Tour to the North and Down East, Written by Himself* (Philadelphia: E. L. Cary, 1835), 41; Quigley, "Southern Slavery," 271; Foner, *Business and Slavery*, 12.

23. Quoted in Michael O'Brien, *Conjectures of Order: Intellectual Life and the American South, 1810–1860* (Chapel Hill: UNC Press, 2004), 1:47; Franklin, *Southern Odyssey*, 101.

24. James De Bow, "Editorial," *De Bow's Review* 11 (Nov. 1851), 544.

25. Quigley, "Southern Slavery," 278.

26. Agenor de Gasparin, *The Uprising of a Great People: The United States in 1861* (1861; rpr. Freeport, NY: Books for Libraries, 1969), 76–77.

27. Abram J. Dittenhoefer, *How We Elected Lincoln: Personal Recollections* (New York: Harper and Brothers, 1916), 1–2.

28. Ibid., 2–3.

29. Burrows and Wallace, *Gotham*, 674, 677.

30. Eric Foner, *Gateway to Freedom: The Hidden History of the Underground Railroad* (New York: W. W. Norton, 2015), 194, 210, 150.

31. Ibid., 126–27.

32. Ibid., 127.

33. Burrows and Wallace, *Gotham*, 347, 349.

34. Ibid., 479.

35. Fred Hobson, *Tell about the South: The Southern Rage to Explain* (Baton Rouge: LSU Press, 1983), 20.

36. Hinton Rowan Helper, *The Impending Crisis of the South: How to Meet It* (New York: A. B. Burdick, 1860), 34–35.

37. Ibid., 35, 41.

38. Ibid., 117; Robert B. Downs, *Books That Changed the South* (Chapel Hill: University of North Carolina, 1977), 122.

39. Helper, *Impending Crisis*, 34; Downs, *Books That Changed the South*, 123. For a full description of the reception to Helper's *Impending Crisis* see David Brown's *Southern Outcast: Hinton Rowan Helper and The Impending Crisis of the South* (Baton Rouge: LSU Press, 2006), 124–51.

40. Joseph Gustaitis, "Eyewitness to War," Historynet.com; James W. Wall, "Hinton Rowan Helper," in *Dictionary of North Carolina Biography*, ed. William S. Powell (Chapel Hill: UNC Press, 1979–1996).

41. Helper, *Impending Crisis*, 35; Hobson, *Tell about the South*, 54.

42. Burrows and Wallace, *Gotham,* 860–63.

43. Ibid., 854–60.

44. Bertram Wyatt-Brown, *Yankee Saints and Southern Sinners* (Baton Rouge: LSU Press, 1985), 187.

45. Russell Shorto, *The Island at the Center of the World: The Epic Story of Dutch Manhattan and the Forgotten Colony That Shaped America* (New York: Doubleday, 2004), 6; Andrew Burnaby, *Travels through the Middle Settlements in North America in the Years 1759 and 1760* (Ithaca, NY: Great Seal Books, 1960), 80.

46. James Henry Hammond, "Speech of Hon. James H. Hammond, of South Carolina, on the Admission of Kansas," March 4, 1858. Americanantiquarian.org.

47. Ibid.

48. Burrows and Wallace, *Gotham,* 414, 605, 770–72.

49. Michael E. Woods, "'Mudsills versus Chivalry!': Class Conflict and Total War in the Occupied South," filsonhistorical.org., 4–5.

50. *Gotham,* 517–18, 772.

51. Hammond, "Speech."

52. Walter Johnson, *River of Dark Dreams: Slavery and Empire in the Cotton Kingdom* (Boston: Harvard U. Press, 2013), 12.

53. Ibid., 168, 160.

54. Edward E. Baptist, *The Half Has Never Been Told: Slavery and the Making of American Capitalism* (New York: Basic Books, 2014), xxi.

55. "Execrable New York," *Richmond Daily Dispatch,* April 24, 1861; Charleston *Courier,* April 27, 1861.

TWO

THE GREATEST EMPORIUM OF THE WESTERN HEMISPHERE

1. Arthur Morson, letters to Arthur Alexander Morson, 17 September 1818, 21 September 1818, Morson Papers, Southern Historical Collection, University of North Carolina.

2. Bettina Manzo, ed., "A Virginian in New York: The Diary of St. George Tucker July-August, 1786," *New York History* 67 (April, 1986), 181–82.

3. Ibid., 186, 193, 189.

4. Ibid., 193, 194.

5. Ibid., 196.

6. J. A. Maxwell, letter to Adam Alexander, August 4, 1822, Adam Alexander Papers, Duke University; Judith Page Rives Diary, August 12, 1829, Duke University.

7. J. A. Maxwell, letter to Adam Alexander, August 4, 1822.

8. Daniel Allen Penick Diary, 1821–1822, Daniel Allen Penick Papers, Southern Historical Collection, University of North Carolina; Agnes Tinsley Diary, August 31, 1824, Daniel Allen Penick Papers, Southern Historical Collection, University of North Carolina.

9. William Elliott, letter to his wife, July 29, 1823, Elliott-Gonzales Family Papers, Southern Historical Collection, University of North Carolina; Elliot, letter to his wife, July 24, 1828.

10. Quoted in John Hope Franklin, *A Southern Odyssey: Travelers in the Antebellum North* (Baton Rouge: LSU Press, 1976), 38.

11. James Jeffreys, letter to his wife, April 9, 1826, Mrs. James M. Jeffreys Letters, Duke University.

12. William Elliott, letter to his wife, 29 July 1823.

13. Agnes Tinsley Diary, September 2, 1824; Elizabeth Ruffin Diary, 37, 17, 19, Harrison Henry Cocke Papers, Southern Historical Collection, University of North Carolina.

14. J. C. Myers, *Sketches on a Tour through the Northern and Eastern States, the Canadas and Nova Scotia* (Harrisonburg, VA.: J. H. Wartmann and Bros., 1849), 49-50, 79; "University of New York: National Medical School," [unsigned] *Southern Literary Messenger* 7 (July-August 1841), 552.

15. "University of New York," 553.

16. Ibid., 552.

17. Davy Crockett, *An account of Col. Crockett's Tour to the North and Down East, Written by Himself* (Philadelphia: E. L. Carey and H. Hart, 1835), 41; Burrows and Wallace, *Gotham*, 478.

18. Crockett, *An Account of Col. Crockett's Tour,* 48, 49.

19. Ibid., 50.

20. John McQueen, "Admission of California," House of Representatives, 31st Congress, 1st Session, appendix to the *Congressional Globe* (1850), 735.

21. Ibid.

22. Paul Hamilton Hayne, letter to his wife, 1854, Hayne Papers, Duke University; Pickett quoted in O'Brien, *Conjectures of Order* (Chapel Hill, UNC Press, 2004), 1:36.

23. J. T. Harrison, letter, August 15, 1853, James Thomas Harrison Papers, Southern Historical collection, University of North Carolina.

24. Ibid.

25. William Adams, diary entry, June 11, 1858, William Adams Diary, Duke University.

26. Francis Hawks quoted in O'Brien, *Conjectures of Order,* 1:43-44.

27. "Danger of Worldly Pleasures," *Southern Lady's Companion* 2 (May 1849): 44.

28. Clement Claiborne Clay, letter to Hugh Clay, July 22, 1850, Clement Claiborne Clay Letters, Duke University.

29. Ibid.

30. James Pickett quoted in O'Brien, *Conjectures of Order,* 1: 36.

31. Meyers, *Sketches on a Tour,* 50-51; Elizabeth Ruffin Diary, 37.

32. Quoted in Franklin, *A Southern Odyssey,* 20.

33. Meyers, *Sketches on a Tour,* 51.

34. Quoted in Barrows and Wallace, *Gotham,* 695.

35. *The Diary of Philip Hone, 1828-1851,* ed. Allan Nevins (New York, Dodd Mead, 1927), 201-2.

36. Ibid., 202, 395.

37. Ibid., 896-97.

38. Ibid., 730; O'Brien, *Conjectures of Order,* I: 36.

39. "Southern Travel and Travelers," *De Bow's Review* 21 (September 1856): 323.

40. Franklin, *A Southern Odyssey,* 110.

41. Paul Hamilton Hayne, letter to Susan Hayne, July 3, 1843.

42. Abram F. Rightor, letter to Andrew McCollum, August 19, 1851, Andrew McCollum Papers, Southern Historical Collection, University of North Carolina.

43. Sarah Gayle Crawford, diary entry, August.—September 1853, Gayle and Crawford Family Papers, Southern Historical Collection, University of North Carolina.

44. Quoted in O'Brien, *Conjectures of Order,* 1:36.

45. John Stewart Oxley, letter to Tom Henry, October 1, 1853, Gustavus Henry Papers, Southern Historical Collection, University of North Carolina.

46. Burrows and Wallace, *Gotham,* 671–72; Sue Henry, letter to her mother, October 9, 1853, Gustavus Henry Papers.

47. Ibid; Sarah Gayle Crawford, diary entry, 26 July 1853.

48. Sue Henry, letter to her mother, October 9, 1853, Gustavus Henry Papers, Southern Historical Collection, University of North Carolina.

49. Letter, September 21, 1859, Cheves-Wagner Papers, Southern Historical Collection, University of North Carolina.

50. Sarah Gayle Crawford, diary entry, summer 1853.

51. William Elliott, letter to his wife, October 16, 1828.

52. John Stewart Oxley, letter to Tom Henry, October 1, 1853.

53. Ibid.; Sue Henry, letter to her mother, October 9, 1853.

54. Virginia Clay-Clopton, *A Belle of the Fifties: Memoirs of Mrs. Clay of Alabama* (New York: Doubleday, Page, 1905), 102.

55. Ibid., 102, 101.

56. Burrows and Wallace, *Gotham,* 815; Clay-Clopton, *Belle of the Fifties,* 102.

57. Burrows and Wallace, *Gotham,* 456; Sarah Gayle Crawford, diary entry, 29 July 1853.

58. Sarah Gayle Crawford, diary entry, 28 July 1853; Burrows and Wallace, *Gotham,* 721, 688.

59. Sue Henry, letter to her mother, October 9, 1853.

60. Berlin and Harris, "Uncovering, Discovering, and Recovering," 23.

61. Burrows and Wallace, *Gotham,* 645

62. James T. Harrison, letter, July 16, 1853; Burrows and Wallace, *Gotham,* 644.

63. Sarah Gayle Crawford, diary entry, July 26, 1853; Sue Henry, letter to her mother, October 9, 1853.

64. Burrows and Wallace, *Gotham,* 669.

65. James T. Harrison, letter, July 17, 1853; John Stewart Oxley, letter to Tom Henry, October 1, 1853; Sarah Gayle Crawford, diary entry, August–September 1853; Benjamin Silliman and C. R. Goodrich, eds., *The World of Science, Art, and Industry, Illustrated from Examples in the New York Exhibition, 1853–54* (New York: G. P. Putnam, 1854), 8.

66. "Memories of Home Travels," *Southern Literary Messenger* 20 (January 1854): 29.

67. Alfred Mordecai, letter to Samuel Mordecai, November 11, 1853, Jacob Mordecai Correspondence, Duke University.

68. Ellen Mordecai, letter to Samuel Mordecai, November 17, 1853, Jacob Mordecai Correspondence, Duke University.

69. James T. Harrison, letter, 15 August 1853.

70. Ibid.

71. Kate Carney, diary entries, September 4–11, 1859, Kate S. Carney Diary, Southern Historical Collection, University of North Carolina.

72. Ibid., September 4, 1859, September 16, 1859.

73. "Editor's Table," *Southern Literary Messenger* 31 (November 1860): 391.

THREE

EARLY FICTIONAL APPRAISALS
OF NEW YORK CITY

1. Burrows and Wallace, *Gotham*, 674.

2. Sven Beckert, *Empire of Cotton: A Global History* (New York: Alfred A. Knopf, 2014), 229.

3. See Ritchie D. Watson's *The Cavalier in Virginia Fiction* (Baton Rouge: LSU Press, 1983), and *Yeoman versus Cavalier: The Old Southwest's Fictional Road to Rebellion* (Baton Rouge: LSU Press, 1993).

4. Caruthers quoted in O'Brien, *Conjectures of Order,* 1:48; Curtis Carroll Davis, "William Alexander Caruthers," in *Fifty Southern Writers before 1900,* ed. Robert Bain and Joseph Flora (New York: Greenwood, 1987), 87.

5. William Alexander Caruthers, *The Kentuckian in New York, or, the Adventures of Three Southerns, by a Virginian* (1834: rpr. Gregg Press, Ridgewood, N J:, 1968), 1:76, hereafter cited in the text by volume and page number.

6. Walter Blair, *Native American Humor, 1800–1900* (New York: American Book, 1937), 82.

7. Hennig Cohen and Willian B. Dillingham, eds., *The Humor of the Old Southwest* (Boston: Houghton Mifflin, 1964), xvi.

8. Burrows and Wallace, *Gotham,* 591.

9. Arthur Hobson Quinn, *Edgar Allan Poe: A Critical Biography* (New York: D. Appleton-Century, 1941), 405.

10. Burrows and Wallace, *Gotham,* 700.

11. Jacob E. Spannuth and Thomas Ollive Mabbot, eds., *Doings of Gotham: Poe's Contributions to "The Columbia Spy"* (Pottsville, PA: Jacob E. Spannuth, 1929), 65, 31, 60, 61.

12. Burrows and Wallace, *Gotham,* 700; Spannuth and Mabbot, *Doings of Gotham,* 25, 40.

13. Spannuth and Mabbot, *Doings of Gotham,* 40, 25, 40–41, 25–26.

14. Ibid., 59, 65, 59.

15. Ibid., 32.

16. Ibid., 48.

17. Ibid.; Burrows and Wallace, *Gotham,* 723.

18. Burrows and Wallace, *Gotham,* 701–2.

19. Edgar Allan Poe, "Mellonta Tauta," in *Complete Stories and Poems of Edgar Allan Poe* (New York: Doubleday, 1966), 373–83.

20. Ibid., 381.

21. William Tappan Thompson, *Major Jones's Courtship and Travels,* 2 vols. (Philadelphia: T. B. Peterson, 1848), 2: 8, hereafter cited in the text by volume and page number.

FOUR
BLOTTED FROM THE LIST OF CITIES

1. William M. Bobo, *Glimpses of New-York City, by a South Carolinian* (Charleston: J. J. McCarter, 1852), 9, hereafter cited in the text by page number.

2. Richmond *Examiner,* January 6, 1860.

3. Ibid.

4. Mrs. Henry R. Schoolcraft, *The Black Gauntlet: A Tale of Plantation Life in South Carolina* (Philadelphia: J. B. Lippincott, 1860), iii, hereafter cited in the text by page number.

5. For a more detailed description of the Brooks-Sumner caning see Ritchie D. Watson's, *Normans and Saxons: Southern Race Mythology and the Intellectual History of the American Civil War* (Baton Rouge: LSU Press, 2008), 1–16.

6. "Union with the Northern States Necessarily Destructive of Southern Liberty," *Charleston Mercury,* January 18, 1861.

7. Mrs. V. G. Cowdin, *Ellen; or, the Fanatic's Daughter* (Mobile: S. H. Goetzel, 1860), 6. Hereafter cited in the text by page number.

8. Jennifer Rae Greeson, *Our South: Geographic Fantasy and the Rise of National Literature* (Cambridge, MA: Harvard University Press, 2010), 124.

9. Ibid., 125.

10. Ibid., 128–29.

11. Walter Johnson, *River of Dark Dreams: Slavery and Empire in the Cotton Kingdom,* (Cambridge, MA: Harvard University Press, 2013), 195.

12. A. Clarkson, "The Basis of Northern Hostility to the South," *De Bow's Review* 28 (1860), 13; "Northern Mind and Character," *Southern Literary Messenger* 31 (1860), 345.

13. Charleston *Courier,* April 27, 1861.

14. William Kauffman Scarborough, ed., *The Diary of Edmund Ruffin,* 3 vols. (Baton Rouge: LSU Press, 1972–1990), 1:122.

15. *Charleston Courier* April 27, 1861.; Fred Hobson, *Tell about the South: The Southern Rage to Explain* (Baton Rouge: LSU Press, 1983), 27.

16. John Beauchamp Jones, *Border War: A Tale of Disunion* (New York: Rudd and Carleton, 1859). See Frederick R. Lapides, "John Beauchamp Jones: A Southern View of the Abolitionists," *Journal of the Rutgers University Libraries* 33 (1970), 64–65; Scarborough, *Diary of Edmund Ruffin,* 1:407–8.

17. Ibid., 415–16, 437–38.

18. Edmund Ruffin, *Anticipations of the Future, to Serve as Lessons for the Present Time* (Richmond: S. W. Randolph, 1860), 126, 134, hereafter cited in the text by page number.

19. Scarborough, *Diary of Edmund Ruffin,* 1:463; *Southern Literary Messenger* 31 (October 1860), 320.

20. Scarborough, *Diary of Edmund Ruffin,* 1:554, 536, 554.

21. Burrows and Wallace, *Gotham,* 895. All quoted come from volume 2.

22. Ibid.

23. Scarborough, *Diary of Edmund Ruffin,* 3:70–71.

24. Ibid., 3:71–72.

25. Burrows and Wallace, *Gotham,* 899.

26. B.L.H., "Minnesota as Seen by Travelers: An English Visitor of the Civil War Period," *Minnesota History* 9 (September 1928), 270; George T. Borrett, *Letters from Canada and the United States* (London: J. E. Adlard, 1865), 275.

27. Ibid., 277.

28. Scarborough, *Diary of Edmund Ruffin,* 3:949–50; "Edmund Ruffin Fires His Final Shot of the War," Civil War Profiles.com, June 17, 2015.

29. "The New Inquisition," *New York Tribune,* March 22, 1861, 4.

30. Ibid.

31. "A Woman's Story," *New York Tribune,* March 22, 1861, 7.

32. "The New Inquisition." *New York Tribune,* March 22, 1861, 4.

33. Paul Starobin, *Madness Rules the Hour: Charleston, 1860, and the Mania for War* (New York: Public Affairs, 2017), 122–25, 176.

34. *Charleston Courier* April 27, 1861.

FIVE

WILLIAM GILMORE SIMMS, WILLIAM CULLEN BRYANT, AND THE BREAKING OF THE HINGE OF UNION

1. *The Letters of William Gilmore Simms,* ed. Mary C. Simms Oliphant (Columbia, SC: University of South Carolina Press, 1952), 3:423–24, 429, 431.

2. Ibid., 3:454; Jon Wakelyn, *The Politics of a Literary Man: William Gilmore Simms* (Westport, CT: Greenwood, 1973), 55; John Caldwell Guilds, *Simms: A Literary Life* (Fayetteville: University of Arkansas Press, 1992), 241.

3. John Hope Franklin, *A Southern Odyssey: Travellers in the Antebellum North* (Baton Rouge: Louisiana State University Press, 1976), 103

4. Charles H. Brown, *William Cullen Bryant* (New York: Charles Scribner, 1971), 203–4; *Letters of William Gilmore Simms,* 1:xciv.

5. Howard R. Floan, *The South in Northern Eyes: 1831 to 1861* (New York: McGraw-Hill, 1958), 148–49.

6. *The Letters of William Cullen Bryant,* ed. William Cullen Bryant II (New York: Fordham University Press, 1977–84), 2:139; *Letters of William Gilmore Simms,* 1:213–14.

7. John C. Guilds, "Bryant in the South: A New Letter to Simms," *Georgia Historical Quarterly* 37(June 1952), 142; William Cullen Bryant, "A Tour in the Old South," in *Prose Writings of William Cullen Bryant,* ed. Parke Godwin (New York: Russell and Russell, 1964), 2:29.

8. Ibid.

9. *Letters of William Gilmore Simms,* 1:345–46.

10. William Cullen Bryant, "A Tour in the Old South," 29–30.

11. William Cullen Bryant, "Simms," in *Homes of American Authors; Comprising Anecdotal, Personal, and Descriptive Sketches* (New York: G. P. Putnam, 1853), 258–59; Parke Godwin, *A Biography of William Cullen Bryant, with Extracts from His Private Correspondence* (New York: D. Appleton, 1883), 1:407–8.

12. Floan, The *South in Northern Eyes,* 150; *Letters of William Gilmore Simms,* 1:355, 150.

13. Bryant, "A Tour in the Old South," 31; Bryant, "Simms," 257.

14. Bryant, "A Tour in the Old South," 32.

15. Ibid., 34; *Letters of William Cullen Bryant*, 2:257.

16. Bryant, "A Tour in the Old South," 34.

17. Godwin, *Biography of William Cullen Bryant*, 329.

18. Wakelyn, *The Politics of a Literary Man*, 29–30; Brown, *William Cullen Bryant*, 213.

19. Brown, *William Cullen Bryant*, 213–14.

20. Ibid., 214.

21. Erika Thrubis, "Exchange Articles Carried by the New York *Evening Post*," in *The Antebellum Press: Setting the Stage for Civil War*, ed. David B. Sachsman (New York: Routledge, 2019), 245.

22. Bryant, "Abolitionist Riots," in *Prose Writings of William Cullen Bryant*, 1:377–78.

23. Wakelyn, *Politics of a Literary Man*, 31–32.

24. Ibid., 61.

25. Ibid.

26. *Letters of William Gilmore Simms*, 1:lxxvii–lxxviii.

27. Simms, "Miss Martineau on Slavery," *Southern Literary Quarterly* 3 (November 1837), 643.

28. Ibid., 645.

29. Ibid., 647.

30. Ibid., 654, 656.

31. Ibid., 656–57.

32. Wakelyn, *Politics of a Literary Man*, 65.

33. Brown, *William Cullen Bryant*, 331–32.

34. William Cullen Bryant, *Power for Sanity: Selected Editorials of William Cullen Bryant, 1829–1861*, ed. William Cullen Bryant II (New York: Fordham University Press, 1994), 266–67.

35. Simms, *Letters*, 3:76.

36. Bryant, "The Auburn Conventions," *New York Evening Post*, September 27, 1854.

37. *Letters of William Cullen Bryant*, 3:540; Bryant, "The Auburn Conventions."

38. Bryant, "More Nebraska Settlers," *New York Evening Post*, October 12, 1854.

39. Bryant, *Power for Sanity*, 287; Brown, *William Cullen Bryant*, 380–81.

40. Simms, *Letters*, 3:191.

41. Bryant, "Simms," 259; Simms, *Letters*, 3:191.

42. Simms, *Letters*, 3:415–16.

43. Ibid.

44. William Peterfield Trent, *William Gilmore Simms* (Boston: Houghton, Mifflin, 1892), 219.

45. Simms, *Letters*, 3:416, 423.

46. Ibid., 433, 434.

47. Preston Brooks, "Statement to Sumner," *Congressional Globe*, 34th Cong., 1st sess., 1349–50; Robert L. Meriwether, "Preston Brooks on the Caning of Charles Sumner," *South Carolina Historical and Genealogical Magazine* 52 (1951), 2–3.

48. Meriwether, "Preston Brooks on the Caning of Charles Sumner," 3.

49. David Donald, *Charles Sumner and the Coming of the Civil War* (New York: Knopf, 1974), 297.

50. Charles Sumner, *The Crime against Kansas* (1856; rpr. New York: Arno, 1969), 8.

51. Ibid., 9–10.

52. Donald, *Sumner and the Coming of the Civil War,* 286; Sumner, *Crime against Kansas,* 85.

53. Sumner, *Crime against Kansas,* 87.

54. Donald, *Sumner and the Coming of the Civil War,* 287.

55. Ibid., 288–89.

56. Horace Greeley, *New York Daily Tribune,* May 21, 1856, 4; Donald, *Sumner and the Coming of Civil War,* 288.

57. Donald, *Sumner and the Coming of the Civil War,* 301, 304.

58. Henry Wadsworth Longfellow, letter to Charles Sumner, May 24, 1856, Longfellow Letters, Harvard University; Donald, *Sumner and the Coming of the Civil War,* 299; "The Sumner Case," *Littel's Living Age* 50 (1856): 376.

59. Philip S. Foner, *Business and Slavery: The New York Merchants and the Irrepressible Conflict* (Chapel Hill: University of North Carolina Press, 1941), 104–5.

60. George Templeton Strong, *The Diary of George Templeton Strong,* ed. Allan Nevins and Milton Halsey Thomas (New York: MacMillan, 1952), 274–75.

61. Foner, *Business and Slavery,* 105.

62. Bryant, *Power for Sanity,* 289–90.

63. Ibid.

64. Simms, *Letters,* 3:437.

65. Ibid., 440.

66. Ibid., 446–47.

67. Ibid., 440.

68. Ibid., 441–42.

69. Guilds, *Simms: A Literary Life,* 125.

70. Simms, *Letters,* 3:454–55.

71. Simms, *Letters,* 3:424; William Gilmore Simms, "South Carolina in the Revolution: A Lecture," in *Letters,* 3:521–49.

72. Simms, "South Carolina in the Revolution," 521–22.

73. Ibid., 547–49.

74. Ibid., 456.

75. Quoted in Simms, *Letters,* 3:456.

76. Quoted in Simms, *Letters,* 3:457.

77. Ibid.

78. Philip Paxton, *The Wonderful Adventures of Captain Priest: A Tale of but Few Incidents* (New York: Redfield, 1855), 334.

79. Quoted in Simms, *Letters,* 3:457–58.

80. Quoted in Simms, Letters, 3:458; Preston Brooks Archives, University of South Carolina.

81. Simms, *Letters,* 3:467.

82. Ibid.

83. Quoted in Simms, Letters, 3:459.

84. Ibid., 462–63.

85. Bryant quoted in Simms, Letters 3:467–68.

86. Quoted in Simms, Letters, 3:459.

87. Ibid., 467–68; Miriam Shillingsburg, "Simms's Failed Lecture Tour of 1856: The Mind of the North," in *"Long Years of Neglect": The Work and Reputation of William Gilmore Simms*, ed. John Caldwell Guilds (Fayetteville: University of Arkansas Press, 1988), 188.

88. Quoted in Simms, *Letters,* 3:459, 463.

89. Simms Letters 3: 463.

90. James Hammond quoted in Simms, Letters, 3:465.

91. Ibid., 465–468.

92. Ibid., 469, 474.

93. Guilds, *Simms: A Literary Life,* 385.

94. Quoted in Shillingsburg, "Simms's Failed Lecture Tour," 189.

95. Ibid., 190.

96. Ibid., 193.

97. Ibid., 192.

98. Ibid., 198, 197.

SIX

EXECRABLE NEW YORK

1. Quoted in Philip S. Foner, *Business and Slavery: The New York Merchants and the Irrepressible Conflict* (Chapel Hill: University of North Carolina Press, 1941), 12.

2. "Late Elections," *New Orleans Daily Crescent,* October 13, 1860, in *Southern Editorials on Secession,* ed. Dwight L. Dumond (New York: Century, 1931), 187–88.

3. James Philemon Holcombe, *The Election of a Black Republican President* (Richmond: C. H. Wynne, 1860).

4. "Late Elections," *New Orleans Daily Crescent,* 188; New Orleans *Daily Picayune,* September 19, 1860, quoted in Donald E. Reynolds, *Editors Make War: Southern Newspapers in the Secession Crisis* (Nashville: Vanderbilt University Press, 1966), 120.

5. Quoted in Burrows and Wallace, *Gotham,* 864.

6. Ibid., 865; quoted in Foner, *Business and Slavery,* 206.

7. Burrows and Wallace, *Gotham,* 865.

8. *The Diary of George Templeton Strong,* ed. Allan Nevins and Milton H. Thomas (New York: MacMillan, 1952), 3:56–57.

9. Ibid., 3:67.

10. Burrows and Wallace, *Gotham,* 865–66; Michael Zakim, "Dialectics of Merchant Capital: New York City Businessmen and the Secession Crisis of 1860–61," *New York History* 87 (2006): 78.

11. Paul Starobin, *Madness Rules the Hour: Charleston, 1860, and the Mania for War* (New York: Public Affairs, 2017), 189–90.

12. Sven Beckert, *Empire of Cotton: A Global History* (New York: Alfred A. Knopf, 2014), 96.

13. "The Law," *Richmond Examiner,* January 6, 1861.

14. "Southern Policy," *Vicksburg Daily Whig,* January 18, 1861, in Dumond, *Southern Editorials,* 13–14.

15. "South Carolina's Mission to Virginia," *De Bow's Review* 29 (December 1860): 777.

16. "Commercial Relations between the North and South," *New York Times,* December 7, 1860, in *Northern Editorials on Secession,* ed. Howard Cecil Perkins (Gloucester, MA: Peter Smith, 1964), 2:567.

17. Ibid., 569.

18. Ibid., 569, 571.

19. *Charleston Courier,* November 26, 1860; *Charleston Mercury,* December 3, 1860.

20. *Charleston Mercury,* December 3, 1860; Quoted in *Charleston Courier,* December 6, 1860.

21. Charleston *Mercury,* Dec. 11, 1860.

22. *Charleston Courier,* December 13, 1860, February 15, 1861.

23. Fernando Wood, "Message," in *New York Times,* January 8, 1861.

24. Ibid.

25. *New York Daily News,* December 22, 1860, in Perkins, *Northern Editorials,* 1:396; Burrows and Wallace, *Gotham,* 868.

26. Foner, *Business and Slavery,* 288; *New York Journal of Commerce,* January 8, 1861, in Perkins, *Northern Editorials,* 1:403–4.

27. Burrows and Wallace, *Gotham,* 868.

28. Ibid., 866; Zakim, "Dialectics of Merchant Capital," 70–71.

29. Foner, *Business and Slavery,* 299, 314.

30. William Howard Russell, *My Diary North and South* (Boston: Burnham, 1863), 370; *New York Tribune,* March 25, 1861, 7.

31. *The Diary of George Templeton Strong,* ed. Allan Nevins and Milton Halsey Thomas (New York: MacMillan, 1952), 3:105–109.

32. Foner, *Business and Slavery,* 304.

33. Ibid., 305.

34. *Diary of George Templeton Strong,* 3:119.

35. Ibid., 122–23.

36. Sidney Webster to Caleb Cushing, April 15, 1861, April 17, 1861, Caleb Cushing Papers, Library of Congress.

37. Ezra White to Gideon Welles, April 17, 1861; Nathaniel Niles to Gideon Welles, April 15, 1861, Gideon Welles Papers, Library of Congress.

38. Russell, *My Diary North and South,* 370.

39. *Diary of George Templeton Strong,* 3:133.

40. Maria Lydig Daly, *Diary of a Union Lady* (New York: Funk and Wagnalls, 1962), xxxii, 14–15.

41. Ibid., xli, 12.

42. "The People and the Issue," *New York Times,* April 15, 1861, 4.

43. David Silkenat, "In the Civil War, Surrendering Was often an Act of Honor," Historynet.com, October 2019.

44. Ibid.

45. Ibid.; Oren Gross Diary, April 21, 1861, New York Public Library.

46. Daly, *Diary,* 11–12.

47. Silkenat, "In the Civil War"; *Diary of George Templeton Strong,* 3:127.

48. Silkenat, "In the Civil War"; Oren Gross Diary, April 20, 1861; *Diary of George Templeton Strong,* 3:127.

49. *Diary of George Templeton Strong,* 3:135; Truman Smith, letter to Gideon Welles, April 27, 1861, Gideon Welles Papers, Library of Congress.

50. Russell, *My Diary North and South,* 116; Charleston *Courier,* April 27, 1861.

51. Daly, *Diary,* 6.

52. Charleston *Courier,* April 23, 1861.

53. Russell, *My Diary North and South,* 371; Charleston *Courier,* April 24, 1861.

54. Charleston *Courier,* April 25, 1861.

55. Charleston *Courier,* April 29, 1861.

56. "Execrable New York," *Richmond Daily Dispatch,* April 24, 1861.

57. Ibid.

58. *Charleston Courier,* April 27, 1861; Milton Willis to his mother, Willis Family Papers, South Carolina Historical Society.

59. Foner, *Business and Slavery,* 317.

60. New York *Tribune,* May 13, 1861, 7.

61. Georges Fisch, *Nine Months in the United States during the Crisis* (London: James Nisbet, 1863), 160–62.

62. Burrows and Wallace, *Gotham,* 872–77.

63. Ibid.

INDEX

INDEX

New York City (*continued*)
to London, 5; sentiment against Preston Brooks in, 167; as a slave city, 4–5; slow evolution of the antislavery movement in, 8; southern predictions of New York City's economic collapse, 123–24, 195, 197, 198, 201, 203, 218–19; squalor underlying the luxury of, 42; sympathy towards southern economic interests and general support of the slave system, 7–8, 10, 17; working class toleration of slavery in, 26. *See also* New York City, and the cotton trade; New York City, early southern fictional appraisals of; New York City, southern tourism to

New York City, and the cotton trade, 202; centrality of New York City to the cotton trade, 3; conviction of southerner fire-eaters that New York's dependence on southern cotton rendered the city economically vulnerable, 118–19, 192–93; and the cotton trade with South Carolina, 196–97; exports and the massive expansion of New York banks, 3; increasing cotton exports of, 2–3; legalization of the cotton trade by Congress with the South, 131; southern cotton traders' debts to New York City creditors, 192–94

New York City: early southern fictional appraisals of, 68–70; and romantic fictions, 69–70; and southern cultivation of New York publishers, 69–70

New York City, southern tourism to, 36–38, 51, 52–53; conflicted views of New York City by, 46–47; cultural opportunities available to, 57–61; demographics of, 53; exclusive hotels frequented by, 53–55; extensive shopping of by tourists, 55–56; general condescending view of New York City, 44; influence of plantation culture on southern tourists, 47–48; musical

opportunities available to, 57–58; negative views of New York by tourists, 39–41, 43–44; potential danger of southerners traveling to New York City, 93

New York City Chamber of Commerce, 213; petition of calling for "mutual concessions" from both North and South concerning southern debts, 193

New York Daily News, 199–200

New York Democratic Party, 156, 157, 190

New York Herald, 15, 128–29, 131, 178, 181, 200, 204, 205; support of for the American Civil War, 206

"New York Kidnapping Club," 9

New York Times, 15, 178, 195

New York Tribune, 15, 16, 27, 133, 178, 179, 181, 189, 200, 204, 218

New York Vigilance Committee, 16

Norfolk Day Book, 197, 214

Notes on the State of Virginia (Jefferson), 73

Orr, James, 169, 170

O'Sullivan, John, 10

"Outrage on Mr. Sumner, The" (Bryant), 167–68

Oxley, John Stewart, 54, 55, 57–58, 63, 64

Panic of 1857, 119, 187, 192

Partisan, The (W. G. Simms), 137, 172

paternalism, 30; racist paternalism, 128; in the South, 126

Paulding, James Kirke, 137

Paxton, Philip, 176

Penick, Daniel Allen, 35

Philadelphia, 2, 8, 9, 10

Phillips, Wendell, 14

Pickett, Albert James, 42, 46, 47, 50, 69

Poe, Edgar Allan, 25, 70, 82–83, 102; disenchantment with New York's municipal government, 85; opinion of Brooklyn, 85; opinion of Manhattan, 84; positive view of New York's transformation into Americas richest urban area